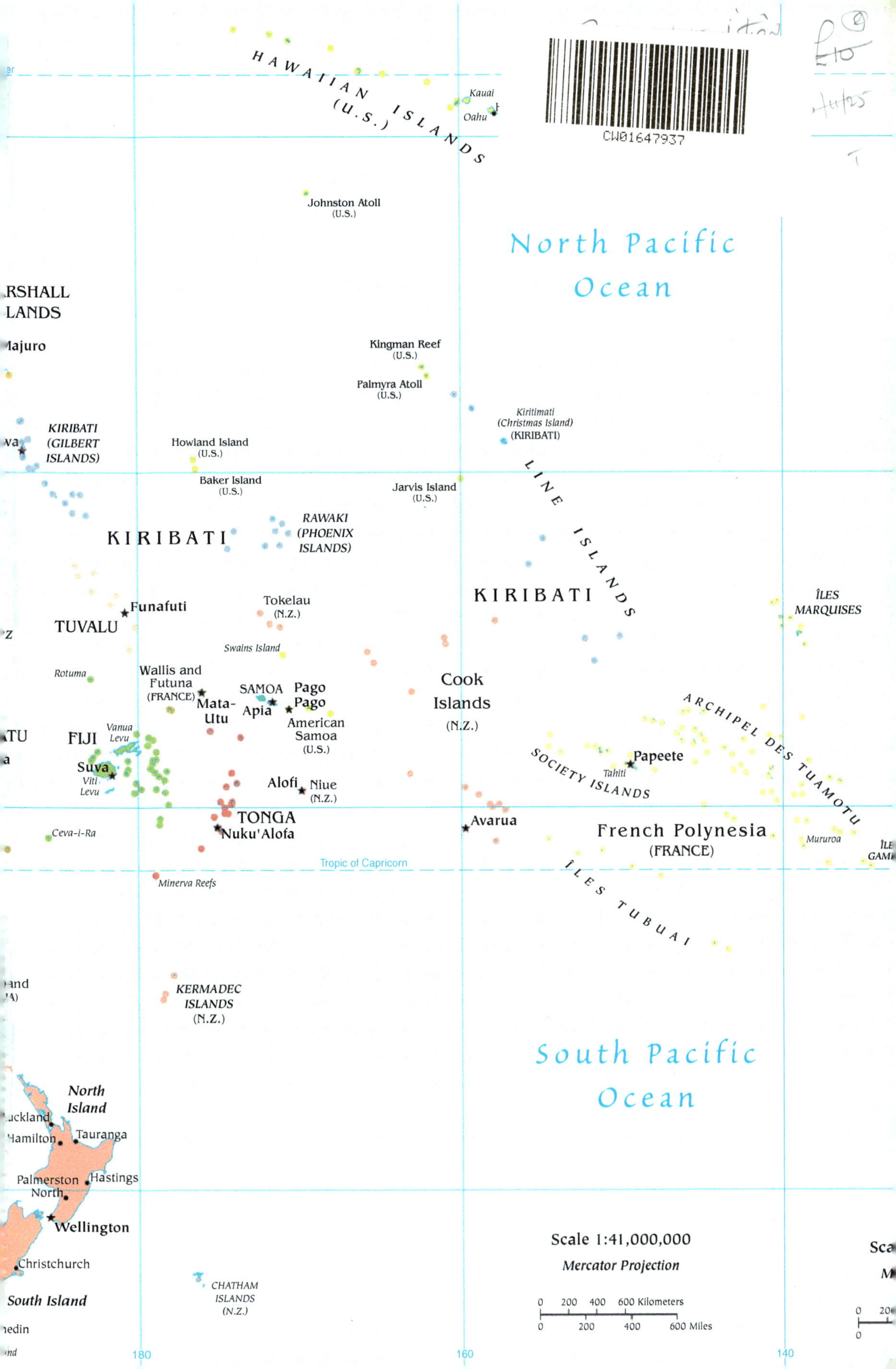
HAWAIIAN ISLANDS
(U.S.)
Kauai
Oahu
Johnston Atoll
(U.S.)
North Pacific
Ocean
RSHALL
LANDS
Majuro
Kingman Reef
(U.S.)
Palmyra Atoll
(U.S.)
Kiritimati
(Christmas Island)
(KIRIBATI)
KIRIBATI
(GILBERT
ISLANDS)
Howland Island
(U.S.)
Baker Island
(U.S.)
Jarvis Island
(U.S.)
LINE ISLANDS
KIRIBATI
RAWAKI
(PHOENIX
ISLANDS)
KIRIBATI
Tokelau
(N.Z.)
ÎLES
MARQUISES
Funafuti
TUVALU
Swains Island
Rotuma
Wallis and
Futuna
(FRANCE)
Mata-
Utu
SAMOA
Apia
Pago
Pago
American
Samoa
(U.S.)
Cook
Islands
(N.Z.)
ARCHIPEL DES TUAMOTU
SOCIETY ISLANDS
Papeete
Tahiti
FIJI
Vanua
Levu
Suva
Viti
Levu
Alofi
Niue
(N.Z.)
TONGA
Nuku'Alofa
Avarua
French Polynesia
(FRANCE)
Mururoa
Ceva-i-Ra
Tropic of Capricorn
ÎLES TUBUAI
Minerva Reefs
KERMADEC
ISLANDS
(N.Z.)
South Pacific
Ocean
North
Island
Auckland
Hamilton
Tauranga
Palmerston
North
Hastings
Wellington
Christchurch
South Island
CHATHAM
ISLANDS
(N.Z.)
Scale 1:41,000,000
Mercator Projection
0 200 400 600 Kilometers
0 200 400 600 Miles
180
160
140

Acknowledgements

The late Joyce Brown, without whom I would not have gone on this adventure.

Particular thanks to Hilary and Dick Tulloch and Hilary and Glenn Kennedy.

Also, Janet Artherton and staff at Belfast Central Library; Graeme Hill, Dianne Barnes, Carol Churches and everyone in Bathurst, NSW; Paul Clements; Anne Craig; Ian Pearce; Mary Delargy, Linenhall Library; Bernie Donaghy, Colin Neighbourhood Partnership, and all at Cloona House; Reid Echols (Utexas); Lawrence and Monika Fernandes; Jack Foster; Brian Garrett; Denis McCoy; Jaki de Boussac; Henline Mala and the Chief Librarian Margaret Terry, National Museum of Vanuatu; Barbara Mayne; Sam Mordey, Wanganui River Cruises; Harry Nikiau and Hugh Lowe in Tanna; Sigatoka River Jet Boat people, Fiji; Damien Simeon and everyone in South West Bay, Malekula; Andrew Storey; Jane West, Matt Capper, Mr Roko, Etu and the villagers I visited in Fiji.

And last, but certainly not least, Averill Buchannan for her advice and editorial skills.

For Terence,
with best wishes
Diane Greenhill.

First published in 2022 by
Cuan Beach Press
17 Cuan Beach
Killyleagh, Co. Down
BT30 9QU
E: diana@gleadhill.com

ISBN 978-1-3999-2030-8

Design by
Colin The Designer
213 Clabby Road,
Clabby, Fivemiletown
Co. Tyrone, BT75 0RD
T: 028 8954 5032
E: hello@colinthedesigner.com

www.colinthedesigner.com

Printed by
CPI Antony Rowe
Bumpers Farm Industrial Estate
Chippenham
Wiltshire
SN14 6LH
T: +44 (0)12 4965 9705

www.cpi-print.co.uk

Dedicated to the memory
of Joyce Brown

... the wondrously tall journalist Miss Beatrice Grimshaw is about to pay another visit to the islands to study black nature in all its painted nudity, and as she carries a gun and a good camera some startling things are to be expected in the future

Table Talk (Melbourne, May 1907)[1]

1 *Table Talk* (Melbourne, Victoria), 23 May 1907, p. 24.

Contents

Preface

From the small coastal town of Wewak on Papua New Guinea's north coast, to Ambunti on the Sepik River, our flight in a tiny six-seater aeroplane, was magic. Off into the unknown and west away from the early morning sun; flying over glittering threads of water meandering through the dark green forest; the Hunstein Range of mountains lying in the distance, rugged and mysterious.

In 1994 my nephew Andrew Storey went to live and work in Papua New Guinea. Being an inveterate traveller myself, I was excited by the possibility of going to visit him and do some exploring in this relatively unknown part of the world.

I knew that European exploration of Papua New Guinea had been quite recent – indeed the Central Highlands were only discovered in the 1930s – and that ritualised cannibalism, i.e. honouring dead ancestors by eating them, still took place. Papua New Guinea's remote and wild character is possibly tied to its dramatic geography with towering mountains, rushing rivers and plunging ravines keeping the indigenous people separate from one another. That in such a relatively small island over 840 languages and as many cultural and racial groups have developed, must be some indication of the ruggedness of the landscape.

Andrew is a freshwater biologist, and was at that time employed by Ok Tedi Copper Mine Ltd. to assess impacts from the discharge of tailings and waste rock from the mine into the river system. The Ok Tedi is a tributary of the Fly River eventually flowing into the Gulf of Papua in a large delta.

I had very much wanted to go up the Fly River as Andrew knew it so well, but he said it was not possible as there had been a lot of physical unrest in the area; so instead he suggested the Sepik River.

Andrew's brother David, and mother – my sister Trish – joined me in planning this exciting adventure, and by the spring of 1995 we were ready to go.

Luckily, I tucked a new notebook into my rucksack.

We arrived at Ambunti Lodge, some 200 nautical miles from the coast, and met Alois Mateus who had organised our river trip. The Sepik was in flood. We thought it was supposed to be the dry season, but in fact that was academic; it was wet – very, very wet. There, in the water lay our transport, a dug-out canoe, about 30ft long and 3ft wide and equipped with a decent looking outboard engine. We had two Papuan men with us, Dion, young and energetic, speaking quite good English, and Moses, who was older and our skipper, with very little English. Each of us had a comfortable wicker chair fitting nicely into the width of the boat.

Finally settled, feeling like the 'African Queen' – only Papuan – off we went up the fast-running river, past tall pit-pit grass (wild sugar cane), yellow convolvulus, and dozens of plants I had no knowledge of. I felt totally euphoric. We passed villages of wooden houses on stilts, with thatched roofs of sago palm leaves. We watched a big grey eagle with a white chest, right beside us catching his fish dinner with unerring accuracy. There were women fishing and washing, men making canoes, and lots of little children running hither and thither. Onwards we went, into a tributary, and then into another, passing Dion's home. We travelled through high grasses with a channel just wide enough for our boat. There were birds singing, butterflies of enormous size, and large bright blue dragonflies.

Children with frightened baby at our white faces

At last, tied to a tree, we had stopped for a lunch of crisps, warm orange squash, and a banana each. Although still very hot, it was lovely under the trees – frequently hung with exotic orchids – and so peaceful with just the sound of the river rushing past. The blue sky, dotted with small white clouds, stretched above us. There was a *haus tambaran* here where were stored the carvings that represent the various spirits. These houses are mainly men-only clubs and women are only allowed into some parts of them. They are beautifully made with high, elegant, sweeping roofs. Here, we were charged one *kina* to take a photograph – these locals had got the tourist idea already. Everyone was friendly, kids giggling and pointing to us, and a baby crying with fright at the appearance of our white faces. Were we that unusual? Could Trish and I possibly be the first white women up the Middle Sepik?

No, of course we were not the first. We were disabused of this fanciful honour some twenty years later when I learned that another Irishwoman – Beatrice Grimshaw – had achieved this accolade over ninety years before, in 1923.

Not one renowned for being coy, Beatrice Ethel Grimshaw entered – and more or less took over – my life, in Portaferry Sailing Club, on the shores of Strangford Lough, County Down, in February 2015.

I had been giving a talk on my waterborne adventures, which included the voyage I had made up the Sepik River in 1995. When I finished my talk, a man – who turned out to be Jack Foster, Professor Emeritus of English at Queen's University Belfast – approached me out of the audience and asked if I had ever heard of Beatrice Grimshaw; born near Dunmurry, Co. Antrim, in 1870. When he told me she had lived in Papua New Guinea for twenty-seven years in the early 1900s I was amazed. Papua New Guinea is not an easy place to live in – hot, humid, full of mosquitoes, and well known for its fearsome cannibals, even when I was there in 1995. It was a *very* unusual spot for a Victorian woman to make her abode.

Naturally enough, when I arrived home after my talk I googled Beatrice Grimshaw and found that she had published six non-fiction travel books and more than forty novels and collections of short stories. Many of the novels were serialised and reprinted numerous times, as well as translated into several languages; two were made into films. Countless articles and several poems were among her publications. I was fascinated, and straight away sent for one of her books about Papua New Guinea and two others about her odysseys across the South Pacific. I loved her travel writing. Even the era's ladylike Victorian reserve could not conceal her obvious excitement and lively descriptions as she painted explicit pictures of her exotic surroundings.

That was just the start of a very long, frequently frustrating affair with the elusive Miss Grimshaw. But I was hooked.

Early on I discovered that we had one or two things in common. To start with, we were both Aquarians, albeit born in very different eras – Beatrice's birthday was the 3rd February; mine was the 1st and we were both middle children. She rode her pony and cycled as did I. There was more; both our families were heavily involved with the linen industry, but sadly Beatrice and I had fathers who spent family money with carefree abandon, the gradual straitened circumstances forcing our families into selling our homes and moving to smaller houses, eventually financed by mothers and grandparents. Maybe this background was what made us independent daughters, and gave us such wanderlust.

For both of us, our big adventures abroad started by crossing the Atlantic from Liverpool to New York. Our ships would have called at Cobh – or Queenstown as it was called in Beatrice's day. I wonder had she also watched, while her ship sailed away from our home country of Ireland, the many shades of green slipping gently into the distance, and had she been as emotional as I was?

Passagers disembarking in New York

I began my search for Beatrice in earnest at the Public Record Office of Northern Ireland (PRONI), where I dug into boxes and flipped the pages of enormous ledgers in the hope of finding information. At Belfast Central Library I borrowed and read books about Victorian women travellers and writers, but her name appeared nowhere.

She wasn't even in *The Virago Book of Women Travellers*, which contains entries for fifty-six women.[2]

I was lucky to be given, by Jack Foster, an interesting extract from his book *Irish Novels 1890–1940* in which he discusses Beatrice Grimshaw's writing. I got hold of Eugénie and Hugh Laracy's article, 'Beatrice Grimshaw: Pride and Prejudice in Papua' and Susan Gardner's 'A "'Vert to Australianism": Beatrice Grimshaw and the Bicentenary'.[3] But it was the late Dr A. A. Kelly's *Wandering Women: Two Centuries of Travel out of Ireland* that planted the seed which would sprout to take over my life. In the twenty-page entry on Beatrice, Dr Kelly wrote: 'Books about adventurous women have all neglected Beatrice Grimshaw (1871–1953) ... This remarkable woman deserves a biography.'

Cloona House, today

I had soon become so curious about Beatrice that I went to see her old home Cloona, built by her father, Nicholas, and where Beatrice was born in 1870.

Around the same time, in the spring of 2015, my friend Joyce Brown and I were casually chatting about visiting some of the Pacific Islands. Now that I was becoming more and more interested in Beatrice Grimshaw, and as Joyce originally came from New Zealand, we thought we might try and follow Beatrice's adventures across the Pacific. It took us quite a long time to find just the right ship. Then we struck gold: we discovered the *Astor*, which sailed from Tilbury in October 2016, arriving in Auckland at the end of November. The ship went through the Panama Canal, which I had always wanted to do anyway, and was the route which Beatrice eventually took, but in the other direction. It also called at some of the islands Beatrice had visited. It was perfect! We soon were booked and the deposit paid.

That summer, while I was rootling around on the internet, I came across some emails about one of Beatrice's forebears. They were obviously written by someone who knew a lot about the Grimshaw family, and I decided to try and contact the person who had written the emails. After a lot of detective work I discovered Hilary Tulloch (nee Grimshaw) – a distant cousin of Beatrice, and to my good fortune she lived in Dublin.

2 Mary Morris, ed. *The Virago Book of Women Travellers* (London: Virago, 1994).

3 Eugénie and Hugh Laracy, 'Beatrice Grimshaw: Pride and Prejudice in Papua', *Journal of Pacific History*, Vol. 12, No. 3 (1977), pp. 154–175; Susan Gardner, 'A "'Vert to Australianism": Beatrice Grimshaw and the Bicentenary', in *Hecate: An Interdisciplinary of Women's Liberation*, Vol. 13, No. 2 (30 November 1987), pp. 31–68.

She and her husband and two friends who were interested in genealogy far outpaced me in digging up archival information.

One day, standing at the door of my living room, and seeing in the thin early morning sunshine, the mayhem of papers before me. This constituted the material I had gathered up on Beatrice. But I hadn't actually started writing anything, always hoping to find some letters she might have written home, or other family documents. But I found none of these.

What I did discover, was that Beatrice was a remarkable woman who led a fascinating life in a world that is very different to our own. In accordance with her era, many of her remarks seem arrogant today, and shockingly racist although frequently leavened by a great sense of humour. However, I thought her story should be told as she was a pioneer in several different fields: as a cyclist, as a female professional journalist and author, as a colonial planter in Papua and – most of all – as a lone traveller in the Oceanic world.

As the time approached for our departure, I finalised some details. With the help of Jane West of the Fiji Tourism Office, I found a company that could take me in Beatrice's footsteps through Fiji on a trek from Ba to Sigatoka. I also discovered a travel office in Vanuatu with a contact in South West Bay on the island of Malekula where Beatrice had stayed with the local missionary. Meanwhile I sent emails to a number of newspapers in towns where I thought Beatrice might have been known, asking them to publish a letter explaining that I was doing research on Beatrice Grimshaw and if anyone knew anything about her to please get in touch with me.

Through this route, Graham Hill, a historian in Bathurst, New South Wales, contacted me. I already knew that Beatrice eventually went to live in NSW where she died in 1953, and was in an unmarked grave. However, coincidentally, and totally independent of me, this historical group were hoping to erect a plaque marking Beatrice's grave, with an unveiling in early January 2017. I was invited to attend this ceremony as guest of honour. Needless to say, I accepted with alacrity.

Joyce and I set off in October 2016. By then I was excited about the prospect of following my heroine as far as I could. Obviously I was not going to be able to cover her lifetime of travel in just three months, but in the process I hoped to weave my own story with Beatrice's.

So, in fact, this is a tale of two travellers as I shadowed Beatrice Grimshaw around Belfast, Dublin and France, and onwards to the South Pacific, New Zealand and Australia.

Joyce and me departing England

Chapter 1: The Grimshaw Family

> I am a Victorian. I was born in the Seventies, in a big lonely country house five miles – a whole hour's journey – from Belfast. I was governessed and schooled and colleged. I was taught to ride and play games. I was taught to behave. To write notes for Mamma. To do the flowers. To be polite but not too polite to Young Gentlemen. To accept flowers, sweets and books from them, but no more. To rise swiftly with the rest of the six daughters and sons when Papa came into the breakfast-room, to kiss him ceremoniously, and rush to wait upon him. He liked it, and we liked it.[4]

George Benn, in his *History of the Town of Belfast*, records an Easter Monday fête on Cave Hill when 'the Grimshaws were represented that day by forty individuals of the name' and notes that at the time of writing 'the family, once so numerous and all potent in Whitehouse' no longer had representatives 'in the village or near it'.[5]

The Grimshaw family were of yeoman stock in Lancashire, the family being traceable back to the reign of Henry II of England in the twelfth century. In the eighteenth century, one of the Grimshaw descendants became, like his father, involved in textile manufacture, establishing a cotton spinning business on the Isle of Man and then, around 1776, moving his family to Whitehouse, just north of Belfast in County Antrim. By the 1820s the Grimshaw families were involved in a variety of influential activities across the developing city of Belfast. One of this extensive family was Conway Blizzard Grimshaw (1789–1869). He was Beatrice Grimshaw's grandfather. Beatrice's father, Nicholas William, was born in 1829.

By the 1800s, Belfast was expanding to become the largest industrial city in Ireland. The area around the White Linen Hall in Donegall Square – today's City Hall – began to establish itself as the town centre during this era, although High Street remained the main business district. In the 1860s, the American Civil War devastated cotton production, enabling linen to take over, with Belfast quickly establishing itself as the greatest linen producer in the world, the Grimshaw family playing a part in the industrialisation of Belfast.

In 1886, Beatrice's father and his older brother, O'Donnell (1825–1907) owned properties in Church Lane, and in High Street near Castle Place from where they ran their wine trade. Although these properties were worth a lot in rent and real estate, various mortgages were taken out by the brothers, using the properties as security.

4 Beatrice Grimshaw, 'How I Found Adventure', *Blue Book* (April 1939). This article is the closest Beatrice ever came to writing her biography. Available < http://web.archive.org/web/20110709082848/http://pulprack.com/arch/2003/02/beatrice_grimsh.html >. Last accessed: 16 June 2018.

5 George Benn, *A History of the Town of Belfast From 1799 Till 1810* (London: Marcus Ward, 1880), p. 215.

Against this backdrop of financial disarray, Nicholas Grimshaw married, on 29th January 1861, Eleanor Thomson Newsam, daughter of James Ramsey Newsam, a merchant of Belfast, and Jane Simpson Newsam. The newly married couple lived in Pakenham Place, near Bedford Street in Belfast. Their first child, Ella, was born there in 1863. She lived just seven months. Her sister Maud was born in 1864, and Ramsey in 1866. Ramsey also tragically died, aged not quite a year old. Emma was born in 1867.

In that same year, Nicholas leased land at Ballycullo, near Dunmurry in Co. Antrim, and built 'Cloona', which was to be the family home. This was where Beatrice Ethel was born in 1870, the fifth of eight children, followed by Nichola in 1872, Osborne in 1875 and Adrian Ramsey in 1876.

Cloona, I had discovered, meant a great deal to Beatrice throughout her life, and I decided to visit her old home. En route I explored the nearby Colin Glen Forest Park in the foothills of Slievenacloy and Divis Mountain. It has always been a river glen and it gave me a good idea of how the natural countryside might have been in the days when the land-owners enjoyed hunting and shooting in the locale.

The glen is under a mile as the crow flies from Cloona House which was not too difficult to find, just off the Old Colin Road. I had phoned ahead explaining my quest and was warmly welcomed when I arrived at the house. As I was shown around, I was very conscious of Beatrice's presence, playing with her siblings, riding their ponies, and growing up into well-behaved Victorian children. Much of the house is unchanged with old shutters and elegant plasterwork around the ceilings.

The house is a listed building, described by the Environment and Heritage Department as:

> Substantial, well-proportioned, two-storey gentleman's residence of 1868–69 in typical mid-Victorian Italianate fashion, with red brick walls and stone dressings, some canted and full-height square bays, a projecting single-storey porch, and a slated hipped roof with overhang on brackets. Originally built for mill-owner [Nicholas] William Grimshaw, the property was in the hands of the army for much of the 20th century, but is now a community centre.

Above the front door there is a stone with a coat of arms. I photographed it, and on closer examination found it was a monogram of NWG – Nicholas William Grimshaw's initials. There is also presumed to be a family motto of 'Per Libertate Patriae', meaning 'For the Liberty of my Country'.

Nowadays, Cloona is owned by the Roman Catholic Church and houses the Colin Neighbourhood Partnership, a community organisation that works collaboratively with other organisations within the Colin Glen area.

These early days at Cloona appeared to be a time of plenty for the Grimshaw family. Everything was safe and stable. The children's mother presided over the kitchen and the housekeeping, arranging the day's meals with Cook, and always seeing that there was enough in the pantry to get them through a siege. With five miles to travel to the town and no telephones or motor cars, one had to look ahead. Laundry also had to be sorted with the help of a servant (nobody called them maids in those days). There were frilled chemises and hole-and-stiletto worked drawers (knickers) and petticoats. Mrs Grimshaw was never idle.

Then there was the entertaining. Friends and acquaintances often visited Cloona in the afternoon, arriving in carriages, heard a long way off rumbling up the rough drive. Ladies would be the first to enter the hall, followed by bewhiskered gentlemen wearing white waistcoats showing off their large gold watch chains. Refreshments of port and sherry would be handed round, accompanied by plum cake and seed cake. This would be followed by hours of talk. But, unlike the rest of the family, Beatrice loathed these parties where nobody talked about anything really 'serious'.

However, on 8th March 1877, an advertisement appeared in *The Belfast Newsletter* advertising a sale by auction of everything at Cloona. From horses and carriages, saddles and guns, to furniture from every room in the house, even the servants' apartments.

But not everything was sold. For the next twenty plus years, the Grimshaws came and went to less grandiose accommodations as their finances fluctuated, and while they were absent, different tenants lived at Cloona.

Later that year, the Grimshaws went to live in Caen in Normandy, and Cloona was let to a Mr James Boyd. I could find out nothing about the family's time in France, except part of a letter to Nicholas' solicitor, L'Estrange and Brett, in which he writes, 'We are sojourning in St Honorine La Chardronette'. Whether this was where the family lived outside Caen, or if it was the venue for a holiday is unclear. What is known is that Beatrice, and presumably her siblings, went to school at Le Pension Retaillaud in Caen.

There was no mention of Grimshaws in the Belfast newspapers from March 1877 to November 1881.

Diana in France 2016

Keen to visit as many places as I could where I knew Beatrice had been, I went to Caen with my friend and brother-in-law, Denis, in the summer of 2016.

We explored some of the city before setting off to find the village of St Honorine where Nicholas Grimshaw wrote the above note. St Honorine was a very unprepossessing 1950s-type satellite town for Caen.

Anglican Church, St Honerine la Chardronette

We wandered around the churchyard of the little Episcopal Church, which was much older than all the houses. It was quite disappointing until we met a local man who asked if he could help us. It transpired that the original town had been bombed to rubble by the Allies during the Second World War, thus wrecking any house in which the Grimshaw family might have lived, but avoiding the little church as it was a good landmark for the Canadian Air Force at the time. The man got the key for the church, so at least we could go and see where the Grimshaws had presumably worshipped.

The family returned to Cloona in 1881, when Nicholas and a Mr McFadden bought the Tavanagh Linen Factory in Co. Armagh. However, on 1st November 1887, Cloona was again advertised to let in *The Belfast Newsletter*, and on 9th December 1887 there was a sale by public auction of land adjoining Cloona, 'the property of N Grimshaw Esq'.

By 1888–1889, Alfred Jaffe, JP, was renting and living at Cloona.

So where was the Grimshaw family residing now? In *The Belfast Newsletter*, of 13th October 1890, there was a mention of 'Mrs Nicholas Grimshaw of *University Square*, providing clothing for the Home for Destitute Little Girls', and by 1891, the family had moved less than half a mile to 19 College Gardens, an end of terrace three storey house, somewhat smaller than University Square, and very much smaller than Cloona. Eventually, their financial situation having gone from bad to worse and, with Nicholas and O'Donnell heavily in debt, all their properties had to be sold. In 1896 Cloona was purchased by its then tenant, William Augustus Ferrar. The Grimshaws would never live there again.

Home for the family was now in Portrush Co Antrim, where Eleanor Grimshaw, Nicholas' wife, had bought a house.

No matter how bad things were financially, Nicholas always had time for his son Osborne and his future, writing a letter in 1898 from his new home in Portrush to the Marquess of Dufferin and Ava:

My Lord Marquess,

I am taking the liberty of writing to you to ask if you will do me the great kindness to give a letter to my son Osborne Grimshaw who is living in Canada, stating that you know the family and that they are respectable. My uncle was Robert Grimshaw, my father, Conway Blizzard Grimshaw, whom I believe you knew. My name is N.W. Grimshaw, I am a magistrate. My son is very steady, a good linguist, and would do anything he undertook well and conscientiously. Your name is so widely known and respected in Canada that a line from you would carry great weight. With my apology for trespassing on your Lordship's time.

Your obedient servant.

N.W. Grimshaw.[6]

On 4th October 1898, Beatrice's elder sister, Maud Osborne, married Francis Howard Sinclair, a well-known doctor and yachtsman from Belfast. The ceremony took place at Holy Trinity Church, Portrush. Nichola, her younger sister, was the sole bridesmaid. There is a wonderful list of extravagant presents from the good and the great. Beatrice's present was an inlaid drawing-room chair.

6 N.W. Grimshaw, Portrush, Co. Antrim, to Lord Dufferin, 25 July 1898, PRONI, D1071/H/B/G/437.

Chapter 2: Beatrice, the Early Years

According to *Catholic Authors*, Beatrice was 'taught by private governesses and tutors and later attended the Pension Retaillaud, Caen, Normandy'.7 By 1886, when she was sixteen, she was attending the Ladies' Collegiate College at Lower Crescent in Belfast.[8] There is no record of a place of education for Maud, Emma or Nichola, while Osborne attended Rossall School in Lancashire, and Adrian Ramsey went to the Royal Belfast Academical Institution (better known as Inst).

In 1887, Queen Victoria's Jubilee Year, the Ladies' Collegiate College changed its name by Royal Command to Victoria College and School, so Beatrice was certainly there for the great occasion.

By that time she was already honing her poetic skills, and the poem 'Our Calisthenic Class' was published in the *Walsall Advertiser* on 4th September 1886:

Our Calisthenic Class

I.—Opening Day.
'Step out, young ladies! hold yourselves quite straight
My teaching is no good without you trying.
Don't shrug your shoulders, thinking that it's Fate
That keeps your limbs in wrong directions flying.
I hope to teach you how to move with grace;
To make you sylphs, instead of elephants;
Yet, when I give the simple order—'Face!'
Each girl stands still, and with amazement pants.
With balls I now will give an exercise

(In which I hope you soon will be proficient;)
You throw them down, then catch them as they rise,
Raising your arms to get the force sufficient.
Now, have you all got balls? then raise, let fall!
Catch! ah, how stupid! only nine or ten
Of thirty girls, have each one caught her ball.
Come, we must persevere, and try again.'
Thus drags the hour away, and when at last
The welcome words, 'Young ladies, you may go,'

7 Matthew Hoehn, ed., 'Beatrice Grimshaw' (by M. S.), in *Catholic Authors: Contemporary Biographical Sketches, 1930–1947*. (Newark, NJ, St. Mary's Abbey, 1948), pp. 293–5.

8 Founded by Mrs Margaret Byers in 1859 in Wellington Place, Belfast, Victoria College, as it is now known, is one of the longest established girls' schools in the British Isles. It soon acquired a high reputation for academic excellence and sporting prowess. The college moved to Lower Crescent 1874.

Are heard, the girls rush out in joyful haste,
Like arrows shot from quickly-bending bow.

II.—Closing day
A class that steps with care, and bows with grace,
A class that postures, slides, and moves in time,
Marching with measured, slow, and steady pace,
Moving together with the music's chime.
The girls, too, curtsey as they leave the room,
And pass on up the stairs with chatter gay,
Though o'er each face there comes a shade of gloom,
As they remember 'tis the last 'Class Day.'

* * * * * *

Adieu! chère Madame Sylvestre – but not adieu,
'Tis au revoir – until next comes September,
And every pleasant hour we've spent with you
Will be a thought to cherish and remember.
B. E. Grimshaw, Ladies' Collegiate College, Ireland.[9]

After leaving Victoria, in January 1887 Beatrice became a student at Bedford College, London, and studied the college's full-time course, which covered up to seven subjects but didn't lead to a formal qualification. She took Maths, Chemistry, English Language, Latin, Greek and English History in the first term. In the second (Easter) term she dropped English History and started Physics, and then in the third term (Michaelmas) she took up French as well, at which she must already have been almost fluent. She left Bedford College in December 1887.

Four years later, Beatrice had an article entitled 'In the Far North', published in the *Bedford College Magazine*.[10] She already saw herself as a journalist and describes the town to where her family eventually moved, through the eyes of a travel writer. Portrush, she says, consists of three or four main streets and a couple of terraces up in the north of County Antrim. It was a good place to go for summer holidays, with bracing salt-laden winds coming from Iceland and Newfoundland.

One might stay at the big aristocratic hotel or some of the smaller lodgings. After breakfast one could go for a bathe. If not a very proficient swimmer, there was a little sandy cove called the Ladies' Bay where there was a row of bathing boxes. But strong swimmers could use the deep-water bathing place, possessing two or three boxes and an iron ladder with a small diving board. It was always wise to check the tide and be aware of the big rolling waves, which could be dangerous.

9 Beatrice Grimshaw, *Walsall Advertiser*, 4th September 1886.

10 'In the Far North', *Bedford College Magazine*, December 1891.

It was also possible to enjoy a game of golf on the four-mile course. The links were very pretty with lots of wild flowers in the springtime. In the afternoons a trip to the Giants' Causeway was always popular. This involved taking a picnic lunch and using either the steam or the electric railway. Beatrice and her friends always travelled third class as the carriages were open and one could lean out and see the cliffs below. 'Only the Sassenach tourists go first class!' she said.

Arriving at the Causeway, it was usual to explore the strange basalt rock formations. Portrush was a casual place to stay, she wrote, and very out-of-doors. One could eat oranges in the street, live without gloves, and only wear boots on Sundays, as 'sand hoppers' were allowed during the week. In the evenings, a walk up to Ramore Head might be enjoyed, watching the sunset over the waves. Beatrice finishes her tour-guide article by encouraging 'those who love the ocean and its surroundings, as there is no pleasanter place for a summer or a winter stay.'

Beatrice, circa 1889

In 1890, Beatrice enrolled at Queen's College Belfast (later Queen's University) for the academic year 1890–91. By then, living nearby, she did not have far to go to get to her studies.

She said she wanted a future involved with sport. Being keen on both horses and athletics, Beatrice frequently went to horse racing and athletics meetings with a view to being a sports journalist. She was also sociable and, riding her bicycle, enjoyed exploring Belfast and its environs:

> I went to dances and waltzed to 'The Blue Danube', 'Sweethearts', and 'Estudiantina'. I bought a bicycle, with difficulty. I rode it unchaperoned, miles and miles beyond the limits possible to the soberly trotting horses. The world opened before me.[11]

By 1891 I wonder did Beatrice foresee the impending financial disasters. At any rate, that year, she kicked over the traces and went to live in Dublin:

> And as soon as my twenty-first birthday dawned, I went away from home, to see what the world might give to daughters who revolted. What it gave me first was the offer of a journalistic post.
>
> There were maps of far-away places, maps with tantalising blanks in them; maps of the huge Pacific, coloured an entrancing blue. I swore that I would go there.[12]

11 Beatrice Grimshaw, 'How I Found Adventure', *Blue Book* (April 1939).

12 Beatrice Grimshaw, 'How I Found Adventure', *Blue Book* (April 1939).

Chapter 3: Dublin

Her parents had hoped that Beatrice would become a classics lecturer at a woman's college. Very early, however, their daughter decided that she wished to write. Her parents, somewhat reluctantly, saw her off to Dublin where she first lived in number 6, Fitzgibbon Street:

> It was the dining-room of a set of rooms in Number 6, Fitzgibbon Street, Dublin. It was in the nineties, and a summer day.
>
> From the back window you could see ... a bit of high white wall, outlined against a sky that occasionally was blue. On that summer day a dream, from the white wall and the blue sky, took birth; a dream of things longed for, never seen. One could almost see those things. One could almost fancy, behind that un-European-looking scrap of shining wall, against the blue that might have been Mediterranean, or Pacific, the trembling of tall palms.[13]

But it wasn't long before Beatrice moved on to 18 Upper Merrion Street. She had written a letter to Richard J. McCready, the editor of *The Irish Cyclist*, expressing her interest in cycling and journalism.

Members of the staff of the Irish Cyclist

13 Beatrice Grimshaw, *Isles of Adventure: From Java to New Caledonia but Principally Papua* (1930. Boston & New York: Houghton Mifflin, 1931), p. 1. Hereafter *Isles of Adventure*.

Beatrice, being aware that her own feminine name might deny her the job, signed her letter, 'Belsize'. (The Belsize Road in Lisburn is near to where Cloona is situated.) To begin with, Beatrice was an occasional contributor to the magazine. She appears to have been made a permanent staff member in 1892, writing at that time under the pseudonym Graphis or simply, 'G', or sometimes with no signature at all. Appointed to the post of sub-editor in 1893, her rise through the ranks of this otherwise all-male magazine was rapid.

Beatrice, at the Irish Cyclist

Her boss, Richard McCready, praised her literary style and ability to tackle any subject. She learned all about cycles and the organising of the paper, to the extent that if her boss was away, she was capable of running the business.

Beatrice described herself as being 'very young and rather brazen and full of the "beans" that go with a good muscular system'.[14] She audaciously, started teaching the rest of the staff how to go about their jobs, describing it as fun, but how she got away with it is quite amazing. One time she had a visitor to the offices with a long complaint. When he was ushered into her office, and she asked what could she do for him, he was left quite speechless, obviously wondering what was the world coming to now with female editors.

Beatrice had been born into the Church of Ireland, but some time around 1893 or 1894, she converted to Catholicism and, to mark the occasion, published the poem 'To Myself' in *The Irish Monthly:*

To Myself.
If thy wouldst to thyself be true
And reach that higher goal,
Unseen, unknown, yet felt, whereto
Though leadest on thy soul:
If thou wouldst read the tangled lore
Of human life and scene,
And faithful follow evermore
Fair knowledge of thy Queen:
Be brave! Bear out thy toil and smart—
A crown in store hath Time;
Tread down the weakness of thy heart,
And upwards, onwards climb!
If loving, loved, thy spirit yet
A loneliness has known,
If thou the soul hast never met
That speaks unto thy own—
Yet bear! Though happiest are they
Who lean on friendly hand,
It is the strongest soul that may
Alone unshrinking stand.
Though the dark maze of human life

14 Grimshaw, *Isles of Adventure*, p. 2.

Lie heavy on thy heart,
Shrink not, nor fail before that strife
In which thou hast thy part.
Fight out thy fight, and dare to speak;
One light thou hast in view—
Men may be false, and flesh is weak,
But God is strong and true.

Beatrice Grimshaw.[15]

In 1893, while continuing to write for *The Irish Cyclist*, Grimshaw joined the staff on the magazine's sister publication, *The Social Review*. She was with the paper approximately two years when she was promoted to editor. Again her quick brain and business acumen stood her in good stead.

One aspect of the bicycle's revolutionary impact is that it enabled women to challenge prevailing notions about women's physical frailty. It was considered scandalous for women to 'scorch' (go very fast) on their bicycles; those guilty of such behaviour were described by the more sedate as being 'fast', and those few Irish women who wore 'bloomers' or 'rational clothes' when cycling, were subjected to fierce ridicule. Initially, cycling clubs were reluctant to admit women so the ladies formed all-female cycling clubs. But gradually attitudes changed and mixed clubs slowly emerged.

In 1893, Beatrice, a member of the Ohne Hast Cycling Club, claimed that she set a world record for a 24-hour cycle by a woman by riding some 212 miles on a Rover bicycle, beating the previous record by some five miles. She describes the event:

> I left my rooms at eleven o'clock at night; rode through the dark alone, with provisions packed on the bicycle, and an ankle-length skirt encumbering my limbs. Checks were necessary for world records. I got my first on leaving; my next, far out on the central plains of Ireland at 5 a.m., from a police barracks. From eight o'clock on through the 'proper' hours I was paced from time to time by various enthusiastic friends.[16]

The newspapers of the day featured the performance, keeping silent as to whom the pacers might have been. When one considers the roads in the 1890s, riding a bicycle at all was a feat of endurance. The surfaces of even the main roads would have been Macadam (named for John Loudon McAdam). On site, stones were broken into very

15 *The Irish Monthly*, vol. 21 (Dec. 1893), pp. 654.

16 Grimshaw, *Isles of Adventure*, p. 7.

small pieces, the quality of the road dependent upon how carefully the stones had been spread over the surface.[17]

In Ireland, polo on bicycles became hugely popular. It took a little longer to catch on in England, but when it did, clubs began to crop up throughout the country. In 1898, Richard McCready brought two Irish teams to Catford, London, to demonstrate the superiority of the Irish game. He also played an unprecedented trump card by including a woman – Miss Wheeler! (I wonder could that have been yet another pseudonym for Beatrice who was still working for *The Irish Cyclist*). After her team won, it was reported that her presence 'unmistakably proved the safety of the game'. And while it was an audacious move by McCready it also demonstrated the growing popularity of cycle polo among women.

Beatrice's first novel, *Broken Away*, was published in 1897 by John Lane in London and New York. It is a romance about an assertive young woman who was also a cyclist, rather like herself.

In 1898, *The Irish Cyclist* was bought by its editor, Richard McCready. In a supplement McCready remarks:

One of Beatrice's "homes" in Dublin

> The Irish Cyclist was all in all to me. My affection for it had very little of the commercial element in it, and I viewed with dismay the mere idea of letting it go out of my hands. Under such circumstances I consented to pay £1500 for my brother Alex's two-fifths share. Of this, Mr Kyle purchased one-fifth. So the shares then stood as follows: R. J. McCready, three-fifths. W. P. (Percy) French, one-fifth. S. Kyle, one-fifth.[18]

In 1899 Beatrice moved to 51 Great George Street. She stayed put here until, according to the 1901 census, she finally moved to Fitzwilliam Street Upper.

I was keen to see for myself some of the places where Beatrice had lived and worked so I went to Dublin and met the Tullochs. I was interested to see where Beatrice had made her home and grown from a student to become a competent journalist and editor, equipped with skills to support herself and fulfil her dream of travelling the world.

17 Later on, tar was mixed with the stones, thus creating tarmacadam, or tarmac.

18 *The Irish Cyclist*, 19th January 1898.

Chapter 4: From England to Tahiti

By 1902, Beatrice had left Ireland and was working in Liverpool as Publicity Manager for Cunard, and in September she crossed the Atlantic for the first time, on board the SS *Saxonia*, to Boston and New York, staying for ten days.

Beatrice then moved to London where she enjoyed working as a freelance journalist and immigration promoter. But she could not settle in London. From her early days in Dublin she had harboured a desire to see the Pacific.

Using her entrepreneurial skills, and with great ingenuity she had visiting cards engraved with her name and calling herself an Advertising Expert. Armed with these and wearing her best dress, she visited shipping offices, suggesting that if they paid her way round the world she would guarantee plenty of newspaper advertising. Amazing though it sounds nowadays, the biggest shipping companies consented to support a young and totally unknown woman all over the Atlantic and Pacific, so long as she could assure them of newspaper editorials:

> I made a London newspaper commission me; I went. Long ago, when travel was travel, and the South Seas unknown to tourists; when the charm of the island world was still unbroken I went to all the chief island groups, and lived in most; I saw the inner New Hebrides, Solomons, and New Guinea, at their rawest and fiercest.[19]

Even more audacious, she accepted government and company commissions in 1904 and 1905 to write tourist publicity for the Cook Islands, Tonga, Samoa, Niue and New Zealand, and on the prospects for settlers in Fiji.

19 Beatrice Grimshaw, 'How I Found Adventure', *Blue Book* (April 1939).

Cunard ship on tow

In 1904, on commission from *The Times* (London) and the *Daily Graphic* and, equipped with her letters and free passes she set off from Liverpool on 23rd January on board the SS *Etruria*, destination New York. Beatrice describes her departure from Liverpool:

> So, like the fairy tales, 'it all came true', and one bright winter afternoon a Cunard liner bore me away from the streets and shops and drab-coloured, huddled houses of Liverpool, down the muddy Mersey – off round the world.
>
> There were thousands of people on the quay, come to see the famous boat away, for it was Saturday afternoon, and the town took holiday.[20]

The following day, about fifty additional passengers from all over the world boarded the ship in Ireland, at Queenstown, (Cobh) in Cork Harbour. Every person going to the United States had to declare the amount of American dollars they were carrying. Many had savings of less than $50 on which to start their new lives. The saloon passengers, of whom Beatrice was one, all declared they had more than US$50.

Mariposa 1907

I have been unable to find any descriptions of her travels across the Atlantic, her arrival in New York, or her trip across the United States which must have been quite an adventure. She would likely have taken a train from New York to Chicago, then the Santa Fe Railroad across the States to San Francisco.

But what we do know is that on 11th February 1904 she boarded the SS *Mariposa*, a liner owned by the Oceanic Steamship Company, bound for the Pacific Ocean and Tahiti.

Diana on Board The *Astor*, 2016

In bright sunshine Joyce and I sailed away from Tilbury docks, London, on Sunday 16th October 2016. With thoughts of Beatrice in my head, who made a similar journey over one hundred years before, I felt quite emotional as we watched a flock of seagulls hanging motionless on the breeze while we sailed down the dirty brown River Thames. I stayed on deck for a long time watching the passing scene.

20 Beatrice Grimshaw, *In the Strange South Seas* (London: Hutchinson, 1907), p. 13.

By the time we went below to our cabin the low sun was streaming in through the large square porthole, and towards evening we could make out the White Cliffs of Dover.

Even through the Bay of Biscay the seas were calm with just a little more roll, and the sun still shone becoming warmer and warmer as we sailed south.

There was great excitement on board one day when it was discovered that we had a peregrine falcon aboard. Sure enough, there it was high up on the forward superstructure. We were watching when off it went, low over the sea, scooping up a small bird that we hadn't even noticed, bringing it back to eat, scattering feathers all over the decks.

Our first port of call was Madeira. We made up behind an enormous P&O cruise ship, looking like an apartment block, capable of taking around 3,000 persons. Once ashore we just wandered through Funchal and went to see the famous Reid's Palace Hotel. After beers and sandwiches on the balcony, we ignored the notice telling us it was out of bounds to non-residents and explored the rather formal but very pretty gardens, with fabulous views over the bay. I don't know if Beatrice ever went there. It's certainly possible as it's en route to the Canary Islands.

Oh, the sea, the sea. How we loved watching the great Atlantic as the glorious translucent purple-blue near the ship gradually faded to pale blue further away. I had sworn never, ever, to go on a cruise, but here I was with my friend Joyce, being transported from Ireland to the South Pacific. The weather remained benign as we gently sailed south-west across this huge ocean. From the forward deck, turning round you could see very nearly the whole 360 degrees of this blue, slightly ruffled disc. Maybe the world is flat after all! We saw no other vessels until we approached Antigua, and then early one morning I looked out of our porthole to find the pilot boat directly outside our cabin. The crew gave me a happy and slightly startled wave as they took the pilot on board.

We did a tour of the island, setting off with a group of about twenty-four others in three jeeps to see the interior of Antigua. The tour took us crashing up unmade roads, past little farms, tiny poor houses and green rugged hills, until at last we ended up at the coast to enjoy a gorgeous swim at a lovely beach.

Leaving Antigua in the early evening, Joyce and I stood in the bows as we slipped away from the dock. We watched, on tenterhooks, as we dodged floating pontoons, only just avoiding two of them – the captain shouting ferocious orders to the navigator and helm. Then we turned and made out to sea on a northerly heading.

What a view we had! The low sun threw glorious shades of pink, salmon, crimson and gold onto the huge cumulous clouds, always changing as the sun gently sank in the west. Three frigate birds circled languidly around the awestruck passengers as we watched, transported by the glory of the scene being played out as gradually the pinks faded to grey. An hour later and it was all over.

Evening entertainment on board The Astor

By 6 o'clock we were in total darkness. Walking aft, we came across an enormous leaving party in full swing – music, people clapping and cheering – from the sublime to the ridiculous.

The following day we arrived in Saint Lucia and again we joined a crowd for a tour; this was in a small bus. From the capital, Castries, we motored to Soufriere, passing through a couple of little local fishing villages which I would have loved exploring, At Soufriere we boarded a catamaran for the return trip to Castries by sea with a great view of the Pitons – two mountainous volcanic plugs, or spires, and passing high cliffs with almost no habitation, except for a few holiday homes perched on jaw-dropping ledges above the sea. We eventually poked into a bay, dropped anchor and a flight of steps was lowered into the water so that anyone who wanted a swim could do so. Of course we couldn't resist the lure of the warm Caribbean and were among the first to take the plunge.

The next day we left the Caribbean Islands and set off for the Panama Canal, passing many container ships on the way. Once again, we were back shadowing Beatrice, who came through the canal in the opposite direction in 1926, although, surprisingly she didn't write anything about her experience.

Diana Traverses The Panama Canal, 2016

In September 1513, the Spanish conquistador Vasco Núñez de Balboa led a party of men into the interior of what is now Panama, to search for the rumoured Great Ocean across the mountains, and on September 25th Balboa climbed a hill, and turning one way and then the other could see both oceans quite clearly. In Balboa's party was an engineer, Alvaro de Savedra, who suggested in a report to the Spanish King Charles V that it might be possible to build a canal. However, although a survey was made, no canal was built.

At the end of the seventeenth century a Scottish adventurer, William Paterson, produced a bold plan. If ports could be established on both coasts of the Panama isthmus, cargoes could be transferred over the narrow strip of land, saving ships the long and dangerous voyage around Cape Horn. His plan was perfect enough to envisage not just a road but, in time, a waterway.

However, Paterson's foray into the country was a failure, attributed to the hostile local population, and the harsh living conditions – particularly malaria from the abundant mosquitoes which killed hundreds.

For years, the above vicissitudes hampered all attempts at building a canal. However by the late nineteenth century, technological advances and commercial pressure allowed construction to begin in earnest. An initial attempt by France to build a sea-level canal failed after a great deal of excavation. This enabled the United States to complete the present canal in 1913. They had implemented some sanitation practices, including draining wetlands and dumping oil into lakes to keep mosquitoes from breeding, these methods saving thousands of lives. The canal was open to shipping in 1914. The 2007 Panama Canal expansion project began operation in 2016 – the new locks allowing transit of larger ships, which the original locks could not accommodate.

We were due to arrive there on the 2nd of November, sometime in the early morning. As is normal for me I kept waking up and looking out at the dark sea. The closer we got to the canal, more and more brightly lit up ships were gathering. Although I had set my alarm clock for 6.30, I could wait no longer, and eventually about 5.45 I quietly got up and dressed. Grabbing my binoculars and camera I made for the upper deck. Seeing nobody on the way I thought I would be the only person in the bows, so was surprised to find quite a few – also curious souls – lined up along the railing. Taking my place amongst them, I gazed ahead at the dark sky.

Looking south-east one could see the lights of Colon on the horizon. Gradually behind the city, the sky began to lighten, the palest pink, gradually suffusing to brighter pink.

As we approached the navigation lights, I went to get Joyce from our cabin. We stayed watching as very slowly we made our way up Limon Bay, under the Atlantic Bridge, collecting our pilot, and on to the Gatun Locks – watching transfixed as two tiny rowing boats set off from each side of the dock to take our lines and thence to the 'mules'. Although we went ahead totally under our own power, the 'mules' – electrically motorised vehicles on tracks – kept us straight. Any deviation of the ship could cause it to come into contact with the stone sides of the locks, doing expensive damage to both the lock walls, and to the ship. The *Astor* was quite a small ship, but coming towards us was a huge freighter with – apparently – only two inches to spare on either side.

Having navigated the locks, we dropped anchor in Gatun Lake as we were ahead of schedule. It was lovely place. We could see the navigation lights winding away into the distance, evidently following the original river bed, now kept dredged where necessary. Little green islands dotted the water, inhabited only by birds.

After a while we continued watching our progress through the three Miraflores Locks, taking us down to sea level. Through the canal-side trees we could see the lights of the huge city of Panama. Then under the Bridge of the America's – linking North America to South America – and on into the Pacific Ocean.

Ten hours later, after exiting the canal, we sailed almost due south, until we rounded Punta Mariato to starboard, and then almost due north, passing Costa Rica, Nicaragua, a tiny bit of the Honduran coast, El Salvador and Guatemala, and thence to Mexico and Acapulco, places, I am pretty certain, Beatrice never visited.

However, I had been to Acapulco at the height of its fame in the 1950s. And so on the evening of our arrival at the port, I took Joyce and our onboard friends to the well-known restaurant at La Quebrada. Arriving there at dusk the cliffs were floodlit. We drank margaritas and had a meal while watching the divers with their spectacular show, diving hundreds of feet down into the sea below.

The following day we set sail again. It was very hot and there was very little wind. We must have been more or less in the doldrums. Then followed two or three days of dark, windy and wet weather. The rain, when it came, was torrential – the sea no longer blue but iron grey, scattered with white topped broken waves.

It was very easy on board to just do absolutely nothing – stay late in bed, or even all day; read endlessly; eat and drink endlessly. But we went to many of the interesting talks, and listened to the Diamond Duo, a pretty Russian couple with their delightful piano and violin playing. I learned to dance the tango with my borrowed partner, Brian. Earlier, we had had some fun selecting congenial folk with whom to dine in the evening, and were lucky to find a trio of English 'yachties' who, surprisingly, had once sailed into Strangford Lough.

From time to time we saw shoals of flying fish. They would rise up from the depths, skittering across the wavelets looking as though someone had thrown a handful of silver coins, glittering in the bright sunlight, to fall back into the sea as soon as they came into contact with a larger wave.

We crossed the equator at 10.20 a.m. on Saturday 12th November, a perfect, cloudless day. There was a great party, with our captain taking the part of King Neptune.

I also, at last, started writing about Beatrice.

Chapter 5: Tahiti

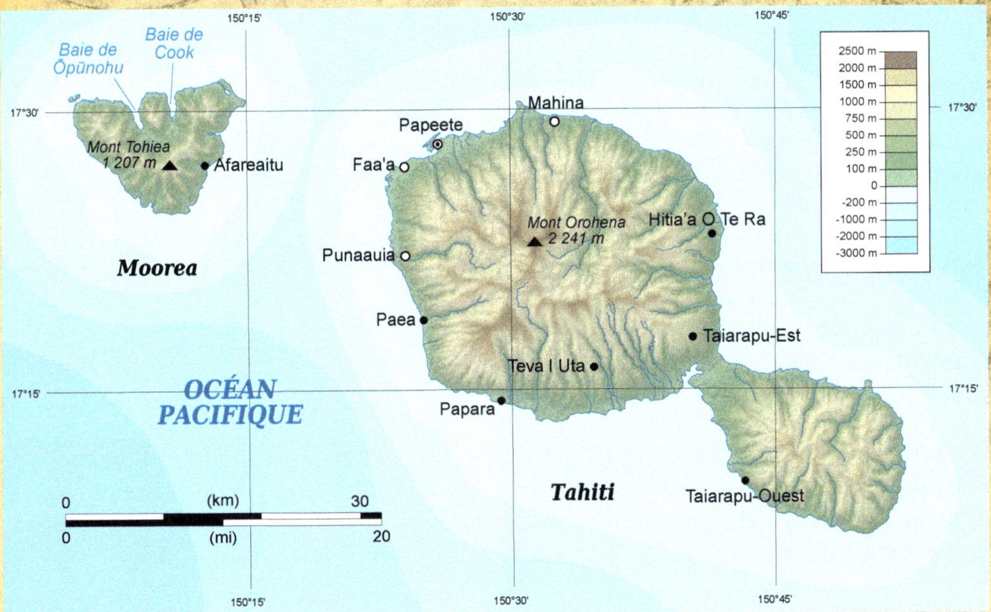

Beatrice stood with other eager passengers on the promenade deck of the SS *Mariposa* watching while the captain, looking through his telescope, pointed out the low-lying Tiki Hau, their first Pacific island. Was it as good as they had anticipated? The general consensus of opinion was yes, but not how they imagined it.

Tiki Hau is a large coral atoll, fringed with coconut palms, surrounding a placid lagoon seventeen miles long, and now part of French Polynesia. Beatrice and her friends had imagined a mountainous place covered with tropical vegetation and tumbling waterfalls. There are plenty of islands like this, but they had to wait another few days until reaching Tahiti.

At last, one morning in the pearly light of dawn, Tahiti came into sight, her spire-like mountains exactly what Beatrice had imagined.

Explored by Captain James Cook in the eighteenth century, Tahiti is the largest island in French Polynesia, the South Pacific archipelago. Shaped like a figure-8, it is divided into Tahiti Nui (the larger, western section) and Tahiti Iti (the eastern half). With black-sand beaches, lagoons, waterfalls and two extinct volcanoes, today it is a popular vacation destination. The capital, Papeete, is situated on the north-west coast of Tahiti Nui.

Beneath a sparkle of red-roofed houses, the ship dropped anchor in a calm bay dotted with the local dug-out canoes. The wharf was thronged with people, and a strange scent of perfumed coconut oil emanated from the land:

Smells are surer than sounds or sights
To make your heart-strings crack—
They start those awful voices o' nights
That whisper, 'Old man, come back![21]

So the passengers from the SS *Mariposa* landed in Papeete, the capital. They were in the South Seas at last. Here were the waving palms laden with immense clusters of nuts; here were the wonderful bananas, with broad green leaves ten and twelve feet long, enshrouding bunches of fruit that were each a good load for a man; here were the rare stephanotis, tuberose, gardenia; and here were trees with wonderful scarlet flowers.

Of course none of these plants grew outdoors in Ireland and Beatrice was overwhelmed by the exotic tropical flowers and fruit, most of which she had never seen before. It is easy to understand her vivid and excited descriptions of everything.

She and several of the other passengers from the ship stayed in a little hotel – a bungalow situated on a green lawn surrounded by flowering plants. The proprietress was a half-caste local woman with bare feet and long flowing black hair. Her dress was a simple long muslin gown, her hair kept more or less in place by wearing a wreath of gardenia and tuberose.

'L', as Beatrice referred to her landlady, was a great hostess. The food was delicious, and the drink flowed – not that Miss Grimshaw enjoyed any alcoholic beverages. Sometimes the men of her party became rather too well refreshed, and sometimes arguments and even the odd fight broke out, but nothing too serious or long-lasting.

Very early, one warm balmy morning, 'L' persuaded Beatrice to accompany her to the market. She dressed Beatrice in like fashion, but was not allowed to let her hair fall loose. That would have been a bit too much like Tahitian custom for Beatrice. It was still dark when they reached the market, lamps and torches casting flickering shadows over everything. Most of the wares for sale were fish, flowers and fruit. But *what* fish, flowers and fruit. The fish were of every colour, size and shape. The fruits were various types of banana, pineapples, custard apples, mangoes, avocado pears, papaya, guava, and all costing next to nothing. Gradually more people started to arrive. Beautiful young women, and strange-looking mountain men dressed in a shirt and kilt or *pareo* which is the uniform of all Tahitian men. They were there to sell the *fei*, or wild banana, found only on the rocky outcrops of the mountains.

In the town of Papeete, alongside the beach, ran a one-sided street of shops. Each little building was surrounded with its own plethora of flowering plants and climbers twisting their way up and over the tin roofs. Along the beach-side of the main street lay a green slope of grass running down to the waters of the bay,

21 Grimshaw, *In the Strange South Seas*, p. 17.

with frangipani trees giving shade to the native population as they lazed on the grass. Further along the bay, a river flowed into the sea where many folk went to bathe in its cool, fresh water. There were cafes and restaurants, run in the Parisian style.

Many of the schooners that came in to Papeete were pearling boats returning from the Paumutus – a group of islands where some of the richest pearl beds in the world could be found. Beatrice found these sailing vessels very attractive, and would have loved to have gone off in one to adventure among the pearl islands, but sometimes the boats never came back. The Paumutus are low lying, and going aground on the coral reefs often caused tragic shipwrecks.

Mariposa departing Tahiti

Diana in Tahiti 2016

I could find no record of Beatrice Grimshaw visiting the Marquesas Islands, which would have been virtually en route from San Francisco to Tahiti, but she doesn't mention them. Of course her ship was not a cruise ship for pleasure, but a passenger and cargo vessel, only putting in at working ports.

Our ship, the *Astor*, however, stopped off for a day at Nuku Hiva, the main island in the Marquesas group and I was determined to be up on deck, not just for our arrival, but for the first glimpse of Nuku Hiva – my very first Pacific island, and part of one of the most remote groups of islands in the world – and set my alarm clock for 6.30 a.m. I need not have worried; as ever, I slept badly, and from 4 a.m. was wide awake, looking out the window every fifteen minutes or so, lit by the moon shining a long beam across my bed. By 5 a.m. I turned off the alarm clock, got dressed as quietly as possible so as not to wake Joyce, and ventured up on deck.

It had been raining heavily, soaking the decks as I made my solitary way to the bow in light drizzle and waited for either the dawn or a sight of the island. In a few minutes, one other passenger came to join me. Gradually, before dawn, out of the mist we were able to discern land – initially just a grey blur, but noticeable above a bright strip of sea. The cloudy sky kept changing colour with intermittent patches of blue shining through the shades of grey. All around us the sky was angry with dark ragged clouds pouring out torrential rain. Where we were, it was now dry and dramatic, as we steamed ahead as though on a magic path, towards the almost ethereal cliffs of Nuku Hiva.

Girl from Nuku Hiva, Marqueses Islands

We spent a delightful day ashore here with another couple, driving across the island with a local guide in his jeep.

At Anchor, Moorea

Now, at last I was catching up with Beatrice. For once I was a bit late arriving on deck for our approach into Papeete, It didn't matter too much as one half of the island was covered with low cloud hanging over the mountains and right down to sea level. A straggling line of cloud hid the rising sun, until soon it parted a little to reveal the early light. It was very stormy at the bows, the wind whining through the ship's superstructure, battering me and whipping my hair across my face, the heavy seas making it hard to walk in a straight line. Very different conditions from Beatrice's.

Joyce, after a hard Climb!

I could totally understand her love affair with these tropical islands, so very different from her native Ireland.

She wouldn't recognise the Papeete of today – a busy waterfront with cranes and containers, another large sailing cruiser at the dock, and dozens of yachts in the modern marina. There is just one road going right round the island. Joyce and I had opted to go for an organised trip, down the west coast, en route passing numerous road-side stalls selling delicious-looking fruits and flowers. Our guide welcomed us with a 'hello' in pidgin/Tahitian of something that sounded like 'lulonha'.

Flower Market, Papeete

Young Resident

The word stemmed from the early days of the British on the island when the natives had to bow to their invaders, and had been taught to say 'your honour', so 'lulonha' wasn't a bad imitation.

Our first stop was the Museum of Tahiti and its islands. I asked about Beatrice from the museum guide who, of course, had never heard of her. The museum itself was excellent, going way back to the early inhabitants, with displays of their household implements, their fishing and canoes, and the arrival of Captain Cook. To my surprise and joy, there was also a photo of the *Mariposa* – Beatrice's ship – which I was allowed to photograph. It was all very well exhibited and most interesting.

On the way back to Papeete we visited a *Marae de Arahuraha*. The ancient Polynesians were polytheists, and they travelled to these temples to honour their gods and ask them to influence events such as the quality of their harvests or victories against enemies.

Only at a temple (*marae*) could the gods (*atua*) be called to earth by priests (*tahu'a*) to embody sculpted idols and give men *mana*, the divine strength responsible for health, fertility and more. The *marae* rituals involved making offerings to the gods as *mana* was only given in exchange for something else. Since the best gifts would entice generosity (plentiful fishing, victory in battle) from the gods, the biggest gift was that of human flesh. This *Marae de Arahuraha* had been totally destroyed by the Christians who arrived about twenty years after Cook landed here, but it was rebuilt by the man who owned the land between 1950 and 1980 – thirty years labour.

Later, we wandered through the beautiful Parc Bougainville, situated between the road and the sea, and where the locals still reclined on the grassy slopes. We did a bit of shopping mainly in the market, full of stalls selling fish, fruit, and vast quantities of brilliantly coloured and perfumed flowers. I purchased a shark's tooth on a string! We also went to visit two places that Beatrice would certainly have seen, and probably visited: Notre Dame Cathedral, completed in 1875, with its idiosyncratic mixture of French and Polynesian design. We also went to see the extravagant town hall, built as a replica of the Palace of Queen Pōmare IV. Beatrice would have seen the original palace, built in the French colonial style.

Not quite so Young Resident

Chapter 6: The Cook Islands

After a few weeks in Tahiti, in March 1904, the steamer arrived, and carried Beatrice off to the Cook Islands.[22] Although Atiu is the largest of the Cook archipelago, Rarotonga is the principal island. This vast, scattered group of islands stretches between the most southerly island of Mangaia lying almost 900 miles south of Penrhyn, the most northerly island.

A hundred years before Beatrice's visit to Rarotonga the natives were cannibals, raiding neighbouring islands and eating their captives. In 1817, John Williams and his wife Mary voyaged to the Society Islands which included Tahiti. Here, John and Mary established their first missionary post, and from there they visited a number of the Polynesian island chains. They used Tahitian converts to carry their message of God to the Cook islanders, and in August 1823, a ship with the Reverend Williams on board, arrived at Rarotonga. They were the first missionaries there.

Although a government house had been planned as accommodation for Beatrice, it was not ready, and so she found an empty house where she thought she could 'self cater'. However, very soon a group of local people called to visit her, and invited her to go

22 Joyce and I passed close by the south of the islands on our trip in 2016 but we didn't put in there.

and stay with them. Of course they were total strangers to each other, but as Beatrice remembered from experience:

> We were not in chilly England, where a whole countryside must discuss your personal history, family connections, probable income, and religious views, for a good six months before deciding whether you are likely to be an acquisition or not, and calling accordingly.[23]

She had heard of colonial hospitality, but had no idea what it meant as she moved in with these friendly folk doing their best to make her feel at home. However, things were not altogether as they seemed. After the family had gone to bed and Beatrice was writing letters, she realised that she was not alone. A great horde of cockroaches – as large as mice and with waving horns – came to keep her company, proceeding to run over the floor and walls making a horrible clicking noise. As if this was not enough, an army of large spiders appeared, their long silent legs conveying them along in pursuit of beetles which they caught and noisily crunched.

Beatrice's travels in the South Seas were not only for her own pleasure – of which there was no end. Her honest raison d'être for her visits to the Pacific Islands was to discover, as far as possible, what the prospects were like for would-be settlers. In order to make a living, some practical information was necessary. So Beatrice spent some time exploring such queries as to what the cost of living might be. What society was there, and what type of person might be suitable for island life. But frequently, by her own admission, she lingered over the life and the ways of the Rarotongan, admitting to having missed things she should have studied – but didn't.

Certainly, in the early 1900s, the British possessions in the South Seas were crying out for settlers. Planting would be the main reason for settling. Tropical fruits, vanilla, coffee, cotton, coconuts and vegetables grew almost wild here. But it was a very long way from home, and many of the young men who went there found that life was too easy, and ended up as beachcombers, spending money without replenishing it. Also, naturally enough, local trading interests were unreceptive to settlers invading their territory.

Although a religious person herself, Miss Grimshaw was ambivalent about missionaries. On the one hand they civilised the islands and made them safer to live in. On the other hand she deplored the irresponsible authority exercised by many semi-educated men, expecting totally primitive people to grasp 'civilisation' in one giant leap. Infectious diseases previously unknown in the islands, introduced by these white men, had brought the native populations tumbling, with measles and consumption (tuberculosis) the worst culprits. Few Rarotongans lived to very old age, accepting the inevitable without resistance.

Within a few days of Beatrice's sojourn with her adoptive family, she was invited to pay a visit to Queen Makea, being made aware that it would be looked upon as an

23 Grimshaw, *In the Strange South Seas*, p. 53.

insult for her not to make her presence known. She walked there with her hostess to translate. The queen received her visitors in a pretty little thatched house, near her palace. Queen Makea was not long a widow and wore a plain black dress, loose from the neck. She was around seventy years old, tall and very stout, yet extremely dignified. Her dark eyes took in everything with a shrewdness and judgement of everything around her. She was known to be wise and fair, and still held much power in her hands:

> I was friends with the old Queen of the Cook Islands, the late Makea Takau, a real monarch, six feet three in height, who ruled her islands with an iron sceptre. Her Prince Consort, Ngamaru, was less civilised than she; it was his way to threaten people who offended him, by making the 'cannibal sign' at them – rapidly drawing his clenched fist across his teeth; the significance being: 'I will tear you with my teeth![24]

As for Makea Takau, she used most courteously to tell an enemy, 'I do not expect to see you after Wednesday', and the enemy walked away and obediently died on Wednesday – of nothing at all!

The once beautiful queen, as a princess, (of whom Beatrice afterwards wrote stories entitled 'Queen Vaiti') had been as fiery as a female dragon. She had often captained her father's recruiting schooner, running it like a bucko mate of whaling days.

On another day Beatrice drove in a fast little horse-drawn buggy, round the island to visit the more minor Queen Tinomana. The pathway was white sand circling the bright lagoon. On one side rose the forest, rich and green and gorgeous. And on the other side palms and thick undergrowth hardly veiled the vivid gleam of the emerald lagoon lying within the white-toothed barrier reef, where all day long the surf of the great Pacific creamed and frothed.

The drive was about six miles long before they reached the queen's village; her 'palace' not quite as smart as Queen Makea's. Again, her normal residence was in a little creeper-wreathed cottage, scented by a frangipani tree in the garden. Tinomana also received her guests from an ironwood bench where she sat most of the day. She was also elderly but no longer beautiful, but Beatrice could see how she would have been in her youth when she fell in love with the grey-haired man standing by her side.

Going for picnics was a very popular pastime in Rarotonga. Bathing picnics were especially enjoyable when a few ladies would go to the lagoon where the water was shallow and warm and one could spend hours swimming, and then lie for another hour on the coral sand. (The all-concealing bathing dresses kept the ladies so well covered, they didn't get sunburnt). When it was time to change, they would stand against a large rock until the wet bathing dress was half dry. This was supposed to prevent chills! Beatrice's reaction to this was typical:

24 Beatrice Grimshaw, 'How I Found Adventure', *Blue Book* (April 1939).

> I think myself that one would have to hunt a chill very hard indeed in the hot season in Rarotonga before catching it; it is not a place where one hears of 'chill' troubles.[25]

A reefing picnic was one of Beatrice's favourite outings. One needed to be equipped with a short reefing skirt, cut rather daringly to the knees, and stout old shoes for walking on the corals which were very rough. Someone, probably a Rarotongan, would paddle the party out to the reef in a canoe, over the changing colours of the lagoon. Under the keel, as they shot forward were wonderful water-bouquets of purple, pink and pearl; great lacy fans of ivory; frilled and fluted fairy shells, streamers of brilliant weed and some peacock and parrot-coloured fish that fluttered through these wonderful water gardens.

After a while, they would leave the canoe and start walking about, carefully avoiding the wicked black spiky sea urchins. It was the myriad colours and shapes of the shells that the party was interested in. Amongst these lovely treasures there were sometimes eels, and other biting or stinging fish hiding in the holes in the coral. It was foolhardy ever to put one's hand into a reef pool. Back on shore, tea would be prepared, the native girls kindly offering to lend some of their spare, loose-fitting Mother Hubbard dresses to the wet white folk. Intended to cover as much skin as possible, these dresses were introduced by missionaries in Polynesia to 'civilise' those whom they considered half-naked savages.

This question of dress frequently raised its head. The native loose robe was very much cooler and, according to the doctors, much healthier than the corseted dresses of the *papalangi* (whites). Nevertheless, the Europeans stuck to their own dress for fear of becoming too native. Only if a woman was ill was it acceptable for her to wear the cooler garment. Beatrice, herself, wrote that she was very much in favour of the native dress, but did not appear to change from her tight British blouses and corsets.

Housekeeping in the South Sea Islands was uncomplicated. With the exception of some important officials, the standard of living was very modest. Most people had either one or two servants, or none at all, and dressed and ate very simply, women frequently making their own clothes.

After the dress, came, as ever, the question of servants. White servants simply did not exist, and native girls becoming married at a very young age, also were unavailable. So native boys and men were the only resource. They were hard-working, honest and cheerful, and could work in the garden, (almost everyone grew much of their own fruit and vegetables), clean, fetch wood and water, prepare coconuts, do the washing-up and prepare vegetables. So the cooking, laying of the table, and tidying had to be done by the woman of the house. Beatrice allowed that in fact she didn't think doing these not-too-onerous tasks did the women any harm at all.

Most of the South Sea Islands' white's houses were built of coral concrete – bricks made from a mix of crushed coral and sand – and sometimes of wood, and with imported windows and doors. (The native houses didn't have walls, so no necessity for doors and windows).

25 Grimshaw, *In the Strange South Seas*, p. 97.

The veranda would have been the most popular part of the house, used by everyone for living in. Indoors, the high-pitched roof rose above a number of partitions separating the different rooms, thus allowing a current of air to circulate round the house. Some of the houses had tin roofs while most of the older ones had a thatch of pandanus leaves – a much cooler option. The floor would have been covered with native mats also made from the pandanus tree, and the furniture would be bamboo.

On the whole, Beatrice reckoned, the difficulties of housekeeping were somewhat less than at home and the cost certainly much smaller. She was of the opinion that:

> white families would benefit both in comfort and in pocket, by adopting the native style of house, which is, as already mentioned, a structure of small sticks or poles set very closely and strongly, but not filled in. The roof is always thatched. In such a house, the air circulates freely without any draught, and there is a pleasant, diffused light during the daytime. At night, when native houses are more-or-less transparent, the privacy-loving white can draw thin cotton curtains across his walls until the lights are put out.[26]

Beatrice's month on Rarotonga was running out, and on 3rd April 1904, a little late arriving, the three-masted topsail schooner the *Countess Ranfurly* bore her away:

> In those days I roamed the South Seas in a schooner long since sunk among the corals – the Countess Ranfurly, captained by a little white daredevil who afterward became famous in another quarter of the world as an Antarctic explorer. Any passenger he took had to work passage as well as pay; I learned to go aloft, to 'hand, reef and steer,' and to use the sixteen-foot oar in the whaleboat. We found a pearl lagoon on one occasion, and when we reached the nearest island port, anarchy almost broke out among its few white inhabitants' they all wanted to secure the chart that marked off the lagoon, and I had to convey it across the island in the dead of night, to place it in safe hands.[27]

The 'daredevil' was Frank Arthur Worsley, DSO and bar, and OBE, later to be Commander R.N.R. He was born in Akaroa, New Zealand, in 1872, and joined the New Zealand Shipping Company in 1888, serving aboard several vessels running trade routes between New Zealand, England and the South Pacific.

The *Countess Ranfurly* was his first command. He did indeed eventually go to the Antarctic with Shackleton, as captain of the *Endurance* where he became renowned for his brilliant navigation enabling him to bring Shackleton and Tom Crean in the *James Caird* safely from Elephant Island to South Georgia. He was so audacious in his command that Beatrice frequently referred to him as 'the pirate'.

26 Grimshaw, *In the Strange South Seas*, p. 110.

27 Grimshaw, 'How I Found Adventure', *Blue Book* (April 1939).

Beatrice was destined to make the *Countess* her home for the following few months, in order to visit the outer islands of the Cook group – Savage Island, Penrhyn, Malden, Rakahanga and Manahiki. The ship was built in 1901 in Whanganui, New Zealand, and according to Beatrice no other schooner could touch her for speed, size, or (alas) pitching and rolling. Her ninety-five foot masts when the sails were set, made a conspicuous show. Her white 112 ft hull gleamed, and the bright work and the varnished woodwork, were immaculate.

This was a totally new experience for Beatrice, and one that excited her from the start. However when the captain showed her the cabin she was allotted, she was immediately horrified at the tiny room. The floor space was totally covered with her boxes. Her bunk, she described, was about the size of a coffin. The filthy porthole was partly below sea level, and the oily smell from the engine room nearby added to by the smell of copra from the hold, caused her to feel sick. The captain kindly asked if there was anything else she would like as they didn't normally have female passengers on board, but he would do everything he could to please her.

She would have liked to ask for a different cabin with thirty feet more room, but she kept her mouth shut, closed the door, sat down on her bunk and 'said things for quite ten minutes, that would not have passed muster in a Sunday School'.[28] What had she expected? A sparkling little sea parlour, smelling of rope and brine, a porthole looking out on deck, and another window fitted in the stern that overhung the horizon? With great strength of mind, she knew she just had to get on with it as, by this time, there was no way of backing out. For three days Beatrice felt unwell, but by the third day she was feeling a lot better, and going out on deck saw they were about to land on the island of Mitiaro.

Mitiaro, Aitutaki, Mangaia and Atiu

The *Countess* dropped anchor and everyone went ashore. Beatrice spent the day here exploring the little town and surrounding countryside. Mitiaro was known for producing dried bananas. As the steamers never called at this island, it was impossible for them to export fresh fruit, but the dried bananas lasted a long time, and were sometimes shipped by schooner to New Zealand where, it was said, they rivalled dried figs for flavour.

The following bright sunny day they weighed anchor and set off for Aitutaki. They had to negotiate an opening in the reef, with the boatmen having to pull hard against the outward rush of the tide, then to row easily across the lagoon and to the little wharf. As usual there was an excited crowd to meet them, Beatrice heading a procession adorned with necklaces of flowers and berries, and given bananas and coconuts to eat.

28 Grimshaw, *In the Strange South Seas*, p. 121.

The *Tau Ariki* – or chieftainess, whom Beatrice had met in Rarotonga – invited her to dine and stay the night. Unsurprisingly, it did not take more than a second for Beatrice to accept her kind offer of hospitality. Tau was married to a white ex-Schooner mate, and was well travelled having been to Auckland – the ambition of all Cook Islanders.

Beatrice was given a room to herself with a large bed and, to her horror, a large uncurtained glass window with a view on to the main street, and consequently, an unimpeded view from the street back into the bedroom. The only way she could keep her modesty was to undress in the dark. She was given an empty kerosene tin full of water for washing. Tau offered Beatrice several choices of garment to wear in bed. One was far too big covered with ruffles and frills. When Beatrice remarked about this, she was given a *pareo*, the native kilt which of course only covered her bottom half. After refusing a diaphanous muslin robe as being indecent, eventually this difficult person was happy to accept a cotton day gown, and peace at last reigned in the *Tau*'s house.

In the morning, Beatrice and the captain of the *Countess* decided they would like to go shark fishing. But shark fishing in Aitutaki is totally different from shark fishing as you or I would know it, with a line and hook well baited with a nice piece of rotten meat. On the island, when the lagoon water became really warm, some of the sharks would leave the lagoon for the open sea through a gap in the reef, but others swam along the reef until they found a hole large enough to conceal most of their body, and they lay there in the cool shade with just its tail sticking out. A diver would stroke the shark, lulling it into a relaxed state. Then he would slip a noose over the tail, swim to the surface and get into the boat. He and the rest of the crew would pull the rope tight with the noose round the shark's tail, and they would haul the captive shark on board.

Unfortunately, the day Beatrice and Captain Worsley organised a boat, it was a bit breezy creating a ripple on the water and everyone said it would be too difficult to see the sharks. Undaunted, the pair decided to go anyway, setting off across the lagoon to the reef. The diver went overboard with his rope and noose, and swam down to the bottom. Beatrice wondered anxiously what they did with the shark once it was in the boat.

It was much calmer in the lee of the reef, and they could see quite clearly the slim brown body of Oki the diver, silhouetted against the sandy bottom. Beatrice grew more and more worried as the seconds ticked by, sure that he must be at the point of death. But Oki knew exactly what he was doing and seemed quite relaxed when he finally shot to the surface, gloomily stating the obvious that 'No shark stop'. It was a great disappointment.

The island of Mangaia was the next port. However, this island is a complete coral atoll with no gap in the surrounding reef for entry into the lagoon. Consequently the schooner had to anchor outside the reef and the passengers were transported in the local dug-out canoe:

> It is most excellent fun and a new thing in sensations. As the little dug-out … rushes shoreward on the crest of a foaming roller, you watch with rather anxious interest

the movements of the dusky boatman, who poises his paddle in the air, waits, looks, and strikes the water always at exactly the right moment ...

There is the reef right in front, a pearly shadow in the blue, with up-springing spears of ivory, bared like the teeth of a tiger, when the wave rolls back. Are we going to jump that? We are indeed. The boatman lifts his paddle – we sweep upwards on the sloping blue satin neck of a curling wave. ... Another wave, a monster this time, swinging us up into the air as if we were a couple of grasshoppers out paddling in a walnut shell ... The wave roars with us; the wicked white fangs gleam on either hand: our rough thick keel scrapes agonisingly on the coral, and there is a smother of foam and tumbling blue and bursting green all about the cranky little craft. Bump! ... over we go, and we are in the smooth, safe, shallow green water inside, and across the reef. And here are a dozen men of Mangaia, splashing about in the lagoon, ready to pick up the visitor in their powerful arms as soon as the canoe grounds in the shallow water, and carry her ashore.

That is how one lands in Mangaia.[29]

Atiu was the next island visited. Here, the captain of the schooner took his passengers in one of the large whale boats from the ship, through the waves breaking on the reef, where he deposited them to a very wet landing.

There was a good deal of locally made lime juice to be taken from Atiu to the schooner, amusing Beatrice as she watched some of the men rolling the casks of juice down the beach and into the sea where the ebb tide gradually took them across the lagoon, to the reef, where the sailors off the Countess collected them for stowage on board.

The *Countess* set sail that same night passing Mauke, Maunwai, and Takutea.

The trade winds in this area were quite fickle, and many changes of sail and direction had to be negotiated. But nobody seemed to mind. Sometimes when the wind dropped they trawled for albacore and bonito, everyone shrieking with delight when a fresh fish was landed. They watched the Southern Cross by night among the myriad other stars, and lay about on the poop deck by day, yarning for hours about wild tales of frontier life, and adventures in unknown seas. Enough stories to write in a book, Beatrice thought, as she talked to her companion:

'Do you care much for reading?'

'Well no,' answers the bare-footed officer lying with his head in a coil of rope; 'books aren't very interesting, are they?'[30]

Along with the calm days and nights, sometimes the wind blew hard and it was all hands on deck.

29 Grimshaw, *In the Strange South Seas*, p. 140.

30 Grimshaw, *In the Strange South Seas*, p. 157.

There were times when sailing past unknown islands, Beatrice would sleep with one eye open, and her hand on her revolver, not knowing who might try boarding the little schooner.

Beveridge Reef

The *Countess Ranfurly* returned to Rarotonga and the Commissioners and the First Mate left the ship. A few days later Beatrice was reading her book when the skipper said he needed a break and told Beatrice it was almost eight bells, and time she did her trick at the wheel. She was appalled, saying she had no idea how to steer a boat:

> 'That's your misfortune, not your fault,' said the pirate kindly. 'You'll never have to say that again. There's eight bells now – come along. J—[the bosun] and I have had too much of the wheel, and now we're well away from land is your time to learn.'[31]

For the next week Beatrice spent part of each day with the wheel in her hands, watching the compass and the sails, ensuring they would not sail too close to the wind. She noticed with some amusement that their wake could have competed with a snake for all the curves they left. She learned how to lower the whale boats and to row them. Encouraged by her new prowess, she bravely climbed up to the cross-trees, and to descend on the rat-lines or the back-stay, wearing the flannel gymnasium dress she had brought for mountaineering. She loved it up there on a bright morning. She was strong and athletic, and, with a good head for heights never became dizzy, soon enabling her to take many photographs from her lofty perch.

They were about 150 miles from Niue when the captain asked Beatrice did she want to see something that he had only seen once before. Of course she wanted to see whatever it was he had in mind. She was told to keep a sharp lookout as they were going to pass by Beveridge Reef. Captain Worsley said the reef was incorrectly charted and there had been many shipwrecks, so he wanted to set it right. Later in the day, they spotted the reef. With no land above the surface, the only way of spotting the reef, was by the waves breaking over it. Although becoming dark, and with rain squalls, through the breaking surf two abandoned anchors were almost always visible.

They got closer and closer, everyone fascinated by the fearful look of it, and Beatrice was able to take some photographs. The crew were beginning to swing out one of the boats, when eight huge sharks appeared, cruising around the schooner. The captain said he was going to land on the reef and that there was absolutely no chance of his taking Beatrice with him. It was far too dangerous, and he just might not be able to get back to the schooner. They had the boat in the water, and the captain and three of the men were in her, when a rogue wave slapped her against the side of the schooner, and in a flash she capsized, throwing the four men into the sea where, luckily, they were able to cling on to the keel of the overturned boat.

31 Grimshaw, *In the Strange South Seas*, p. 171.

The next half hour was a total nightmare for all. The wind was rising and night was falling. The only way to keep the sharks off was for the four men to keep kicking in the water. The crew were running hither and thither, not accomplishing anything as the new mate and Beatrice tried to lower the other whale boat but not succeeding

Suddenly, in the midst of all this furore, an elderly man, who had been all the time in his cabin, appeared on deck, cursing and swearing and telling them all they were nearly on the reef. After this things got so lively that Beatrice took refuge on top of the deckhouse to keep out of the way. The elderly passenger had obviously been to sea before and quickly took command. The auxiliary engine – which was exactly what was needed – didn't work and, with the strong tide and the wind taking them towards the reef, it really looked as though the Countess's anchors were about to join the other two already abandoned. However, the new boss in taking command, somehow sailed the ship away from the reef, and towards the smaller boat which miraculously had been turned upright, and with the three men baling and the captain paddling it along with one oar, they were able to meet up and take all the men and the damaged boat on board. But that was not enough for Captain Worsley. Nothing daunted, he demanded that they launch the other boat as he still wanted to go onto the reef. This time, however, he was thwarted in his ambitions. Beatrice, the grey passenger and the mate mutinied, by reason that it was far too dark and stormy and the three of them wanted to live.

The *Countess* sailed on towards Niue, the wind never abating, and the ship carrying every last inch of sail, until with a pistol crack, the main square-sail split and began thrashing the main mast with streamers of tattered canvas. The captain had it lowered in a trice, and a new sail raised to a chorus of Māori chants as the men loved all this excitement. Half an hour later, the new sail gave too, most of it flying off into the distance like a huge grey bird. The captain was furious, raging up and down the deck. To arrive in Niue without a full set of sails seemed a huge disgrace. He had no more replacements, and just had to carry on as best he could to yet another difficult landing.

Beatrice was to leave the schooner here, and never saw her 'pirate' captain again.

Niue

It was spring 1904. Niue was one of the least visited islands, still avoiding the typical English traveller of the day. Occasionally, even they would hear the call of the South Seas, but seldom would they have taken to schooner travel, thus missing the most interesting of the islands. Their mode of transport would be the grand liner. As Beatrice writes:

> Hotel dinners, big liners, shops, hired carriages, guides, and picture postcards – these things are death to the spirit of the South Seas. This is the first lesson that the island wanderer must learn. Where every one goes the bloom is off the peach.

> Leave the great ports and the steamers; disregard the advice of every one who knows anything ... take ship on a schooner, it does not much matter where.[32]

Of course she was quite right – even in those days.

An 'ancient mariner' had taken the place of the 'pirate' as captain of the *Duchess*. And what a change it was. He had been on whaling ships before and was as tough as nails and full of the wildest stories and adventures from every corner of the Pacific.

There were about 5,000 natives living on Niue, and around a dozen whites. The capital, Alofi, she loved right from the start as she walked down its grassy main street. The little houses were roofed with pandanus thatch, high and steep. Every house was open to the elements, so Beatrice was able to see their contents of mats and cooking pots, and always the camphorwood box for clothes and treasures. All the houses – natives' and whites' – looked westwards over the blue sea, towards the setting sun. Niue's isolation was almost total. The *Duchess* called twice a year, the mission steamer once a year, and an ancient trade steamer limped across from Tonga once a year or so. There was no regular doctor on Niue, but everyone seemed healthy.

Long before, the islanders had a remarkable form of quarantine. Anyone trying to come ashore was promptly killed. Even sometimes the islanders themselves, who had maybe gone away for some reason, on return would be murdered. It was pretty draconian, but there was certainly no surer form of quarantine.

Beatrice rented a little cottage in the heart of a palm grove, as she settled down to enjoy the life of the island and waited the return of the *Duchess*. The couple who owned the cottage moved out with a few of their possessions, and a friendly white resident was able to round up a bed, a table and some chairs, cups and cutlery. For the two months she occupied the cottage, Beatrice was very happy. She would frequently sit cross-legged on her little veranda, for hours at night watching the stars, or in the moonlight, seeing the shadows thrown by the moon. It was worth losing one's sleep for those wonderful nights.

There were strict manners on Niue. 'Fanage fei' was the greeting to anyone met on the road. It meant 'Where are you going?' Then you must mention your name and the name of your destination, and then repeat the enquiry on your own account. If cantering along on horseback, you would be long past the first enquirer, and have to catch up as you went along. Frequently, the locals wanted to go on to have a good long chat with Beatrice, as she said herself, her manners out riding must have struck Niue as extremely vulgar.

It would seem that Beatrice took these little breaks from travelling to write her books. She mentions while in Niue, she would often write in the mornings in her little house. However, she was always disturbed by the locals calling. They would squat on the floor and silently watch her, none of them seemed put out by her lack of response.

32 Grimshaw, *In the Strange South Seas*, p. 183.

Sometimes they would come and bring dinner. They didn't join in the eating thereof, but would sit and watch as Beatrice struggled to finish these gargantuan meals. Sometimes she gave some of it to Kuru – her landlord – and his wife, but was always disconcerted about how to repay the donor of the repast. Seeking advice, she visited an old resident to discover how to repay the natives for their generosity. He told Beatrice that the islanders do indeed, expect reciprocity. She would certainly be expected to give presents to all the folk she had become friendly with.

One day when the sea was as calm as a sheet of blue glass, and she was finishing her washing-up (there was no shame about the performance of domestic duties) when a couple of local girls appeared on the grass, their beautiful hair flying loose around their shoulders, and their white cotton dresses tied up above their knees. They were going for a swim and asked Beatrice if she would like to accompany them. Of course she would. She fetched her bathing dress and followed the girls from rock to rock until they arrived at the spot from where they intended swimming. The place looked perfect, the deep turquoise sea beckoned. The girls told her there were no sharks in the area, so they stood ready in their differing swimming attire. The prettier and younger of the two native girls had a bright blue scarf wound round her slim, bronze body; Beatrice was not only aware of the beauty of her surroundings, but she frequently remarked about the beauty of the native people – and this was one of them. The other girl was sturdier and 'plain as a pig'. She smoked a huge pipe, chewed tobacco, and laughed like a hyena. A very contrasting pair.

In they went, the two native girls frequently diving underwater and trying to entice Beatrice to follow them. But although a strong swimmer she could not keep up with the girls underwater, and – surprisingly – found the corals frightening, though they were as clear as day. She didn't like the fish either. On the way back to the surface she became aware of some sort of black trailers – maybe tentacles – emerging from the rocks. She raced for the land, to the huge amusement of the girls. One of them was laughingly blowing bubbles on the surface and suggested that Beatrice would join her, which she did. Some days later, Beatrice was recalling her adventure to a friend who told her the black streamers might well have been a devil-fish which was certainly dangerous. Then, when she asked would there likely have been sharks around, and told about the blowing bubbles act, he said that very likely there would have been, as the girls would have been blowing bubbles to distract the sharks:

> 'Surely they wouldn't bathe, if they knew there were any about?'
>
> 'Oh wouldn't they, though! *They* don't mind them. No native is afraid of anything in the sea.'[33]

This, she believed with a pinch of salt. What with that, and having also seen lots of black and white banded snakes, the brave Beatrice became wary of bathing.

33 Grimshaw, *In the Strange South Seas*, p. 203.

That was, until a few weeks later, when she realised she was swimming with a shark nearby. That was enough. She decided there and then to give up bathing in unprotected tropical waters – for ever. She was very sad to say that it was one of the greatest disappointments of the sunny isles of Eden, with its warm, translucent waters, its rainbow-coloured fish, and attractive companions, but they were too dearly paid for, when sharks, devil-fish and snakes had to be included in the party.

It was traditional in the South Sea Islands, for the few white folk – most of them rival traders – to frequently get together. They all lived simply without any extravagances, or keeping up appearances. They mostly made a living without having to worry too much, so everybody seemed relaxed and contented without any of the excitements of European life. That was, until the long-expected steamer arrived. Then everyone shouted and laughed and got dressed in their best as they went to see what the ship had in store for them. Mostly it was the excitement of food, as island provisions would have become very low.

So indeed it was when the *Duchess* arrived once again at Niue, and it was time for Beatrice to take her leave. She had given and received presents, and put her belongings on board as the big sails were hoisted with all the rattling and flapping associated with setting sail, and off they went, a long way northwards to Penrhyn and Malden Island.

The passengers suffered somewhat at the hands of the cook on this long journey. Most of the food he prepared was awful, as Beatrice described one dish as 'tinned rag of a damp and viscous quality'. With tea that tasted of cockroaches (had she ever actually tasted a cockroach?), and biscuits that were full of copra bugs, so that they had to hammer them on the table in the hope the bugs would fall out. However, it was with a stiff upper lip that she remembered that one did not travel on a Pacific schooner expecting the luxuries of a P&O steamer.

It was a rough passage as far as Apia where they took on board forty native passengers. Then they fell into a very bad storm, carrying away their lifeboat, topsail and topgallant; swamped the passengers' cabin, and totally upset the steward who swore he would never go to sea again. It was dramatic, and Beatrice simply loved it. Going out on deck, clinging on to anything she could find, and hoping the captain didn't see her.

The *Duchess* carried benzoline in tins for the little engine, used for coming and going into harbours. Beatrice was somewhat shocked to find that the native's sleeping place was on top of the tins:

> 'Do you mind the dynamite remaining under your bunk?' asked the ancient mariner shortly after we left Samoa.
>
> *'Under my bunk?'*
>
> 'Yes – didn't you know it was there? The explosives safe is let into the deck just beneath the deck cabin.

I'll move it if you're nervous about it – I thought I'd tell you anyways. But it's the best place for it to be, you see, right amidships.' And the ancient mariner ... spat into the deep.

'What do we want with dynamite anyhow?' asked the bewildered passenger ...

'*We* don't want none. The Cook Islands wants it for reefs.'

'Oh leave it where it is – I suppose it's all the same in the end where it starts from, if it did blow up,' says the passenger resignedly. 'What about the benzoline in the hold, though?'

'Every one's got to take chances at sea,' says the captain, easily. 'The mates have orders to keep the natives from smokin' in the hold at night.' [34]

That night Beatrice looked under her bunk and saw the dynamite. Then she looked out at the sea and smelled – for sure – native tobacco. Hmm, natives smoking, benzoline and dynamite, not a happy mix, but *'a la guerre comme a la guerre'*, and one must not tell tales at sea. Nevertheless, she was not the only one to feel relief as they arrived at Mangaia. The natives, plus the dynamite were safely ashore, and on board the *Duchess* – water tanks filled, and a plenitude of fresh fruit.

Malden and Penrhyn

On they went due north, towards Penrhyn, now some thousand miles away. It was hot on deck, but slightly better than below. Beatrice and the crew teased each other with where they could get the best iced drinks. Late one afternoon they very nearly got their wishes, as a huge waterspout suddenly appeared out of the low grey clouds. The black tower of water came nearer and nearer drawing up to itself a huge cone of wild sea until the two joined forming an enormous black pillar of water from sea to sky:

> across the darkening sea, against the threatening copper-crimson sunset, came this gigantic horror, waltzing over leagues of torn up water in a veritable dance of death, like something blind, but mad and cruel, trying to find and shatter our fragile little ship.[35]

Luckily they were able to tack but remained down-wind of the waterspout. One time it was so close that Beatrice had the impression it was looking down on them. The captain afterwards assured her it was more than 300 yards away, but the base of the tower seemed so close it would at any moment swallow them up and spit them out as so much flotsam. Everyone on board was very quiet and ready for the worst.

After the great waterspout drama, life on board continued as normal; everyone going about the business of sailing the ship northwards through calms and breezes, until

34 Grimshaw, *In the Strange South Seas*, pp. 214–5.

35 Grimshaw, *In the Strange South Seas*, p. 217.

after their thousand mile run, and only about four degrees south of the equator, they arrived at Malden.

This island was totally barren, without a tree, and barely a plant to be seen. So why would anybody live there? Beneath a top crust, there lay the rich droppings of millions of sea birds throughout thousands of years. This dung is called *guano*. As a manure *guano* is a highly effective fertiliser due to its exceptionally high content of nitrogen, phosphate and potassium: nutrients essential for plant growth. Fortunes have been made in the transportation and onward production of the fertiliser.

The schooner left off the natives who had been on the schooner, and took away with them the same number who had finished their yearly stint. The managers did a three-year term on the island before being relieved of their duties.

A day or two after leaving Malden, they sighted Penrhyn, lying five degrees south of Malden. This island was famous both in the South Seas and Europe. The reason for this was its pearl-shell and pearls. Also of note were its semi-amphibious natives, a sad leper colony, and its desolate and remote atmosphere. Nothing grew here but a few coconut and pandanus trees, the natives living almost exclusively on coconuts and fish. They were probably the best and most daring swimmers in the world, and would tackle a shark in its own element, killing it with their long knives.

But it was for the pearl and the pearl-shell – or mother-of-pearl – that the native divers were best known. One afternoon, Beatrice went in a pearling sloop, with three native divers, to watch how they worked. The bed over which the boat stopped was about ninety feet from the surface. The men stripped down to their *pareos*, and then sat on the gunwale for some minutes, quietly meditating. The boat's skipper told Beatrice they were 'taking their wind'. Then, after a few minutes, they suddenly sprang into action and dived off down into the sea. While the anxious spectators waited while the minutes ticked by, the divers were deep down looking for the finest shell. When they popped back up onto the surface, they held some of the most beautiful mother-of-pearl. Back on board, they bowed gravely to Beatrice, presenting her with the shells, and, as Beatrice frequently remarked, apparently not one bit embarrassed by their lack of clothing.

Normally the divers would carry a basket each and fill them before coming up to the surface, when each man then searched his 'catch' for pearls in the hope that he would find a large white specimen worth maybe several hundreds of pounds. The likelihood of such a find was small, but nevertheless the small pearls and the shell would be bought by the visiting schooner captains who would sell it all on to traders. Sometimes the divers became paralysed when they dived too deep and for too long a time. Then when they surfaced, they had to be rubbed for hours with sea water in the hope they would recover. Some times they did and sometimes they died.

The sloop's captain then talked about the sharks:

> 'Sharks? Well, I've seen you poppin' at them from the deck of the *Duchess*, so you

> know as well as I do how many there are. Didn't 'it them, even when the fin was up? That's because you 'aven't greased your bullet, I suppose. You want to, if the water isn't to turn it aside.' ...
>
> 'About the divin'? – Well, I think the naked divin' is very near as safe as the machine, takin' all things. Worst of it is, if a *kara mauaa* comes along, the diver can't wait his time till it goes. No, he doesn't stab it – not inside the lagoon, because there's too many of them there, and the blood would bring a whole pack about. He gets under a ledge of rock, and 'opes it'll go away before his wind gives out. If he doesn't, he gets eat.'[36]

What a terrible way to die, Beatrice thought, caught like a rat in a trap, man-eating shark or the fierce *kara mauaa*. Hiding in a cleft of the coral reef with bursting lungs and eyeballs, waiting, and praying the enemy would swim away.

About two miles out in the lagoon was the leper island, or Molokai, where natives afflicted with leprosy were confined. The day Beatrice visited, some of the inhabitants came down to the beach from their little huts, smiling with excitement at seeing the visiting white woman. Nevertheless, it was impossible not to be aware of the terrible illness that had made outcasts of these people. There were in all, nine lepers on the island, but the others either couldn't, or wouldn't, come out of their huts. A boat came at regular intervals with groceries for the lepers, and Beatrice and her trader had brought a large box of oranges which was greeted with enthusiasm, but which the trader said they would distil into alcohol and get roaring drunk and have a bit of fun for once in their miserable lives.

Penrhyn was one island where Beatrice never quite felt relaxed. She found it lonely and depressing with the threat of death all around – death in the waters of the lagoon, death from leprosy – and would never venture alone into the bush without her little American revolver. Although she had been offered the loan of a bungalow for a week, she declined the offer on the grounds that the water was questionable and flies abounded. Consequently, she slept on board the *Duchess* and went ashore during the daytime, but was glad when the schooner was ready to set sail again as they pointed her bows in the direction of merry Manahiki.

Back to Rarotonga

Although they had some very bad weather en route, after a day or two they arrived in Rakahanga and Manahiki. The *Duchess* made short stops at many of the small islands taking on cargo and flitting off again.

They did, however, stay for a couple of days in Manahiki, which had been fun for everyone enjoying plenty of music and dancing. As the *Duchess* spread her sails to flee southwards again, Shalli, the Cingalese steward leant over the rail, listening to the beat of the drums as they tuned up for another night's partying:

36 Grimshaw, *In the Strange South Seas*, pp. 236–7.

> 'He plenty good place, that,' says Shalli mournfully. 'All the time dancing, singing, eating, no working – he all same place as heaven. O my God, I plenty wish I stopping there, I no wanting any heaven then!'[37]

They were bound for Rarotonga once more, where the steamers came with mail and tourists, and where Beatrice would catch a ship onwards. So it was goodbye to the schooner and life on board the *Duchess Ranfurly.*

Beatrice wrote about her stay in Rarotonga for *The World's Work* magazine:

> There is seldom much certainty as to exact time by the clock at Rarotonga since everyone has a different hour; and the day of the month is little heeded. This pleasant disregard of Father Time is the true secret of the fascination of the South Sea Islands. Imagine a civilised country, where people dine out in evening dress, leave cards, and have 'At Home' days, possessed of only one post a month, no telegrams, no trains, or trams! Imagine the peace that comes of knowing that for four whole weeks after the steamer goes away there can be no disturbance in the even current of life; no great events at home or abroad; no hurry, no worry, no responsibility. People keep young long in Rarotonga; smiles are every-day and all-morning wear. Nobody is rich – rich men don't come down to the islands to keep trading stores, or take up small Government appointments – but everyone has enough and extravagance is impossible, since luxuries are unpurchasable on the island. There are no social distinctions save that between the white race and the brown; all the white residents know each other on a common footing of equality, although in England or New Zealand they would probably be split up into half a score of mutually contemptuous sets.[38]

Having left Rarotonga by steamer, it is unclear whether Beatrice stayed any length of time at the Friendly Isles, or went directly to New Zealand. However, she certainly arrived in Auckland, in early November, on board the two-masted Union steamer, *Rotokino*. She then travelled by ship to Wellington, from where she went to Wanganui. After travelling up the Wanganui River; visiting the Rotorua district, and back to Auckland, she then seems to have gone back to the Friendly Islands, for Christmas 1904.

37 Grimshaw, *In the Strange South Seas*, p. 254.

38 Beatrice Grimshaw, 'An Imperial Wonderland. The Hot-Water Country of New Zealand', in *The World's Work*, Vol. 8 (1906), p. 33. Quoted passage taken from *Dundee Evening Telegraph*, 1st June 1905, p. 6. Beatrice also published 'Life on a South Sea Schooner', in *Pall Mall Magazine*, Vol. 36 (1905), pp. 47–58, 147.

Chapter 7: New Zealand

Diana Arrives in Auckland

Disappointingly, the *Astor* did not go to the Cook Islands, even though they are situated between Tahiti and New Zealand, and we must have sailed quite close to some of them. I was frustrated at missing out on these attractive islands, having to be content with sailing on, following Beatrice to New Zealand.

Some days, when the morning sun was shining and it was very hot, and on one side of the ship the sea is blue, benign and bright, but on the other side, the sea takes on the appearance of crumpled molten metal, and the pale sky seems almost completely drained of any colour.

The *Astor* arrived in Auckland on the morning of 27th November 2016. While Joyce spent time with her family, Martin Caughey, a friend of theirs, took me to see the waterfront.

It is fabulous. Now much of it is industrial, with tankers and container ships, and a commercial harbour for ferries and cruise ships. But there is a yacht basin full of the most glorious yachts including Steinlager that won the Whitbread Round the World Race in 1991, the first year my younger son competed. We drove out of Auckland to some of the posh suburbs and walked down to a tiny, beautiful, secluded beach with about ten old wooden houses leaning towards the sea.

Although I had booked a seat in a bus to go south to Wanganui, Martin insisted that he take me there by car. He then decided we could go via Rotorua, where he has a house on one of the lakes. Martin was incredibly kind and generous with his time, but Rotorua was where I had planned *not* to go as I thought it would be very touristy, and I had already had incredible experiences of volcanic activity in Kamchatka in Russia's Far East. However, Martin was so persuasive, that I graciously accepted his invitation.

Martin

Wanganui, 1904

In 1904 Beatrice was commissioned by the Government Tourist Department to tour, and report on, New Zealand, particularly on the geothermal 'wonderland' of the central North Island.

When she arrived in New Zealand, Beatrice discovered that although one could travel by rail to the already famous geyser area of Rotorua, the only means of transport further south was by early Victorian carriage and horses – or boat. As she was keen to visit the pretty area of Wanganui, a town on the west coast of the North Island, and the only way of getting there was to take a ship to Wellington, and then train to the town of Wanganui, she decided to go here first. From Wanganui she would take a river boat north towards Lake Taupo, cross the lake, and thence across country to Rotorua.

Having at last arrived in Wanganui, Beatrice spent a whole day on the Wanganui River, in a little river steamer, gently making its way upstream. It was a very pretty journey; the solitude and the stillness were what entranced her. Every so often they would see a Māori paddling his dug-out canoe, sliding along beneath the willows. The river banks were covered with bright yellow genista, and wild flowers, and behind that the green hills against a backdrop of purple-headed mountains. Every so often they would pass a little village consisting of a few wooden houses and small tin-roofed churches. Beatrice was enchanted by the Māori people. Their olive-skinned good looks, their mostly fluent English, and their manners and bearing she found very appealing.

At the end of the day, the boat ride finished at Pipiriki, with the passengers going ashore for the night to the smart Pipiriki Hotel perched on a promontory overlooking the river. The following morning there was a coach and horses waiting to take them on the next leg of the journey north.

Paddle Steamer, the Waimarie, still in use.

Pipiriki at the end of Beatrice's river trip

All day the big, strong bay horses pulled their burden through muddy roads and frequent showers, up and up to where the tree ferns and mosses grew. Cattle and wild boar having long since escaped from captivity, had then become feral.

Another hotel, in the shape of a little inn appeared in the evening where everyone enjoyed a good dinner. The coach driver, embarrassed by the bad weather, tried to explain that it was not normal for the time of year, late November and December being high summer in New Zealand. His explanations and excuses at its being 'a most exceptional season', amused Beatrice greatly, he sounded so British, just like at home she thought:

> I feel the raspy air of the English spring nipping my face, and hear the familiar music of the old English lie about the spring weather. It is a dear home-like lie, and makes me feel that New Zealand is indeed what it claims to be – the Britain of the Southern Cross.[39]

Another day in the coach followed, now at about 4,000 feet, and in the shadow of Ruapehu volcano. Wild horses, or brumbies, sped across the buff-coloured plains around the coach. Quite soon they were in a valley where, for the first time, Beatrice and her co-travellers noticed a puff of steam coming out of the earth, and a little river with a veil of steam hovering over it. They were, at last in the hot water country.

39 Grimshaw, *In the Strange South Seas*, p. 316.

They were at Tokaanu, and by then, only ninety miles away from Rotorua, but still with Lake Taupo to cross.

Three hours later, a tiny steamer brought Beatrice across beautiful Lake Taupo, and to The Spa Hotel in the town of Taupo. The hotel, one of the country's oldest, had a constant supply of hot water for cooking and bathing and a place to corral their horses.

Here, in Taupo, Beatrice discovered the beautiful Waikato River, lined by banks thickly covered with golden broom. The road took them beside the river, around multiple bends and gorges, past the Huka Falls, to Wairakei.

Here, Beatrice was informed that her life would not be worth living if she did not visit the Geyser Canon. Everyone who had been there, had a different tale to tell, but all agreed that it was a *must*. So off she went to see if all she had heard was true.

A Mr Ingle was her guide for this remarkable day's adventure. Ingle, a respected academic of volcanology talked Beatrice through the mysteries of the earth beneath her feet and the wonders of what she was looking at above ground. Staircases of pink silica; boiling pools of white Fullers' earth; miniature volcanoes and geysers, and sapphire-coloured ponds where one can see fifty feet of scalding depths. The great Wairakei Geyser, casting up huge fountains of boiling steam every seven minutes; and on and on she went seeing these extraordinary wonders. For sure her informants, earlier that morning, had been quite correct.

They saw the marvellous Arateatea Rapids that afternoon, and managed to squeeze out an afternoon for Karapiti to see the Devil's Trumpet, a fierce and roaring jet of steam, known as the Safety Valve of New Zealand. However, with Rotorua still fifty or so miles away, Beatrice, once again took to her coach, and, via the Valley of the Coloured Lakes, made for the famous centre of the 'hot water country'.

Rotorua

Beatrice found the town of Rotorua very attractive with its red roofs, white verandas and wide sandy streets lined with green trees. It was after all a great tourist mecca. Here were a few omnibuses and motor cars and many four-in-hands all going towards the beautiful lakes that lie near the town. Puffs of white steam rose here and there; beside the road, in people's gardens, and on the beach of Lake Rotorua. Rotorua itself, a great source of healing for all sorts of different ills, was – and still is – a thin crust over a mass of hot springs, charged with different minerals, many of which were used in the Government Sanatorium (today a museum). However, for the healthy it was the sights that were the chief attractions, the resident knowledgeable guides taking the sightseers along narrow paths wandering between the fabulous sights.

Some of the more elderly people would have remembered the impression created all over the world in 1886, by the eruption of the volcano Tarawera, and the destruction of New Zealand's pride and joy – the beautiful Pink and White Terraces of Rotomahana.

Beatrice spent a day going to see the track of the eruption. Originally, in 1840, a very basic church had been built near a place called Wairoa, but it was burnt down by the Māori. Then in 1852, a new mission station, and a school were built at Te Mu, and the Model Village – Te Wairoa – were established, catering for the growing number of tourists, there to visit the Pink and White Terraces.

Mt Tarawera erupted in the early hours of the morning in June 1886, followed by the explosion of Lake Rotomahana which buried Te Wairoa Village under a blanket of mud five or six feet deep. So huge was the eruption, as to leave ash four or five inches deep some miles from the town of Rotorua.

En route to the Buried Village, Beatrice passed two beautiful lakes – The Blue Lake and the Green Lake, their colours brought about by different minerals in the water. On coming to what had been Wairoa village, Beatrice saw that it was then a green and silent place of young trees and grass, broken by the remains of the old hotel. She went by boat on Lake Tarawera to see a close-up of the volcano, and by then, the ash-covered pink and white steps.

Diana in New Zealand, 2016

My drive south to Rotorua with Martin was uneventful. The weather was – as with Beatrice – unseasonably windy and chilly, but dry. The Waikato River accompanied us for much of the journey through the green countryside. Places of interest along the way included the wine growing area of Te Kauwhata and the coal mining town of Huntly where we saw the huge coal-driven power station on the banks of the Waikato. The city of Hamilton is carved in two by this mighty river bringing a unique beauty to the town where you can go river boat cruising.

The township of Cambridge is located in the heart of the Waikato's affluent horse breeding district. It is a very pretty town with lovely tree-lined streets and many well preserved heritage buildings.

The Bridge where Beatrice watched Boys diving for Coins. Rotorua

Tiny Geyser beside Lake Rotorua

Just as I thought, Rotorua was very touristy. It seemed to me that the original purpose for going there – the thermal activity – was no longer paramount. A great number of other tourist activities were available as we became aware of huge adverts, shouting their venues as we drove past. You could go on the Hobbiton Film Set tour; you could go parasailing, or on a zip-line through the forest; visit a Glow-worm cave, or of course a Māori village; and of all bizarre pastimes, experience the ZORB Globe: this involved bouncing around inside a 12-foot inflatable, transparent 'balloon', travelling head-over-heels down a hill. Depending upon your sense of adventure, you might choose either a dry or wet version of this sport.

But I did see the Kia Mau Mahara Memorial, and the bridge where Beatrice watched the local boys jumping into the water below for pennies. On the other side of the Memorial is Whakarewarewa, a thermal village where the Māori still live.

This was where a Wahine woman shouted abuse at us as we tried to enter the village, because it was after opening hours. As the main Thermal Area of Te Puia was also closed, we were unable to go there either. However, there were many little fumaroles popping up here and there, through the pavement and the beach which of course look quite eerie, and made me aware of just how close we were to the centre of the earth.

Ohinemutu is a living Māori village with a meeting house and church, set on the shores of Lake Rotorua and home to a sub-tribe of the Te Arawa, and where I saw the canoe which journeyed from the Pacific homeland of Hawaiiki to New Zealand around 1350AD. The location was chosen for its lakeside setting and abundant geothermal energy, used for cooking, bathing and heating. Here, the dead are 'buried' above ground, so that the corpses do not get cooked in the thermally heated underground.

Ohinemutu became the main centre for the Rotorua region in the early 1870s. The large meeting house there, called the Tamatekapua, is named after the captain of one of the voyaging canoes that arrived in New Zealand. The beautiful carving on the outside of the meeting house is exquisitely decorated by hundreds of inlaid shiny *paua* shell, (the Māori name given to abalone), highlighting the eyes of the carved faces. Unfortunately this building was also closed to visitors.

I would have liked to visit the museum in the government gardens, but it was closed due to the recent earthquake at Kaikoura in 2016. This magnificent Elizabethan-style building was built originally as a bath house, and I believe Beatrice used the bath house when she came to Rotorua in 1904.

Now a Museum, originally a Government Sanatorium and Bath House

Martin's lovely House and Garden

An enormous Tulip Tree greeted us at the gateway to Martin's pretty house, with lawns running down to Lake Okareka. Roses tumbled everywhere, and round the tennis court grew flowering shrubs and English cottage garden plants. A flock of uninvited Canada Geese strutted around above the little beach and, to Martin's annoyance, leaving their droppings all over the lawn.

The following day we set off south towards Wanganui. Like Beatrice, we drove past the beautiful Blue Lake – Tikitapu – and the Green Lake – Rotokakahi – which is sacred to the Māori. Motutawa Island in the middle of the lake is the burial ground of many Māori ancestors. The lake is owned by local *Iwi* (tribes).

I learned from Martin about the Buried Village, visited by Beatrice, when Mt Tarawera erupted in the early hours of the morning on June 10th 1886. Our road then took us alongside the Waikato River and again like Beatrice we gazed down at the Huka Falls.

View from Martin's House, Lake Okareka

Lake Taupo, Beatrice crossed by Boat from Pipariki

We soon arrived at Taupo where we stopped for lunch at a café, and continued on to an imposing old hotel built in 1889 called The Terraces Hotel. Leaving Taupo behind, and driving along the shore of the pretty lake for some time, we sadly did not see the three live volcanoes – Mounts Tongariro, Ngauruhoe and Ruapehu – their heads being hidden in the low cloud.

We were by then at quite a high altitude – the scenery becoming more and more bleak; the trees replaced with tussock grasses. In time, as we drove across the Parapara Range we came across the beginning of the Mangawhero River which we crossed and re-crossed as it curved down beside the road. Now the views became stunning; the rushing river over the years had cut a great cleft in the land, creating huge vistas far into the distance.

We were held up frequently by the traffic lights for road works, rebuilding the wreckage caused by the recent earthquake in the South Island. Adding to this, the river had flooded during the winter causing further damage. We arrived at Wanganui in the early evening.

My arrival at Whanganui

I cannot think my two days in Wanganui would have been much like Beatrice's, although Braemar House – my Bed and Breakfast establishment across the road from the river – fitted in well with the Victorian Era, being an old timber house with elegant verandas. I checked in and deposited my rucksack and, joining Martin again, made for his sister-in-law's house. With her husband Ross, they had very kindly invited me to dinner along with Martin. A delightful evening ensued, with me getting a taxi back to my abode, around 10 p.m.

Then, horror of horrors I couldn't find my camera! A sobering, minute search of my room revealed nothing. All I could think was that it was either in Martin's car, or in the taxi. A very sleepless night ensued.

In the morning I told my host Clive, of my loss. He e-mailed Martin, who mailed back saying it wasn't in the car. Then he phoned the taxi company who were sympathetic but said they would have to wait until the taxi driver woke up as he was off duty. There was nothing for it but to forget about the camera and go and enjoy the river trip, literally in the wake of Beatrice. It was a grey day, but I was really looking forward to being, quite possibly, on the very same boat that Beatrice went on – either the *Wairua*, or the paddle steamer, the *Waimarie*. Certainly, these were the two boats working the river while Beatrice was there.

Both boats were built on the Isle of Dogs by Yarrow and Co in London, joining the famous Hatrick and Co, Whanganui River Steamer fleet in November 1904. The two boats were shipped out to Wanganui in kit form to have the topsides and all the woodwork finished on the banks of the river. In order to avoid the many obstacles under the water, a unique form of propulsion is used – the propeller is housed in a tunnel. The water is drawn up into this and then thrust out of the stern past the vessel's rudders, enabling the boat to work in very shallow water.

It was a real Irish day, cool, overcast and drizzling – not normal for that time of year! I walked the few hundred yards to where the old boats were moored; the banks of the Whanganui covered with purple wild sweet-pea and nasturtiums tumbling down towards the water. Young plane trees had been planted along the footpath, their beautiful 'painted-on' trunks glistening in the drizzle. I was early, but Sam Mordey the boat-owner was expecting me as I boarded the *Wairua*. He and his partner were really interested in my quest for Beatrice, as we chatted about her before the other

The Wairua which took me up the Whanganui River, and might have been the boat Beatrice used

passengers came on board for our casting off at 11 a.m. It might well have been the *Wairua* which took Beatrice upriver.

A few pretty houses lined the river bank with gardens running down to the water. Soon the houses ran out and it became hilly and rocky with white cliffs above the water and high peaky hills. The river is tidal up to above Wanganui town, and it was then high water. Even against the wind and ebbing tide we were making eight knots. At 12 p.m. we arrived at the wooden jetty of Upocongaro. We went ashore and I went for a good walk, past The Avoca Hotel and café and up the little Upo River. After weeks of company I was on my own.

I took a few deep breaths and tried not to think about my camera. It was quiet and peaceful with just birdsong breaking the silence. I passed some gardens brimming with roses. They were glorious colours, but not one of them was scented. For me, the whole beauty of a rose is not only to look glorious, but to be perfumed.

After a couple of poached eggs in a café, I walked to a little church with a pointed spire. Evidently, many years ago the shingles, with which the spire had been roofed, had rotted. So the parishioners found some kerosene containers, broke them up and cut them into little tiles with which to renew the spire. The church was built in 1878, so Beatrice would have motored upstream past it.

It was still raining when we returned to Wanganui and I was still disconsolate about my camera, so decided to walk up Victoria Avenue – the main street – and have a look at the Victorian shop-fronts. The first one on the left-hand-side had a splendid red and grey stone and brickwork front, the wording above announcing AE Kitchen. Dispensing Chemist. Est 1858. Further up the street on the right-hand-side and next door to George's Fisheries, was the Embassy Cinema, a brilliant example of an Art Deco frontage. On up and there was a Bank of New South Wales, same era, but no written date. Then, on the corner stood the Rutland Arms Hotel.

I heard later that the Rutland was built in 1849 by Sgt William Spiers-Russell, and is one of the few city hotels to remain on its original site. It was burnt out in 1880, 1903, and 1946, each time rising from the ashes. In 1986 the Rutland closed and all fittings were put up for auction prior to demolition. Luckily, the demolition didn't proceed, and the derelict building was bought in 1993 by two local Wanganui men and restored to its present glory.

Down a side street on my way to find the library and museum (both shut), was a little theatre which, it was evident had at one time been the railway station, and where Beatrice, presumably, would have arrived at from Wellington.

With a heavy heart I returned to Braemar House. Clive met me and said, that no, the taxi driver did not have the camera. Then, as though waiting for the punch line, told me that Martin had phoned again to say that yes, he had found my camera in the car, and would give it to me back in Auckland. Wehey! I could have kissed Clive, the sense of relief was so great. Instead, curbing my emotions, I asked him for a restaurant he could recommend. He told me there was a Thai place up six blocks that he thought was OK. A little later, I wandered up the six blocks and, guided by the delicious smell of Thai cooking, found that the Restaurant was a 'carry-out' place and was not licensed. I ordered a meal and sat down to eat some of it, without the desired glass of wine. Not quite the celebration I had had in mind.

My flight back to Auckland was in a little turbo-prop plane, holding thirty-three people. After about fifteen minutes I could see, emerging from the clouds, the striated snowy top of one of the volcanoes Martin and I had passed on our way south two days previously. Even as I watched, the cloud cover obliterated it from view.

As promised, Martin met me at the airport with my camera, and Joyce had had a lovely few days with her sisters. So we were both happy people as we set off on the next leg of our journey.

The one huge difference between Beatrice's travels and ours was of course air travel, with today's constraints of passports, immigration, customs, and security. None of these impinged on Beatrice's travels. Passports as we know them didn't come into use until 1914. There was no such thing as 'security', and what is more, she would have had porters meeting every ship and train to deal with her large luggage. Now, with a lot of flights in front of us, we had all the modern international travel restrictions to deal with, as we made ready for our trip to Fiji and Vanuatu – Beatrice, again outdoing us by first going to the Friendly Isles.

Chapter 8: Friendly Islands

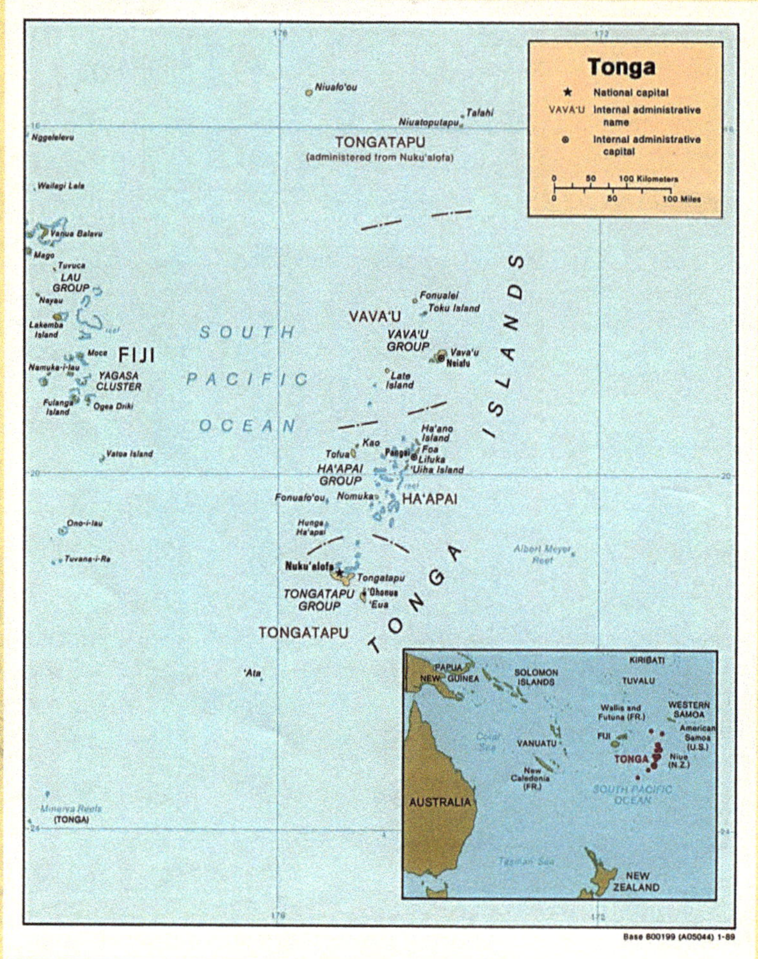

The Friendly Islands, or the Kingdom of Tonga, is today, a Polynesian sovereign state and archipelago comprising 169 islands of which thirty-six are inhabited, and lying almost 1000 miles west of the Cook group. When Beatrice was there, it had been a protectorate of Britain since 1900. Beatrice landed here from the Union steamer, SS *Rotokino*. The Tongans were a partially Christianized, strong, handsome race.

Beyond the wharf at Nukualofa lay the town, consisting of some grassy streets edged by small houses and stores. The native peoples got around their island by horse, or on foot, striding along in their own inimitable style. The sand beside the wharf was silver-white, scattered with huge fluted clam shells. Quite close to the wharf lay the two-storeyed palace, home of the de-throned king – surrounded by graceful verandas and red-coated sentries who marched up and down all day beside the large gates.

Beatrice had been promised an audience with the 'king', George Tubou II. However, before long the invitation was repealed. The reason for this was that Beatrice had become friendly with the High Commissioner of the Western Pacific. He was visiting Tonga to remonstrate with the 'king' on certain governmental inconsistencies, and the very fact that she had met the HC, was enough for George Tubou to consider her an enemy.

This 'king', was not behind the door when choosing a wife. He first of all asked the Emperor of Germany if he could find him a German princess of marriageable age. When this was turned down, he tried a princess of Hawaii, with the same declination. Eventually he proposed to no less than two young princesses of good standing from his own country, named Lavinia and Ofa. Both were happy to oblige, but George was unable to make up his mind which girl to choose. A date was set, and the invitations sent out. The bride at the last minute was decided upon, named as Princess Lavinia. Poor Princess Ofa was devastated at the rebuff. The wedding day reception went at full swing, with a magnificent tiered wedding cake. The 'king', in an act of apology and consolation for not being made his wife, sent the bottom tier of his wedding cake to poor Princess Ofa:

> Princess Ofa was not proud; she had been beating her head on the floor-mats all morning and pulling out handfuls of her long black hair, but when the consolatory cake arrived, she accepted it promptly and ate it.[40]

Princess Lavinia duly gave birth to a daughter, Sālote Mafile'o Pilolevu who became the first Queen regnant and third Monarch of the Kingdom of Tonga from 1918 to her death in 1965. She attended the coronation of Queen Elizabeth in London in 1953.

Tonga enjoyed one of the most pleasant climates on the Pacific Islands. The heat was never excessive and fevers were unheard of, the few white residents enjoying excellent good health. The islands were seldom visited by travellers except for an hour or two during the steamer's time in port, but mostly the English traveller left Tonga out of his or her itinerary, and not a bad thing, according to Beatrice.

There was no hotel. The only place to stay was a public house – not at all suitable for Miss Grimshaw. So she rented a small bungalow almost on the beach beside the cool green water of the lagoon, and where she would set up housekeeping – managing on her own. The little garden held a plethora of fruit and coconut trees, so she lived almost entirely on fruit and vegetables. Most evenings she enjoyed a swim in the lagoon under a star-lit sky, the sea gently rocking one to and fro in the big swell from outside the reef.

Beatrice, as was her wont, frequently went driving with a horse and little buggy to explore the island, one day venturing to a place known as the Wood of the Bats. As she approached the wood, she could hear the shrill chittering and squealing long before

40 Grimshaw, *In the Strange South Seas*, p. 261.

arriving at the wood. But there they were, hundreds of fruit bats – or Flying Foxes, with dark furry bodies as big as cats hanging upside down from the trees. The smell was terrible with all the droppings. But nobody dared to kill them. They were considered sacred to the Tongans, who believed that if ever the bats deserted the island, the country would fall. By night, the bats would fly off to raid the local banana and mango trees.

One day Beatrice was invited to a chief's Kava Party. Kava was – and is – the great national drink of many of the South Sea Islands, made from the hard woody root of the *Piper Methysticum*. It looks like muddy water, is not very intoxicating, and initially does not taste very nice. The root used to be chewed to make it mushy and then spat out and mixed with water, but by Beatrice's time, it was pounded with a stone.

She was the only white person present, everyone squatting on mats in the chief's house, and all well dressed. Beatrice was in a smart *demi-toilette* evening dress, because she was the special guest.

The meagre light from a hurricane lamp threw shadows on the rapt faces of the kava makers as they went through the ceremony. There were chants and responses, all very native, until at last the main kava maker fell back exhausted, the huge bowl of kava ready for consumption in front of him. Then came the calling of names in order of precedence; the chief first; then Beatrice, and so on down through the ranks. She accepted the cup of kava and swallowed it all. The girl who served the kava walked round in a stooped position, it being very bad form to appear higher than the chief. After everyone had been served, the chief held a conversation with Beatrice through an interpreter, explaining the four different ways of drinking kava, each with its own etiquette. They had just enjoyed the highest form, only permitted to chiefs.

Beatrice spent Christmas 1904 in Tonga. It seems she had been recommended being there for the celebrations. She went to Midnight Mass on Christmas Eve at a church near the shore, loving the moonlight shining on the ironwood trees. Someone had spent a lot of time filling half coconut shells with oil, and a wick of twisted fibre, which, when lit provided a clear starry light like a perfect land-based Milky Way. Inside the church, surrounded by the sweet-smelling frangipani, the choral singing was wonderful; the Tongan music, famous for its sheer magnificence and volume. After the Mass Beatrice returned to her little house among the ironwoods and the peaceful sound of the trade winds.

By her own admission, Beatrice was lazy in the Friendly Isles. She took no notes on the politics or economy of the islands, she just simply enjoyed every minute she spent there.

In due course the big Union steamer arrived in port and Beatrice went away with her to Samoa, the island made so famous by Robert Louis Stevenson (he lived there for four years before his death in 1894). The three-day run was broken by stops at the islands of Haapai and Vavau, eventually arriving in Apia, the capital of Samoa.

Chapter 9: Samoa

When Beatrice arrived up on deck she was met by a number of native gentlemen walking about. It was extremely hot with not a breath of wind. But the gentlemen were unaware of the heat, dressed as they were in only a white British bath towel trimmed with red, tied about their waists in the usual South Pacific custom.

There was always a different name for this simple garment, depending which island you were on – in Samoa it was called a *lava-lava*. Beatrice was not one bit blind to the good looks of the native men:

> Coupled to the almost complete absence of clothes, and the copper skins, it was enough to make one perfectly giddy at first. But afterwards, one grew used to it, and even came to compare the average white man's manner disadvantageously with the unsurpassable self-possession and calm of the unclothed native.[41]

At last everyone was ready to go ashore in the usual one-sided seaside town, when suddenly as they were approaching the hotel, a huge waterspout approached, totally transforming the calm of the day. While many of the locals had been dressed in their best to welcome in the strangers off the steamer, suddenly everyone started to undress, running down the street in their *lava-lavas*, clutching their clothes as best they could. Both Beatrice and the rest of her shipmates laughed and laughed at this transformation scene, totally forgetting to try and keep themselves dry, and so arriving at their hotel drenched to the skin.

Beatrice only stayed a few days in Apia before becoming bored with tourist attractions: 'how can one study native customs, dining at a *table d'hote* and living in a great gilt and glass hotel, situated in the midst of a busy street?'[42] So she was delighted when she found she was able to take a little launch to visit a native village at Falepuna, travelling south-west along the coast, enjoying the big rollers tossing the little boat about, and glorying in the views of the blue and green mountains of Upolu.

It was only about twenty miles of a run to their destination and the pretty little port of Falefa where Beatrice thought it was the most glorious spot she had ever visited. She landed on the beach accompanied by a half-caste Samoan woman and a New Zealand girl as they proceeded to their accommodation. This splendid house, built on Samoan lines, was owned by a high chief. There was not a nail in the whole construction, the building being held together by miles and miles of sinnet (plaited coconut fibre). The three travellers were given a great welcome, and a huge feast was laid out for all to enjoy.

Everybody was astonished that this white woman was travelling alone. They had seen white women travelling with their husbands, but never, never venturing from 'Beritania' all alone. So there was some difficulty at first in placing Beatrice according to Samoan etiquette. Eventually – quite possibly because of her height and bearing – she was classed as a male chief, the young chiefs of the district coming in the evenings to call upon her. The women did not call upon her officially, but she had many bathing and fishing excursions in their pleasant company.

41 Grimshaw, *In the Strange South Seas*, p. 283.

42 Grimshaw, *In the Strange South Seas*, p. 284.

Her week's stay, although totally uneventful was very happy. Dawn on a South Sea island was something Beatrice never became blasé about. Her kind hosts would start their day as soon as it was light. Their early mornings were easy. They would get up, put away the mosquito nets and, still clad in the *lava-lava* from the previous night and day, would take soap, a bundle of coconut fibre and a clean *lava-lava*, wander down to the nearest river where they would have a great washing of bodies and *lava-lavas*. Mostly the natives ate just twice a day – around noon, and again some time in the evening. Sometimes Beatrice would get up and go with her young hostess, Kafi, to a lovely spot on the bay shaded by trees from the fierce sun, and where a huge waterfall thundered down the cliff face and into the sea. Here, the two women would swim and dive for hours at a time, sometimes getting into an old canoe and paddling it almost under the spray of the waterfall. Kafi also frequently alarmed her guest while swimming far from land, by calling 'S'ark', in the full knowledge that Beatrice was terrified of the creatures.

Beatrice had stopped carrying a watch or a clock, and soon got to know more or less the time both by the sun and the heat of the day. The Samoan did what he wanted – and no more. There never seemed to be raised voices in a Samoan house. Husbands never came home drunk to ill-use their wives. For sure, the Samoan had his faults – sensuality and indolence were noticeable to the upright Miss Grimshaw, but it was very little, she thought, in comparison with the ordinary European.

One moonlit night Beatrice awoke to the sound of thirty or so women and girls wearing short *lava-lavas*, laughing and splashing about in the sea near her house. Nothing daunted, Beatrice shed one or two of her garments, and ran to join in the fun. It transpired that everyone was engaged in a fishing expedition dragging a huge net through the water; the splashing was to frighten the little fish into the net. As Beatrice joined in, she was entranced by the scene:

> the moon shone down on a cluster of beautiful gold-bronze figures, graceful as statues, stretching out their small pretty hands and wild curly heads, diamond-gemmed with scattered drops of water, over the gathered-in net, now sparkling and quivering with imprisoned life.[43]

The captured fish were then tipped into big woven baskets, and the girls continued with their fishing for most of the night, obviously making sport from the necessity of catching fish. But surprisingly, Beatrice returned to her house after an hour or so, loaded with presents of fish:

> It was quite absurd, but I wanted to go to bed, silly and inferior white person that I was! So I crept under my calico tent, and 'turned in', feeling amid the stir and chatter, the singing and wandering to and fro, of those moonlit small hours,

43 Grimshaw, *In the Strange South Seas*, p. 299.

> exceedingly like a child that has to follow nurse and go to sleep, while all the grown-ups are still enjoying themselves downstairs.[44]

Early one morning, back in her posh hotel, Beatrice was woken by her '*flennie*' – Fangati, the daughter of a chief. A '*flennie*' was a very close friend in Samoan. She was also a young woman of good birth and bearing among whose various duties it was to welcome, entertain, and look after visitors to the town or village.

She had come to invite Beatrice to one of the venues that she most enjoyed. That was bathing in a pool which opened onto a sliding rock over which one plunged thirty feet or so. Beatrice had not intended going over the sliding rock, but as all the others were having fun doing it, dressed in their tiny *lava-lavas*, she got into her extravagant bathing dress, and very hesitantly into the river, then clinging tightly to the rock on either side of her, and looking over her own toes, let herself go:

> It was all over in a minute. Just an unclasping of unwilling hands from the safe black rocks, a fierce tug from the tearing stream, an exceedingly unpleasant instant when one realised that there was no going back now at any price, and that the solid earth had slipped away as it does in the ghastly drop of a nightmare dream; then nothing in the world but a long loud roar, and a desperate holding of the breath, while the helpless body shot down to the bottom of the deep brown pool and up again – and at last, the warm air of heaven filling one's grateful lungs in big gasps as one reached the surface, and swam across to the other side of the pool, firmly resolved on no account to do it again, now that it was over.[45]

They finished the day with a wonderful picnic prepared by the mother of a half cast American/Samoan girl. In the encroaching mauve twilight, the journey home in the buggies was enlivened by everyone singing the sweet, rather sad song, written some years previously by a native Samoan, and by then famous throughout the world – the appropriate – '*Goodbye my Flennie.*'

It would appear that Beatrice must have spent quite some time in Samoa and environs as there are no dates recorded of her movements until April 1905 when she was in Fiji. There was in fact a steamer which called at Apia en route to Sydney, and may well also have called at Fiji, being close by. So it would seem logical that she would have gone to Fiji from Samoa. On the other hand, was there ever anything at all logical about Beatrice's movements?

44 Grimshaw, *In the Strange South Seas*, pp. 299–300.

45 Grimshaw, *In the Strange South Seas*, pp. 309–310.

Chapter 10: Fiji

Viti Levu

Beatrice arrived in Suva, the capital of Fiji, sometime in April 1905. She had been commissioned by the Fijian government 'to see what value the country might be for possible settlers'. The Governor, Sir Everard im Thurn, later declared himself pleased with the resulting publicity.

As ever, when she arrived up on deck, there was the familiar glittering water of the bay, backed by peaks, three and four thousand feet high.

The arrival

A quay ran out from the land where there were custom officials and local people – Fijians, Indians, Samoans, Chinese, natives and whites, all dressed in white and carrying parasols.

Fiji was discovered by Tasman in 1643 and Captain Cook sailed within sight of it in 1774. Bligh, after the mutiny on the Bounty in 1789 also passed by on his extraordinary journey in his little boat en route to Timor, and in 1792, returned in the *Providence* to make some observations. But it was not until 1835 that the first missionaries arrived, ending cannibalism and bringing their own form of civilisation. Cannibalism had been rife in Fiji, exacerbated when the infamous Ratu Seru Epenisa Cakobau – phonetically, King Thakombau – came to power when whites were murdered and war among the natives was continual. In 1855, however, the United States government, incensed by the brutal murder of some shipwrecked sailors, demanded £9,000 compensation, which, of course the native king was quite unable to pay. Then some of the warlike tribes of Tonga threatened to invade Fiji, and it seemed that a Tongan conquest was imminent. Thakombau, now in desperation, asked the British for help – finding he had to decide between being invaded by the Tongans, or handing over the country to Britain. He chose the latter and in 1874 offered Fiji unconditionally to England.

Fiji, when Beatrice was there, was a British Crown Colony. It consisted of 155 islands, the two main islands Viti Levu and Vanua Levu were well watered and well wooded, and could have supported – it was said – three times the population that then existed. The climate was, and is, hot and damp. A day in the capital, Suva, without rain was rare.

Beatrice saw that the Fijian was a mix between Melanesian and Polynesian. They were law abiding pleasant people; splendid singers and dancers; and kept under control by their chiefs and the Armed Native Constabulary. Sadly, the population seemed to be on the decline yet again as a result of diseases brought by white people.

There was a healthy amount of trade from the island, mainly in the exportation of sugar. Bananas were also grown and exported to Australia, as well as peanuts, copra, tea and coffee.

After sight-seeing in Suva, and having seen something of local society – which Beatrice found tiresomely like society at home, although so hospitable and kindly that one had to forgive it – she decided it was time to see just what the native and his life were like, and what value the country might be for possible settlers.

She saw that almost everything grew well on the island, with vanilla, turmeric, and many other herbs and spices growing practically wild. There were thousands of acres unused, and not one hundredth developed.

Beatrice tried to get information about the land and travel from people she met, and from government sources, suggesting that she should go and see for herself. But as always, everyone came up with the same response. A white woman should not go travelling unaccompanied. She enquired why not, and were there still cannibals around. 'Certainly not' was the response to that query. Eventually, she met a government dignitary who was brisk and informative when she asked about riding across the island. He said it was certainly rough, but not too rough:

> 'Certainly, go if you fancy it; you'll have a royal time. The natives are capital fellows; they'll make a queen of you everywhere you go, and you'll see some of the finest scenery in the world. Firearms? Well, you might as well have a Colt with you as not; ... Anything else I can do for you? ... Well, goodbye, and good luck!'[46]

At last someone took her seriously.

Beatrice then had to make preparations for her trip. She didn't hide her excitement when she described this, never having been 'off the road' before. She hoped that by riding, she might be able to cover between twenty and thirty miles a day, so she had to organise a horse to start with. Then saddlery for it; the correct clothes for herself, and a steel trunk to keep it all in. Cooking receptacles and dry goods such as tinned meat, tea, sugar and biscuits were added to the list. Then she engaged Gideon, a retired native soldier of the Governor's armed constabulary, to act as interpreter and guide.

46 Beatrice Grimshaw, *From Fiji to the Cannibal Islands*. Illustrated edition. (London: Eveleigh Nash, 1907), p. 33.

At Ba, the sugar refining town in the north of the island, she found two more carriers – Joni and Nasoni. Here she describes herself as being 'absolutely inflated with pride' as she set off on her borrowed, good Australian horse, and her three retainers walking in her wake, towards the lonely mountain country between Ba and Sigatoka – her final destination.

Beatrice rode all day in the heat of the tropical sun wearing a 'Holland coat' over a cotton blouse. These famous cotton/linen mix coats were made-to-measure in London. They covered one from top to toe – even when riding side-saddle. She also, of course wore a locally made grass hat. Vividly she describes the light:

> But the molten-gold glory of the searching sun at high noon – the minute, photographic clearness of the 'thousand shadowy-pencilled valleys' on the far horizon hills – the fullness of light and life poured out by those blinding rays that strike down through the slender bush foliage as through glass, and bleach the very colour out of the shadeless, quivering sky – these things, to the traveller from the dim grey North, are worth all the heat and glare ... the warm wind in the feathered guinea-grass; the long, unknown track winding ahead into the heart of wild, battlemented, purple hills – this was the beginning of my hundred miles' march through the great island. A happy augury of happy days to come.[47]

All morning she rode over rolling uplands of pandanus prairie, the air growing a little cooler as she attained height, her men loping along, catching up with her each time she stopped to look around. She thought her men a 'dandy trio', dressed in white singlets and coloured '*sulus*' – the local Fijian kilt. They carried both her luggage and their own small boxes with clean clothes and shirt; looking glass and comb, and tobacco. They always went barefoot.

When Beatrice suggested stopping for lunch and a cup of tea, Gideon quietly reminded her that there was no water, and they must continue until they would come to a stream. Beatrice felt a proper fool, remembering to be aware that there were no taps in the Naloto Mountains. Later, when they stopped to make a fire, they had no matches. However, nothing daunted, one of her boys was able to make fire by rubbing a splinter of bamboo up and down in a little hole he had cut in a log. It took some minutes before a small tongue of flame appeared, with the other lad quickly adding dry grass to the flame, and behold, they had fire. Two lessons learned already.

As they continued upwards, the track became so steep that Beatrice had to dismount from her horse and lead him. It was becoming late when they arrived at the summit of the mountain, and Gideon said they would stay at a village called Nandrunga a couple of miles away. So it was then a scramble downhill in the growing dusk. Beatrice was about to sleep in a native village, far from any white people, and as far as she knew, where no white woman had ever visited.

47 Grimshaw, *From Fiji to the Cannibal Islands*, pp. 36–7.

She began to feel quite nervous, and resolved to keep her little revolver beside her – just in case.

In the pitch dark the quartet forded a river and at last came to a high palisade of bamboo, surrounding a cluster of houses. All was silent as they entered through the gate, but her men soon woke up the inhabitants of the biggest house and went to look for a lantern. They then simply took over the house, entering as was the custom by the side door, and chasing the sleepers who watched this invasion with amazement. The house was quite large, standing on a platform of stones and earth, reached by a few steps of coconut logs. Not a nail was to be found – everything laced and tied together by sinnet. The natives prepared a meal for the travellers of banana-leaf platters of baked yam, which Beatrice augmented with a tin of beef. She ate in lonely state until she had had sufficient, when her men and her hosts tucked in to the remains, each one generously offering the delicacies to one another.

It was by now time for bed. Beatrice's men erected her mosquito net over the huge bed, and told the natives that the women might stay in the house with the white lady, but not the men. This, the men found hilarious at the very idea of anyone objecting to sleep in a mixed-sex crowd, while the women fairly crowed in triumph at, for once, getting the best of the deal. So now the tables were turned, and after the men had gone, the women ran about waiting on Beatrice's every whim. They loved her long straight hair and her wonderful clothes. One elderly woman was so taken with Beatrice's pale, smooth skin that she took her arm and gently tried it with her teeth, and, possibly remembering the cannibal days, remarked *'Vinaka na kakana!'* (what good food). Apparently the forearm was the choicest and most tender body-part. Although she was aware of the rats, bats and cats scuttling about, Beatrice slept well surrounded by all the women asleep on the floor, until six o'clock when dawn slid its grey fingers through the slatted walls. The women all woke also, and took Beatrice to the river where they showed her a lovely deep hole to bathe in. She bathed alone as the women sat watching her and singing.

The little village looked wonderfully quaint in the daylight. There were only about a dozen houses all sitting on top of their separate platforms. Everything was new to Beatrice – the scanty *sulus* worn without any upper body clothing and the big frizzled hair dos of the men, displaying a ragged halo at least a foot wide, and so much larger than the neat cut hair of the townsfolk. The men of Fiji were immensely proud of their huge hair, spending hours oiling and shaping it.

In light rain, the quartet set off on their second day's excursion. For many miles there was no sign of habitation, until looking down from a windy height they found Tambale, a tiny village nestling far below.

Gradually the grassland became interspersed with patches of yam or taro, and an odd banana tree.

They were approaching the village of Nambukuya, the principal village of the district where the *mbuli* – or local chief – lived. It reminded Beatrice of Tennyson's 'Island Valley of Avilion' describing it thus:

> I saw it on that golden afternoon, sleeping among the slanting shadows of its rich orange-groves, in the deep round cup of a highland valley. On three sides of the little town the hills rose up like fortress walls of purple porphyry, but on the fourth, the lip of the cup was broken, and through the break one saw, dim and delicate and shadowy-pencilled, the far-off pale blue plains of half a province lying below.[48]

Most of the inhabitants were away working at their gardens. So she boldly jumped her horse over the bars acting as a gate, and into the village. Much of the land was terraced where some large-leaved plants of the Ndalo grew in the water from a little stream, dropping from terrace to terrace until it disappeared. Their noisy arrival roused one or two of the locals who assured them they were expected, as news of the group's journey was the talk of the province. Apparently the *Mbuli* was away on business, and so the wife of the native mission teacher invited the group to stay at their house. Indeed, as Beatrice saw, it was as big as a ballroom and cool as a cave. There were no windows, but through the three doors, beyond the usual raised grassy platform, the different views were exquisite.

Of course there was the usual great excitement from the villagers when they returned from their gardens. But the natives of Nambukuya were polite and considerate, so that when Beatrice lay down for a sleep they slipped away, leaving her alone to take a nap. Later on came another huge feast and another kava festival initiated by the local *Turanga ne Koro* – the head man of the village. By this time Beatrice knew about this custom and was able to speak her replies to the *Turanga*, and able to drink enough of the kava to pass herself. Although she very much disapproved of the quantity drunk by some of the locals, she turned a blind eye – aware of how much her three men enjoyed the ceremony, waking late and still sleepy the following morning.

The travellers stayed for the Sunday services. Three times during the day they assembled in the church – a large native house – for more praying and singing. No work was done except for cooking. It was evident to Beatrice that Sundays were exactly to the liking of the native Fijian; one of their favourite occupations being sitting and chanting in chorus for many hours at a time. It was just bad luck for a white person to find themselves trapped in a church where he, or she, just had to endure it. But Beatrice was restless, and the following morning at daybreak, she roused her men and rode away from the delightful village.

48 Grimshaw, *From Fiji to the Cannibal Islands*, p. 54.

The going was red clay and very slippery. Beatrice's good horse, Tanewa, knew the path, not wanting to go forward. Soon, with Beatrice still riding, and urging him on, he stopped at the top of a steep down-slope, where the path fell away on one side and his hind legs gave way. With a loud grunt, he sat there, looking for anything like a circus horse with his forelegs planted squarely in front of him. Most horses would have struggled, but Tanewa coolly looked round at his mistress still sitting uncomfortably on his slanting back. Beatrice feeling very apologetic dismounted and the horse struggled to his feet to continue their downward trek. All day, back in the saddle, she rode towards the village of Natuatuathoko, Beatrice was aware of how good the land would be for settlers, and resolved to put this to the Governor on her return to Suva.

The Sigatoka River was on their right-hand-side as the quartet approached this mountain fortress, surrounded by orange, lemon and guava trees. The track began gradually rising, leaving the river behind, until in front of them stood a huge Fijian house, fifty or sixty feet high, covered with men re-thatching the roof, who, as soon as they spied the visitors, raised a huge yell in greeting, crying '*sombo, sombo*' (wonderful). They followed her into the town admiring her clothes and her height, and that she must be a chief. Her three men responded with tales of how rich Beatrice was; her father having so many cattle in England that he wanted to bring them to Fiji, and that she was an intimate friend of the King. All the while Beatrice, amused by these fictions, decided that Nambukuya was no longer her favourite village – that honour now belonged to Natuatuathoko:

> Little enchanted town, how you linger in my memory, though I spent only a night and a morning in your wonderful citadel. How often I think of you, as I first saw you from the grassy orange avenue below, perched high upon your green pinnacle like a fairy town in an old-world story-book.[49]

Much as Beatrice had fallen in love with her 'fairy fortress', she had to keep going, and so, after only one night there, she and her men sallied forth, the richer of such generous hospitality.

After Natuatuathoko, the journey became inextricably involved with the Sigatoka River. All day the four of them had to cross and re-cross the tumbling river, in between times climbing up and down the hills that bordered its banks. By dusk the river had become constantly deep and fast flowing. While the men tied Tanewa to a tree, as he was to be returned to his owner the following day, Beatrice decided that as they must ford the river, and as there was no boat to hand, they would have to swim across. This news she relayed to Gideon who, rolling a cigarette, replied 'All right sir'.

49 Grimshaw, *From Fiji to the Cannibal Islands*, p. 75.

Beatrice had prepared for this, and was already wearing her bathing dress under her riding habit which she removed in preparation for the swim:

> 'Plenty s'ark here.'
> I stopped at the laces of the second shoe, and asked anxiously: 'What shark? All same Réwa shark stop here?'
> 'Yes, sir. All same. Plentee.'[50]

For all her bravado, Beatrice really was terrified by sharks and she knew that in the Réwa River they could swim thirty or so miles upstream and bite off arms and legs from careless swimmers. The men didn't seem to mind, but she certainly did. Then quietly, Nasoni mentioned about an *mbili-mbili* coming. Beatrice had no idea what he was talking about, until she looked up and saw a small bamboo raft, paddled by a native, coming across the river from the other side. The *mbili-mbili* was a raft made from bamboo, tied together and used by the locals to take produce, and sometimes people, downstream. After it was unloaded, the raft would be abandoned to make its way to the sea – and oblivion.

However, Beatrice was very glad to see the raft, and having piled her saddle and all her other gear on board set off across the Sigatoka to the town of Lemba Lemba. Here she was met at the water's edge by the *Buli*, or high chief of the district, a huge man with a voice to match, effusive in his greetings, and who helped her ashore. However, the ascent from the river up to the town was almost unscaleable, being almost perpendicular, and very slippery with recent rain. But the *Buli* roared directions at his men, who scurried off bringing back a couple of spades for making steps, while the *Buli* helped Beatrice, as together they climbed up all the way to the top, and into the *Buli*'s house.

Here, as usual, was another great feast, of which Beatrice took her fill before either her host or her three men were allowed to start eating. After everyone had fed, the *Buli* questioned Beatrice's men about her, often roaring with laughter as they embellished one anecdote after another. It was then explained to him, that she would want the whole house to herself that night, with his wife to keep her company. The very idea that he should be turned out of his lordly house in favour of his wife, struck the *Buli* as the funniest thing he had ever heard, laughing so much that his ample belly shook as he bid Beatrice goodnight, and waddled off with Gideon to a neighbouring house, to continue their conversation.

The following morning Beatrice realised she now had no means of transport. Her faithful horse, Tanewa, had been returned to his owner, and the boat that she thought she had organised to come for her had not arrived. So, nothing for it but to take the *mbili-mbili* down-river to the next town. Accordingly, her possessions were

50 Grimshaw, *From Fiji to the Cannibal Islands*, p. 82.

once again lifted on to the raft, and she and her men clambered on board to float gently downstream, using only the punting pole as an oar. The journey was slow, and gradually water seeped in through the bamboo poles wetting Beatrice's feet and some of her belongings, but there was ample time to view their beautiful surroundings, and always the murmuring river winding ahead against a backdrop of soft, mauve hills.

Gradually the little riverside villages became more frequent, until they arrived at Koronisingana in the early afternoon, where news of their approach had brought the local chief to the riverside to welcome them ashore. Beatrice's men shifted her belongings from the *mbili-mbili* to a boat she had hired, and baled it out. The boat had neither engine, nor oars, so again the only means of progress was to use a long bamboo pole as a single oar. When they came to the shallows, as well as punting with the pole, Joni went over the side and pushed the boat; a very novel way of travel.

At Mavua Beatrice was entertained with an excellent *meke-meke*, or song and dance. It went on for some length of time, beginning with some verses about herself, and continuing to chant the saga of all creation. Then, the men all wearing white *sulus*, and decorated with bracelets and coloured grass aigrettes in their hair sat down on mats on the floor where they launched into a graceful 'sitting dance', heads, bodies, arms and hands all swaying in perfect time, and singing throughout, with the most beautiful strong and sonorous voices.

Beatrice and her men had no further stops until they eventually arrived at her journey's end at the town of Sigatoka. Here she stayed at the home of a white magistrate who made her very welcome, while Gideon, Joni and Nasoni found lodging at the local constabulary station.

Beatrice soon left the district for Suva, having a miserable time in a little cutter in terrible weather, arriving at the capital a few days later.

Diana Fiji Trekking, 2016

Joyce, her sisters and I, had flown to Nadi on Fiji's west coast. From here Joyce went with her siblings to a resort on one of the islands off the coast. I, meantime, was picked up by a young man called Matt Capper who ran Talanoa Treks with his wife, Marita.

I had been in touch with Talanoa Treks for some time, organising the trek I wanted to do, shadowing Beatrice, from Ba to Sigatoka. Because Beatrice had ridden this trail, I, too, was offered a horse, but I politely declined the offer. I sent to Matt, the names of all the villages where Beatrice stayed but place names had changed and were unfamiliar. However, Matt had a gentleman working with him called Mr Vilitati Rokovesa – known to all as Mr Roko. He was a mountain man, recognising the old names, and was able to find exactly where the villages were.

Matt, Mr Roko and I set off from Ba in a 4WD. The fine bright weather I had had everywhere since leaving London had disappeared, and although still very warm, we had a light cloud cover. Nevertheless, I could see the Naloto Range which Beatrice had ridden across. Ba was still in the sugar business, although now to a lesser degree than in 1905. In fact, as we drove out of Ba we passed the Rarawai Sugar Mill, originally opened in 1886, and still owned by the The Fiji Sugar Corporation. We drove on through old sugar cane plantations, along an obsolete narrow gauge railway track. It was all very green and lush.

Gradually we made our way uphill, for a time alongside the Ba River, visible to us down in a deep gorge. Eventually we were in high country dotted with pine trees in vast grassland. I could see why Beatrice thought it would be good cattle country. I thought it was not as Beatrice described as 'rolling country', but more severe – steep uplands divided by deep gullies.

FIJI. Base of house where Beatrice stayed at Nadrugu

We arrived at our first village, now called Nadrugu – in Beatrice's time, Nandrunga. As we stepped out of the car, Matt told me the customs I must respect when we visited the villages. First of all I had to wear a '*sulu*' – the traditional kilt. Secondly, I must not wear shoes indoors, and finally, while in the company of a chief who would be sitting down, I must not stand up – i.e. not appear to be taller than him. Matt had brought a *sulu* for me which I wrapped round over my cut-off trousers and bumbag. Not quite the most glamorous of costumes.

It was now time to walk. We parked the car and set off along a very muddy and slippery path, eventually arriving

Garden and view of Mountains at Nadrugu

at the pretty village, nestling under the range of mountains. Mr Roko had already advised the head man of our arrival, so we were expected. We were invited into the chief's house and everyone sat down, bare-footed and cross-legged. The locals all sit comfortably like this, while I find it incredibly uncomfortable, not having been brought up from babyhood to bend my legs and hips in the right places. Nevertheless, I managed to pass myself. Then Mr Roko took off on a long dirge, speaking in a subdued voice. This long talk was called a *sevu-sevu*. Most of the land in Fiji is owned by various people so when you want to visit somewhere you have to have permission from the chief. Then, as Beatrice was familiar with, you present your credentials, introduce yourself and give a present. Traditionally the present is a bundle of kava roots, but it can be anything. Today it was a bar of soap, and this gift is also called a *sevu-sevu*. The chief then replies and hopefully accepts the visitor – in this case me and Matt. The chief then asked me to introduce myself. This took me a bit by surprise, so I just said my name was Diana Gleadhill and I came from Ireland. I then explained the reason for my visit, that I was researching a woman called Beatrice Grimshaw who I knew had visited this village over 110 years ago. I then thanked the chief for his hospitality. Matt then introduced himself in much the same way.

There was some discussion as to whether it was too wet to visit the site where the house had stood when Beatrice stayed the night, but it wasn't quite raining, and so off we went through a lot of undergrowth to where one of the young men climbed up on

Boys showing off, where Beatrice washed

to the rough platform of stones, cutting back the greenery from the top so that I could climb up also, encumbered as I was by the *sulu* wrapped round my legs. Although a far cry from Beatrice's description of the house she had stayed in, it was for sure the correct place, and again I had that odd feeling that I was standing where she had once stood.

We thanked everyone, and returned to the village centre. When Mr Roko had been here a few weeks previously, he had looked to see how Beatrice and her boys could have entered the village on horseback and on foot. He pointed out a narrow path going up into the mountains. This, if continued northwards, would bring one over the Naloto Range, and back towards Ba.

We set off again towards our next village. En route we noticed, down in a valley on our right-hand-side, the tiny village of Tambale, virtually unchanged since Beatrice saw it. Arriving at Numbukuya, now Bukuya, I had to put on my *sulu*, and again sit cross-legged and bare-footed while Mr Roko performed the *sevu-sevu*. This time the *sevu-sevu* was a bundle of kava roots. This ceremony became very familiar to Beatrice; the kava first being offered to the chief, then his guest, before it is offered to the rest of the room.

Tambale village

This was quite an important village as the chief, or *mbuli* lived here. He was a very easy man to talk to – and indeed listen to, as was his wife. Of course we chatted about Beatrice, the chief saying he remembered when he was about three years old, his father taking him to Ba on horseback. Everyone in this central part of Fiji still owned at least one horse as it was the best transport from village to village. Meanwhile the heavens opened. It was raining so heavily that, unfortunately, we were unable to go for the walk to the old village where Beatrice would have stayed.

"Sevu Sevu" at Bukuya, with Chief and Family

I was looking around the house which was quite large with two rooms. Hanging on the wall opposite me were two very beautiful *tapas*, or *masi*. The term *tapa* is international and understood throughout the Pacific Islands. *Tapa* cloths are made of bark fibres, a type of cloth made from the bast, or inner bark strips of the mulberry tree, although several species of breadfruit and fig trees are also used. This is a traditional art form whereby the bast is softened and pounded into sheets of cloth, then bound together using natural starches. In former times the cloth was primarily used for clothing, but now cotton and other textiles have replaced it. The major problem with *tapa* clothing was that the tissue lost its strength when wet and frequently fell apart. *Tapas* are now highly prized for their decorative value and are often found as wall-hangings as I saw in this Fijian house.

I took a photograph of the whole family, and off we went into the rain. We drove eastwards along a ridge which was the watershed between the Ba River and the Sigatoka – towards Nubutautau, where we would spend the night. I took the opportunity of asking Mr Roko about marriage in Fiji, whether it was arranged or not. It seems marriage used to be arranged but not now. However, the prospective groom does ask the bride's father if he might marry his daughter, and there is still a 'bride price' to be arranged. It can vary quite a lot, but might normally consist of a container of kerosene, some pigs and cows, floor mats and a whale's tooth. This latter must nowadays be quite difficult to obtain.

Nubutautau is where Matt has his up-country headquarters, and to where he brings his usual treks for the night if they are not camping.

My "Bure"

There is a community building where everyone eats, and I think where Matt sleeps. I was given the option of sleeping there also, or having a *bure* – or cabin to myself, situated about 100 yards from the rest of the village. I went to have a look at the *bure*, and decided it was so pretty and traditional that I would have it as my own room. The whole building was a wonderful work of art, and all made from local materials. I made up my bed from a stack of narrow, thin mattresses, putting one on top of another and pulling my sleeping sheet from my rucksack. My little travelling pillow on top made it look quite enticing. I lay down and gazed up at the ceiling, wondering at the complexity of its manufacture.

I asked Mr Roko how the *bure* was made. He said that usually the main wooden structure is made from a hardwood tree. There is never a central post, thus ensuring a large open-plan living area. Four hefty posts at each corner are joined with *magimagi*, a fibrous coconut string, rather than nails or bolts, The walls are usually made from split bamboo, sliced and woven together. A raised platform makes up the floor, and this is laid with straw as a cushion, and woven mats for decoration. The high roof is thatched using a reed called *sina* which lasts for around five years before being replaced. To keep the thatching free of insects or animals which might feed on the leaves, a fire is often lit inside which would last a few days, causing clouds of smoke to rise into the thatching, thus fumigating the thatch and keeping it pest-free. I had, anyway, mosquito coils and my headlamp which I had remembered to have at hand.

Because of how the Fijian's organise their clock, it didn't get dark until around eight. As we needed to wait until the men would get home from the fields, our evening meal was not until nearly nine. Everyone almost all the time went barefoot, sometimes wearing flip flops but always slipping them off at the door. The men wore long shorts in the daytime, changing into a clean and immaculate *sulu* in the evening. Grace was said before each meal, and even I was invited to say it once. Unaccustomed as I was to saying grace, the only one I could think of quickly was from school days – 'For what we are about to receive may the Lord make us truly thankful'. As tradition demands, we again sat on the ground to eat. There was an enormous quantity of food, almost everything grown in or around the village, with wonderful vegetables and exotic fruits. Again, I was reminded of Beatrice's words, remarking on how bountiful the land was, and that nobody could possibly ever starve in the Pacific Islands. After eating, I watched while some children played a very popular and noisy game called Vidi Vidi – a sort of cross between Tiddlywinks and Pool.

At last it was time for me to depart for bed. I was warned to watch out for the toads which would be everywhere, and to make sure I closed my half door in case they would waddle in to join me. Sure enough, as I ventured outside, there, as I had been warned, was a veritable army of croaking toads. I dodged them all, and ran to the *bure*, being sure to close the door tight behind me.

The following morning Matt had some disturbing news. The overcast sky and the rain the day before possibly presaged a cyclone which was building up to the north-west. The consequence of the weather forecast was that Matt thought we would have to cut short our itinerary, as being in the mountains during torrential rain and wind would not be ideal. However, he reckoned we could still visit all the villages, and as it was dry that day, we would do the crossing of the Sigatoka River, both on foot, and by *mbili-mbili*. I was thrilled that we were going to have the experience of the *mbili-mbili*.

As soon as breakfast was over, off I went with my guide – Etuate Tesi, known as Etu – for the hike to the Sigatoka River.

To start with our path was very easy across grassy fields, some studded with wild turmeric plants. This is such a useful plant, used for cooking and cosmetics. I asked Etu if the village harvested it for sale, but he said no, that surprisingly there was no market for turmeric. We passed a big mango tree, and gathered up a few fruits to eat. Etu then stopped to examine some wild boar footprints in the damp earth. Wild pigs are quite prevalent here; when I asked did they shoot them, Etu said that, interestingly, they hunted them with dogs.

After a while, going gently downhill, we arrived at a big rock where we had a rest. From here you could see both up and down the river, and about 600 feet far below us to our left, looking as small as ants, we spied Mr Roko and the boys who were making our *mbili-mbili*. Etu told me the slope down to the river was extremely steep and would be slippery after yesterday's rain, and was I sure I wanted to do it.

Etuate Tesi – Etu, my Guide down to the River

I didn't really think I had a choice. This was what I was here for after all. If Beatrice could do it – I could do it.

And so we set off. The path was almost perpendicular in places and deep-set where the rain had turned it into a stream, eroding its way downhill. I couldn't possibly have done it without Etu's help. It took us some time to complete our descent; my total concentration was on Etu's long, muscular legs in front of me, and taking the fingers of his proffered hand from time to time. Sometimes I hesitated, working out my next footfall, but I was really chuffed when Etu remarked on how fit I was and how sure-footed. He described some of the clients he had taken down this hill, some of them he said, were so clumsy. I think all my years of walking in the Mourne Mountains at home stood me in good stead. However, the compliments made me extra aware.

Safely at the bottom – without falling – we met up with Mr Roko and Matt. Here, I found we had to cross the river which was running very swiftly. I have to admit it was quite scary, but again Etu came to the rescue, holding my hand and keeping me upright all the time. It was difficult making out the large rocks doing their best to trip me up under the rushing water – now up to my thighs – which, in turn, was trying to sweep me away. This crossing was in order for me to visit a very old village, with almost no remains visible. It had a sad history from the time of the coming of the missionaries who brought measles with them. The entire village was wiped out, the few remaining still alive, were so sick that they couldn't carry the dead bodies up to their cemetery, and had to bury them under some enormous rocks. By peering through the stones at the entrance, one could still make out some of the bones. While Etu was trying to clear our path, he was stung on the hand by a wasp, his hand becoming red and swollen almost immediately.

I daringly decide to swim across the River

We walked through the sad village and round a bluff of land back to the river. Here it was wider but seemed calmer, so I decided to swim across – fully dressed. However, the current caught me half way across, so I allowed myself to be swept downstream a little way to where there were some rocks and there was the faithful Etu waiting to give me a hand ashore.

We walked down the pebbly beach to where Mr Roko and the boys had finished making the *mbili-mbili*.

There was great excitement with the boys waiting to put the raft in the river and be the first to get on board. These lads were also great entertainment, jumping off some rocks into the river and swimming and laughing, and running back and forth up the beach on bare feet – always sure-footed. Mr Roko and Etu pushed the *mbili-mbili* into the water, with most of the children jumping on also. Mr Roko poled the raft into the deeper water with everyone clapping and cheering.

Then it was my turn. I got safely on board and sat down to enjoy the trip across the river. It was great fun for all, and as Beatrice said, the water of course leaks through the bamboo, but as everyone was already wet, it didn't matter one bit.

Room for More on Board the "Mbili Mbili"

While we were eating our picnic lunch one of the boys produced the big fruit of the cocoa plant, full of sweet slippery beans which we sucked, inside of which is the cocoa. Another lesson for me. After our picnic we left the boys to have fun with the raft while we walked upstream. I thought we were going to go back up the hill to the village, but was told we still had to cross the river again twice, as we couldn't get any further on that side. I couldn't believe it. Two more crossings! But they were easier with the river a little broader and therefore calmer, and I had strong Etu to hang on to. Then we had to hack our way back up the steep sides of the river valley to Nubutautau.

Trek back to our village – Nubutautau

It was slow going, partly because the barely distinguishable path was so overgrown with vegetation which had to be chopped down, and partly for us to stop from time to time to admire and discuss the name of this or that tree, or just to have a breather. Although the climb was tough, it was nothing like as bad as going down.

All the time there was the sound of cicadas 'chirpling' in the trees and the sound of the Sigatoka in the background. There was such a variety of trees and bushes, many of them with scented blossom – lemon, guava and sandalwood. There was always plenty of bird life around. Everywhere, darting about was the Common Myna, and several species of parrot accompanied us back at last to the village after a great day – and it had stayed dry.

I should still have had two days left, but instead of having a day in the village, part time with the ladies, and part time exploring some of the village's historical sites, Matt decided we should leave the following day and visit both of Beatrice's final two villages.

This having been decided, Mr Roko took me that evening to explore the village. He told me, very quietly and very seriously, that this village was where the final murder of a missionary had taken place. The rock recording the incident near where Reverend Baker was killed is still displayed above the village. The sole of his leather sandals, which were also cooked by the cannibal tribe, are in the Fiji Museum in Suva.

The Reverend Thomas Baker (1832–1867) was a Methodist missionary who visited Nubutautau in July 1867, hoping to spread the gospel in the interior of Viti Levu. When Baker met a local chief, he gifted him a British comb and attempted to persuade him to convert to Christianity. When the chief refused, Baker decided to take his comb back, touching the chief's head as he did so, which was an offence in Fijian customs. In pursuing revenge, a dominant coastal chief – the Chief of Bau, cooked up a plot to kill the party, and the body of Thomas Baker being cannibalised and distributed among the villagers.

Baker was killed along with seven Fijian Christian workers. Two men, Aisea and Josefa Nagata, escaped the massacre.

In 2003, Baker's relatives had visited the village for a traditional *matanigasau* – or reconciliation ceremony. This was offered by the descendants of the Reverend Baker's murderers, as an apology for the killing.

That evening, being my last, we had another kava ceremony after our evening meal.

Early the following morning, as it now looked as though the big depression and cyclone were heading towards us, Matt's decision to get downhill made it imperative for us to leave. All the ladies of the village came to say goodbye and my hero Etu gave me such a great handshake and hug. Matt had notified the villages of Natuatuathoko now Nukutau and Nelebaleba, now Lemba Lemba that we would be a day early.

It was a fair drive south to the first village of Nukutau, meeting the chief waiting for us on the side of the road. He was a sturdily built man with a short white beard, and wearing a little hat. He told us his name was Chief Onisimo Naioko and he was the great grandson of Chief Ratu Pemi Qaluvakawalu who would have been Beatrice's host. He told us to drive on down to the river and the boys would come with the horses for the river crossing. Horses? Another river crossing – on a horse? I really *was* following in Beatrice's hoof prints. I can ride, but this was an unexpected experience.

Nothing daunted, Matt – who had never ridden – the chief and I mounted our little horses. Mine was a chestnut mare who was a somewhat recalcitrant about entering the water; I can't say I blamed her. Mr Roko also waded into the river. The water was running fast and was just up to my feet as they hung in the stirrups. I wondered did I remain in the saddle if we started to swim, or did I dismount and swim beside my mare. In the event, it didn't get any deeper, and we scrambled out on the far bank riding alongside the river until we came to a gate through which we rode. On up the hill we went, through thickets of bush and trees with branches hanging at head-height. All I could do was to duck my head, close my eyes, and leave it to the horse to get me to the top.

Up and up we went until the chief stopped, and dismounted. Joining Mr Roko and another man, he climbed some crumbling steps on to a mound of stones. Beatrice's Fairy Fortress. Again, it was covered in undergrowth and bushes, but wielding their long knives they slashed at all the greenery revealing the stonework. As this endeavour was all on my behalf, I couldn't refuse the chief's invitation to climb up and join them. So I slid off my horse and climbed up onto the top of the stone platform – about forty by thirty feet in dimension. I could see why Beatrice had loved this spot. Although there were now trees in the way, and the sky was a murky grey, there would have been the most stunning sight down to the river and the distant view of the mountains. I was so pleased that yet again I was on the same place as Beatrice had been all that time ago. The chief said he was going to clear the bush and make it a venue for tourists. Well ... I wonder?

My horse had been tied up to a tree, so now I needed her again for the ride back down. Up I got and down we rode to the chief's house for yet another gargantuan spread, prepared by two delightful ladies. I asked about provisions such as flour and sugar. Yes, they said, they had to go to the town to get items like that, also salt, tea, onions and spinach – the last two items don't grow well in this area. Apart from these commodities, they could grow everything they needed and they had some hens, and a couple of cows for milk and butter.

By this time I was aware that many of the old villages had been built on the tops of hills, and I asked why they had been replaced by newer villages lower down. Naturally enough the height gave the advantage of being able to see approaching enemies, but with the disadvantage of the women and children having to go a long way to carry water from the rivers up to these fortresses. With the advent of the missionaries and less enmity between the tribes, many of the high villages were abandoned and rebuilt lower down. Today there is running water from a tap in all the villages we visited.

Our meal over, it was time to mount up yet again for the final river crossing. On arriving at the far side, the chief came over to help me dismount. But half way down, my right leg got tangled up in the redundant lead rein, and there I hung for a moment. I had to let the chief take my weight while I extricated my leg from the rope. Ah well, not many of us have been in the arms of a Fijian chief.

Matt, and Chief of village Nukutau, Onisimo Naioko holding my horse after crossing the Sigatoka River

The next village to visit was Lemba Lemba. By the time we arrived there it was pouring. We discovered that the man who was to have been our host, was hosting a group of tourists from Sigatoka River Safaris. They had jetted upstream by boat to visit the village as part of their itinerary. However, Matt announced that we were there and could he spare a few minutes to show us where Beatrice might have stayed. He brought us back up the road 100 yards or so to where he lived, and again was able to show us the foundations of the *bula's* house where Beatrice would have stayed. He showed us where now there is a flight of stone steps from the river for the tourists to use, in place of the muddy slope where the kind *bula* had his men dig steps for Beatrice's use. The rain by now was coming down in stair-rods, so we didn't delay our host and dropped him back with his tourists.

We drove alongside the river towards the town of Sigatoka. The road now was tarmaced and the houses more numerous – the mountains with their little villages were gone. We passed through the village of Koronisingana – now almost a built up township. This was where Beatrice finally said goodbye to her *mbili-mbili* and hired a leaking boat for the remainder of the trip through Mavua, and on to Sigatoka.

The Cyclone

We didn't stop at Mavua or anywhere else until arriving at my hotel, the Tubakula Beach Resort, at the coast on the east side of Sigatoka River. While I was checking in I saw that Matt was still waiting in the car to make sure I was OK. I said my fond farewells to Matt and Mr Roko who had been wonderful hosts, and had taken me exactly where I wanted to go.

Falling coconuts on the roof of my bungalow woke me from a sound sleep in the middle of the night, as the wind and rain howled and crashed preventing me from going back to sleep. Even though the resort staff had moved me back from the beach-front bungalow – afraid that if there was a storm I might get flooded, my imagination ran riot with all the noise, picturing the sea coming in my door. As soon as it was daylight I slipped out of bed and went to the window to see what was happening, to find that the sea was still in its proper place, but the long feathery branches of the coconut palms were being whipped horizontally by the fierce wind, and coconuts were falling, and rolling around in the storm.

I was terribly tired, and was happy doing almost nothing. My day was spent washing some dirty clothes, sleeping and writing up my diary. I rigged up a clothes line in the veranda of the bungalow where the washing enjoyed a good breeze without getting wet. In the afternoon, between showers, I made it down to the waters' edge for a few minutes to have a look at the beach. I had envisioned having a couple of days lazing there, between swims, waiting for Joyce's arrival, but it had no such appeal just then. There is nothing drearier than a South Pacific beach resort in the rain. Pale grey sky and lagoon. Dark grey water beyond the waves breaking on the reef.

When will the next Coconut fall?
Tubakula Beach Resort

This day and the next were lost days while I did a bit of walking, and hibernated in my bungalow – the sole occupant of the resort.

Joyce arrived on the afternoon of the third day having had a lovely time with her sisters, albeit in mixed weather.

Sigatoka River Safari

Because Beatrice had gone by boat down the final part of the Sigatoka River I had wanted to do that also. However, there were no boats doing such trips, and so we had cast around for an alternative way to get on the river. I found that you could get a popular tourist jet boat expedition, upstream and back down again, calling at one of the river villages for lunch (as mentioned above). So Joyce and I had booked ourselves to go on the jet boat the day before leaving Fiji.

We were collected by Sigatoka River Safaris at 8 a.m. and off we went with all our belongings upriver to the starting point. Here we were given light-weight waterproofs and life jackets. There were about 12–15 people on each of two boats – the lightest at the front which was Joyce, me, and a young couple from Hong Kong.

It was not quite raining when we set off, but because of the volume of rain that had already fallen, the river was flowing very fast. It made not a bit of difference to the jet boats as we zoomed up the river, stopping now and then for our driver – another tall and handsome Fijian – to tell us some of the history and customs of the local people. One time, to our amusement, we watched a boy and girl on their way to school floating downstream, their books in plastic buckets which also helped give them buoyancy. It was all great fun, and I had a distinct feeling that Beatrice would have thoroughly enjoyed joining us. It was drizzling when we arrived at the village of Tumbairata, and where we had to walk up the usual steep, slippery path to the village.

After yet another kava ceremony there was a short speech from the chief, welcoming us, and describing some of the village traditions. It was all very nice, but I had had such a truly traditional time in the mountains, and this was nothing like as atmospheric as Mr Roko's *sevu-sevu*. After eating, a guitarist and a drummer started to play, and we all got up and danced – in any way we fancied. We then were treated to some of the most wonderful singing I have ever heard from a non-professional choir. The bass voices were glorious as they sang in harmony, moving me to tears.

Viewed from our boat on the Sigatoka - off to school, books in the bowl

Then the rain really got down to business, falling like javelins from the leaden sky. Our waterproofs were soaked through before we even reached the boats. The ride back to headquarters was unseen by us in the front, the hurtling rain stinging our eyes. Ashore we were all like drowned rats. Luckily Joyce and I had all our clothes with us so we were able to change before driving off to Nadi for the night, where we would catch our ongoing flight.

Before driving away Joyce turned to me and said she thought the rain was great; that she was glad she had experienced it, and that life in Fiji wasn't all blue skies and glamorous resorts. She was right; it was quite something to experience the good and the bad.

We did not follow Beatrice to Vanua Levu, the smaller of Fiji's two main islands.

Beatrice in Vanua Levu

Back in Suva, and having recovered from her cross-country adventure, Beatrice again grew bored by Suvan society and after some deliberation, decided to go to Vanua Levu, the smaller of the two main islands.

So she took a steamer to Lambasa, the principal port on the north coast. There were a couple of stores and a police station, outside of which there were no roads, no shops, no regular mails, and even the native villages were far apart, the inhabitants Beatrice thought, being rougher and wilder in every way.

In those days, the British government tried to keep some sort of curb on the tyrannies of the native chiefs on the *kaisi*, or common people. Even so, the lower classes lived plainly and poorly, whereas the chiefs took anything and everything that took their fancy, and ordering the *kaisi* to work for them without pay. Thirty or forty years previously, the chiefs could slay the *kaisi* at will, but still these poor folk could not leave their villages without permission from their chief. Ambition was impossible; born a *kaisi*, he would for ever be a *kaisi*.

When a chief died, the *kaisi* were slain in dozens and thrown into the grave. When a war canoe was launched, it went down to the sea over the bodies of hundreds of human beings. No wonder the shadow of those hideous days remembered by the elderly, should still rest with the younger generation.

Once again Beatrice had Gideon accompany her, and once again, she hired two more men and a local horse. This horse was not a patch on the lovely Tanewa, shying at the slightest excuse, and worst of all, he hated Beatrice riding side-saddle, trying to rub her off against every tree they passed. The men named him *Somo-somo*, which, somewhat ironically, meant Fiji Flower!

Most of her explorations in Vanua Levu were similar to those in Viti Levu, with beautiful scenery, and discovering land that was available for farming, with forests full of valuable timber for logging. The quartet's nights were not as extravagant as the wonderful times they had had in the main island. Most of their adventures concerned the crossing of rivers, with the difficult *Somo-somo*. One day the party arrived at a river where they had hoped to find an *mbili-mbili* for crossing, but it had disappeared. There was nothing for it but to swim the river:

> I never swam like that before; I never shall again. Imaginary sharks chased my horribly conspicuous red swimming-dress and English skin right up to the bed of greasy mud on which I landed. I was half up the bank before I remembered that my clothes were on the other side ... So I sat in the mud, and screamed to a native woman who was watching the proceedings from the farther shore; and

she (having no fear of sharks, as I, miserable craven of a *'papa-langi'*), put my things on her head and came over at once.[51]

So a very humble Beatrice mounted Somo-somo who was waiting for her, dripping and steaming in the sun, having also swum the river, and rode away to the solitary house of a kind white magistrate and his wife who had offered to have her stay.

Had Beatrice known what lay ahead of them, she would never have expected to ride a horse. There was no visible track. All they could follow was where the undergrowth had been trampled by other travellers. They pushed on over marshy land, frequently fording little streams banked by slippery red clay. Poor *Somo-somo* protested vigorously, bringing to mind the warning Beatrice had been given back in Lambasa – 'Don't get your horse bogged!'

She had dismounted to let the men lead the horse down a gully much the same as those they had already negotiated, and was scrambling up the far side when she heard a terrified cry from Gideon, *'... Missi N-grimshaw! Horsie lie down, by-n'-by he n-dead!..'*[52] Turning round she saw poor *Somo-somo* who had missed jumping the stream, plunging and struggling madly, with terrified eyes and snorting fearfully, already sunk up to his belly in the mud-filled gully. The men were hauling with the reins, obviously getting nowhere; they were as frightened as the horse.

Something had to be done – and quickly. The sides of the gully were terribly steep and it was nearly dusk. Beatrice would have given anything to have sat down with *Somo-somo* and wept. But that was not Beatrice's style. Shouting every un-ladylike obscenity she could think of, the men, shocked, jumped to it. She told them to haul on the leading rope, and to lift the animal's hind quarters with saplings. They cut down a lot of the bush, surrounding him and creating a sort of platform. Beatrice got the lads to flatten part of the steep bank so making a practicable exit. She worked them for an hour, scolding at them like a turkey-hen. At last the team managed to create a fairly solid piece of ground, and the exhausted *Somo-somo*, fought his way out of the mud to stand trembling on the bank. But he was saved.

There followed a long walk in the dusk, and then the dark until the group heard the sound of a white man's voice calling to them. They had finally reached the little settlement Beatrice had been aiming for since leaving Nanduri. Before long, she was enjoying a real meal at a real table in the smallest of three small houses, together with a saw-mill, that made up the settlement of Tumba.

The day after her arrival at Tumba, she went up the river by boat to see the main forest where the logging took place. She had done her homework on the trees and was delighted to find many valuable hardwoods, mostly growing in great profusion.

51 Grimshaw, *From Fiji to the Cannibal Islands*, pp. 117–8.

52 Grimshaw, *From Fiji to the Cannibal Islands*, p. 98.

She loved being in the cool, silent forest; finding brilliant honey-birds hanging on the blossoms; chameleons, wild boars, snakes and centipedes, but dreading the formidable ticks which could bite even through clothing. The wonderful stick insects were invisible of course, except when a native brought one to show her. They really were at the back of beyond.

Here, in some of the little bush houses, heathenism, and devil worship was still practised in spite of the natives being nominally Christian. One character, known as 'Bad Lot' was frequently hanging about Tumba, and was known as a hereditary devil priest. He appeared civilised and spoke good English, having been incarcerated in Suva prison for some years, accused of killing and eating an oppressive chief. Bad Lot had been freed early because he was young, and had apparently been influenced by two older men. He was, during Beatrice's stay, a person of some importance, much admired by his neighbours because he frequently recounted his cannibalistic past. As ever, Beatrice was intrigued by someone who had been a cannibal so recently, and asked him if she might take his photograph. Mr Bad Lot grinned delightedly, and, dressing his head with flowers, posed happily for her.

Just before leaving Vanua Levu, Beatrice was told about a family on the smaller island of Taviuni who had made a great success of cattle ranching, and she should go and visit them.

She was able to get there on a small inter-island steamer. On many of the smaller islands one could find a 'reigning family' of white settlers who owned the island, and made their living planting on a large-scale, copra being the most popular crop. Although many of these islands are remote, they were wonderfully maintained, with a standard of education and refinement surprising to most visitors.

Her hosts began by asking if Beatrice could ride, and if so would she like to partake in bringing some cattle back to the yard from the outlying country, assuring her that it would be no more difficult than cross-country work at home. So, believing all she was told, Beatrice agreed to the idea, looking forward to the following morning. They set off early, Beatrice riding a young and high-spirited thoroughbred. The following few hours were a nightmare; her mount bucked when she held him in, and could do feats in the way of step-dancing at full gallop among the boulders and sudden deep holes. Beatrice did not get thrown that day, but she was very glad that nobody saw the occasions on which she escaped by the skin of her teeth – her head in the scrub and her heart in her mouth. She thought she would never get home alive. She did drive cattle that day – to some extent, at least she looked as though she did. When they had finally driven the cattle up to the stock yards, one of her hosts rode up to congratulate her on her riding (if only he had known):

'I'm glad you had a good time,' he said. 'Rounding-up is really great fun, you know, and we always like our visitors to see it.'

'But mostly,' he added, as an afterthought – 'mostly, you know, they fall off!'

'There, but for the Grace of God, goes John Bunyan,' I murmured as I slipped out of my saddle.'[53]

By this time, Beatrice was due back in Lambasa as the steamer for Suva would soon be arriving. But she was anxious about Gideon's behaviour, which she thought he had probably picked up from some of the less respectable natives in the forest. From being a delightful, cheerful young man, he had become dour, disrespectful and careless. As Beatrice could not leave him behind she decided to teach him a lesson. She talked mostly about her apparent lofty position and the many deeds she had (not) performed, alluding at the same time to Gideon's weak points, vilifying his ancestry and describing him as not good enough as food for a cannibal. She told him to leave her service immediately.

By this time, her cruel words had the big native in tears as he crawled away, collapsing in a heap on the veranda; every time Beatrice passed, asking her could he not stay, to which she heartlessly kept up the reply – *'no, go away'*. The final straw came when Beatrice was invited for tea on the little steamer, and Gideon thought she was going to sail away and leave him behind. His obvious unhappiness almost melted Beatrice's heart, but she kept him waiting until the evening when she finally asked him if he was going to behave, and that he must tell her he was sorry. That was asking a lot of a Fijian who hated, above all, to have to make such an admission, and he hesitated, so that she walked away. Gideon, seeing his last chance disappearing called after her *'I so-re'*. From then onwards, to the end of the trip, Gideon was back to his old cheerful self, travelling back to Suva with Beatrice, where she paid him and gave him a good testimonial, both of them happy with their travels.

Beatrice returned to Sydney from Fiji in August 1905 on board the steamer SS *Pilbarra*.

53 Grimshaw, *From Fiji to the Cannibal Islands*, p. 164.

Chapter 11: New Hebrides / Vanuata

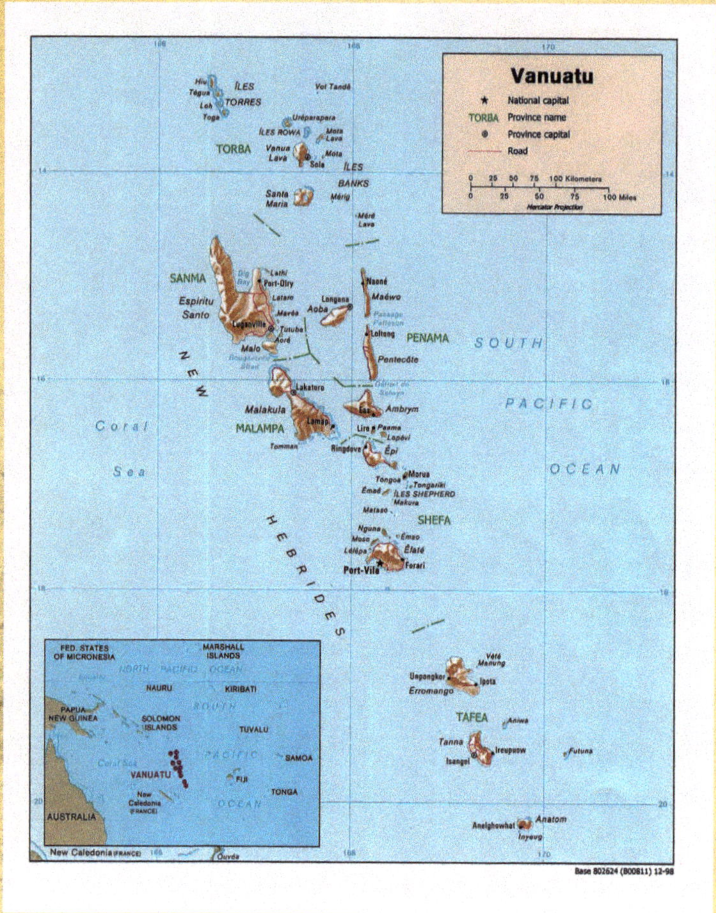

For some time Beatrice had been thinking about going to the New Hebrides (today's Republic of Vanuatu) but as usual, when she enquired about the islands from the people in Sydney, she discovered very little. Most of her questions only succeeded in gloomy accounts that she was not to suppose the New Hebrides were like Fiji, and that there was next to no regard for human life. It was where the natives were cannibals to a man and she would be shot if she went. The Sydney folk thought she was quite mad and would be much better exploring Sydney Harbour. But that was not for Miss Grimshaw.

After leaving the New Hebrides Beatrice wrote that she had had so many adventures that they ceased to seem adventurous. In the New Hebrides, I was caught in a forest fire, and barely escaped into a valley where bones of a recent cannibal feast lay blackening in the smoke. I stood on the shores of Tanna, and watched a recruiting schooner creep cautiously in, afraid to land her boats, while the men of the mountains, fighters and cannibals all, waited with loaded guns beside me, ready to attack the 'blackbirding' crew who had taken away their best.[54]

54 Grimshaw, 'How I Found Adventure', *Blue Book* (April 1939). 'Blackbirding' was a euphemism for enslaving people from New Caledonia, the Loyalty Islands, New Hebrides, (Vanuatu), New Guinea, and the Solomon Islands to work in sugarcane plantations in Fiji and Queensland. This trade ceased at the start of the 20th century. The victims of the trade were called '*Kanakas*', like all the Oceanic people, after the Hawaiian word for 'man'

The New Hebrides, or Vanuatu, is a Pacific island nation of eighty-two islands, located in the South Pacific Ocean. The archipelago, which is of volcanic origin, is some 1,900 miles east of northern Australia.

Beatrice eventually arrived in Port Vila, the capital of Efate Island, in September 1905 after an eight day journey from Sydney in a slow little steamer, the *Induna*, captained by a small, smiling, rosy-faced, man, but where the cook got drunk and struck work.

Beatrice describes arriving in Vila harbour in the morning:

> when the sea is bright with the pale-blue dazzle of sun-smitten tropic latitudes, and the flying-fish are glancing and skipping about our bows, and Vila Harbour – surely the loveliest of all the fairy harbours in the wonderful island world – is opening out before us.[55]

It was as well she thought so much of the harbour, for she was appalled at the town, describing it as a city of magnificent omissions, as there was no hotel, town hall, or any public building.

For about fifty years a tug-of- war had been going on between Britain and France over possession of the New Hebrides group.

The islands were discovered by the Portuguese, De Quiros, in 1605. The subsequent exploring and charting was carried out for the most part by Captain Cook, who named the islands New Hebrides, though the French captains, Carteret and De Bourgainville, also visited the islands during the eighteenth century, exploring certain parts. From 1878 onwards, an infusion of French settlers and missionaries began to flow into the islands, and every effort was made by the French government to strengthen their hold on the country. The result was that the French population now outnumbered the British.

The missionaries in sixty years' work had contrived to tame down a few of the smallest islands, and to make a little impression here and there upon the edges of the larger ones. But, in spite of the work done by the missions, the fact remained that very little progress had been achieved.

Beatrice would have wished to see work carried out by the missions together with a strong and able government which could forbid the sale of poisonous spirits to the natives; disarm the tribes; and compel traders to cease selling rifles and ammunition, impartially punishing all offenders – white or black.

55 Grimshaw, *From Fiji to the Cannibal Islands*, p. 171.

Politics apart, it was the islands again, and Beatrice was glad, for she had learned to love the island world. However, she thought the people were poor substitutes for her idealised native as they paddled silently about the harbour in ill-made log canoes, wearing almost nothing, and most of the men having rifles on their shoulders.

As well as every native having a gun which was meant only for shooting pigeon and flying foxes, dynamite for fishing was sold by the stick as freely as tobacco, and handled with a minimum of care. Beatrice goes on to tell about an instance by the Australian trader with whom she had arranged to board during her stay in Port Vila. He relates his story: 'Dynamite fishing is real good sport, but it's a nice job, mind you ... I'm pretty good at it myself.'[56]

He goes on to invite Beatrice to his back veranda to see what this dynamite fishing was all about. She went out as requested and saw one of the commonest sights in Vila harbour – a canoe lying in the water near the shore with a native putting a match to something, and throwing it into the sea; a dull booming explosion and a fountain of up-driven water, and then a scrambling and scooping over the side of the canoe. 'So that's dynamite fishing?' Beatrice said. With an affirmative, her friend proceeded to explain to her that it worked by putting a bit of fuse onto the end of a stick of dynamite, then you light it and chuck it away, killing a lot of fish. Sometimes of course, accidents would happen. Either the fuse was cut too long and then it entered the sea and was extinguished, or it may have been thrown too high and landed back in the boat with obvious disastrous results, in that many of the local men had only one hand, or were killed. Beatrice's response to this information was very tongue in cheek, saying that there must be a trader in Vila who would have a poor opinion of the courage of an Englishwoman who never learned to fish with dynamite. However, she was still happily possessed of both her arms – and her head.

After a week or two spent in the capital Beatrice made plans to go with two companions to explore part of the island.

Undine Bay in the north of the island, and thirty miles away, was Beatrice's final destination, accompanied by two planters. They rode three borrowed horses carrying their goods with them. The horses were nothing to boast of; Beatrice's was no more than a cart-horse, over sixteen hands, and moved like a hippopotamus. But he was the only four-legged beast to be had for hire in Vila, so choice there was none.

For all Beatrice's travelling, never had she seen:

> such colouring as I saw that day on Mélé Beach, where we rode along the shore before we turned into the forest. It was an immense beach of powdered coral, miles long, and hundreds of yards wide, and it was so exceedingly white in the raging sun that its scoops and shadows were blue of ultramarine, like the shadows

56 Grimshaw, *From Fiji to the Cannibal Islands*, p. 171.

> on a waste of snow ... the mountains far away were blue, the sea was blue, the sky was blue – the shallow lagoon was shot with unnameable hues of changing hyacinth, and Mélé Island, floating on a crystal plain, was one entire and perfect turquoise.[57]

After the beach, Beatrice and her companions rode through the bush for some length of time, along little foot tracks so that they had to go in single file. The silent forest light was dim and green, the sun not able to penetrate the leafage and lianas. Strange reddish, pink and yellow berries showed in the undergrowth, while wild nuts of many kinds, crackled on the ground under the horses' hoofs.

Beatrice spent the night with a local planter and his family. She saw how the family was self-sufficient, and how they made do with what was at hand, seldom seeing other people apart from their black workers. It would have been the planters' sons who would smoke and talk politics with their father, while his daughters would play an old harmonium, and paint pictures to hang about the house. The womenfolk, despite the various fevers and the climate, and the hard work over hot stoves that could not be left to the charge of native servants, never lost their attraction for the isolated plantation life.

Beatrice enjoyed visiting several families in their coffee plantations. She loved the pretty coffee bushes, with their polished dark green leaves, and the scarlet berries, of which the coffee 'bean' formed the stone. But the flowers were the true glory of a plantation. Once a year they would appear, and lasting for three days only, from the bursting of the bud to its dying away – but one day of perfection. All at once, the whole dark shrubbery would break into sprays of delicate white blossoms, the air filled with a hothouse sweetness. Beatrice decided she liked coffee all her life the better for having seen its beautiful beginnings.

She did not recommend that any British youth should emigrate to Efate yet. Beatrice did, however, recommend a tour of the New Hebrides to English travellers:

> I do not assert that nervous maiden aunts, or stout old gentlemen devoted to their dinners and their clubs, would enjoy the somewhat lawless atmosphere of the New Hebridean group ... But those who do not mind undergoing some discomfort and risk, for the sake of marvellous scenery, many adventures, and some of the strangest sights in the whole world, will do well to try these islands when they are tired of the Congo and the Amazon ... And let them not believe the people who assure them that they cannot and must not 'stop over,' or go inland, for they certainly should and can do both of these things.[58]

57 Grimshaw, *From Fiji to the Cannibal Islands*, pp. 191–2.

58 Grimshaw, *From Fiji to the Cannibal Islands*, p. 266.

Meanwhile, the quote below, had appeared in *The San Francisco Call*, July 1905:

> There is a plucky Irish girl named Beatrice Grimshaw who is probably having a higher average of adventures per week at present than any other girl living. Becoming tired of editorial work on an Irish cycling paper, she conceived the idea of setting out, alone, to roam the South Seas, where pirates, cannibals and leper colonies do abound.
>
> News has just been received from her indicating that she is having all the excitement she hoped for. She has kept as far as possible out of the track of monthly mail steamships, travelling about as the sole passenger on irresponsible little schooners to islands where a white woman never had been before ... In a letter written from the Fiji Islands on April 21 ... Miss Grimshaw says: ... 'I intend taking the New Hebrides and Solomons next.'
>
> Miss Grimshaw writes that she has had an amusing reception in one place where the native women had never seen a white woman before. They insisted on touching her to make sure she was real; ... 'The life of these people,' [Miss Grimshaw] says, 'has a peculiar charm. There is no rushing to catch trains or mails ... Time moves leisurely, and it is easier to walk than to run. Food is cheap. The fashions have a comfortable permanence, and existence is free from care.'[59]

Port Vila Museum, 'The Mummy'

Diana in Vanuata

Joyce and I arrived in the early hours of the morning at the main island of Efate, and Port Vila, the capital. Efate is about the third largest island, located more or less in the middle of the islands running north to south. We paid way over the top for a taxi to our hotel – The Melanesian.

The first thing we did the following morning was to go to the museum, which, luckily, was close to our hotel. We hoped we might find someone who would be interested in Beatrice. We brought copies of *From Fiji to the Cannibal Islands* and *A Remarkable Man* (the letters to his mother, of a missionary based in Tanna, in the early 1900s).

Of course we had no appointment and entered the first door we saw.

59 'Plucky Irish Girl on Exploring Trip in the South Seas', *The San Francisco Call*, 2 July 1905, p. 31.

Quite quickly we met the Chief Admin Officer, Henline Mala, who was a bit overcome with our arrival, but brought us to meet the Chief Librarian, Margaret Terry who was thrilled with the books, and my quest shadowing Beatrice Grimshaw. She asked us to sign donation forms and took lots of photos of us. We got their e-mail addresses and went to have a look at the very nice little museum which, although unfortunately not very well lit, was well documented and extremely interesting, with preserved mummies and parts of mummies.

One was of an entire man from Malekula Island. I photographed it and the following description below which was written by the curator in charge, Kaitip Kami, in 2014:

> Rambaramp
>
> *Death Rituals: Our belief in Reincarnation.*
> *A remarkable effigy on Malekula Island.*
>
> *These grotesque figures are to be met with on Malekula Island in the Nieu Hebrides. The natives make them so that the dead chief, or sacred man, may still be able to look on the living; it has also something to do with ancestor worship. (Mr Norman Hardy, British ethnographer and artist, 1895).*
>
> *The way the skull was treated also sheds a revealing light on the worship of the soul of the dead. There can be no doubt whatever, that in Northern Vanuatu the head was regarded as the seat of life and the soul, and consequently, after death, the skull was treated with very special reverence. There is incontrovertible evidence of a skull cult in southern Malekula, where skull masks are made, but only from the skulls of important men or of a dead person who was particularly loved. We believe that the soul lived in the skull's mask. It was the reincarnation of the person in the kingdom of death.*
>
> *Since the native believes that almost all diseases are the result of sorcery¸ he soon gives himself up for lost if he is ill, unless he feels sure that the magic causing the illness can be countervailed by opposing magic. The natives have no particular fear of death. However, there are no great joys in store for him on the other side unless he is a man of high rank, but neither is he to expect unusual punishments. Thus, most natives approach death with considerable resignation.*
>
> *When a man feels he is about to die, he is painted with all the insignia of the rank he may have attained. He wishes to die thus; that spirits may recognise his rank as he passes by. So it sometimes happens that a man is carried out and laid on the ground and wailed and wept over day after day he is spending, lying and writhing and trying to die, starving himself to hasten the end. We may anticipate here, and say that the natives not only believe in a temporary survival of the soul, but also assume that the duration of this continued existence of the soul of a man of high rank survives longer than that of a man of no importance.*

This could be explained by saying that the higher a man's rank, the more mana he – and hence his soul – possesses, and since mana is vitality, his soul lives longer than that of a man with little mana, or rank. His soul does not dissipate so quickly and is also more powerful than the soul of an unimportant man, and for this reason more death ceremonies must be celebrated for him than for an inferior man. The more powerful and feared a man was during his lifetime, the longer the memory of him persists, and the death ceremonies are the expression of this memory. These ceremonial group meals are likely to be sacrificial feasts of sacred food. In Malekula as in Ambrym, the ideas are respected by skull statues, and by tree fern statues. These are the seat of the soul, which are of course, inconsistent with the belief that the soul really goes to Hades, the world of the dead. The feasts are celebrated on the fifth, tenth, and hundredth day after death, depending on the rank of the deceased. In Malekula as in other islands, pigs are sacrificed at these feasts and the wives and nearest relatives of the dead man carry the tusks of these animals around with them, in the form of breast ornaments, but also by armlets. They are therefore sacrificial gifts which are offered to the dead man in order to appease his soul. The sacrificed pigs served in the underworld as evidence that the dead man held a high rank in the Nimangi, and that he is entitled to the same position in Hades and to not be destroyed.

Joyce and I both asked the curator more questions about the local beliefs, and also asked him to 'play' the huge drum made from a hollowed-out tree trunk. It had a wonderful echoing sound carrying far and wide, used to let people in far villages know the news – mostly about deaths.

Mélé Beach near Port Vila where Beatrice went horseback riding

Then, off we set on Beatrice's trail to Mélé Beach. She rode a horse there while we took a local minibus. To begin with we had no idea how to recognise a local bus, but had been told there would be a 'B' on the front and back. That seemed simple enough. But after some time of waiting for a minibus with a 'B' on it, we gave up and asked for help. Aha! The 'B' was on the number plate while we had been looking for a large 'B' painted on the vehicle. We hopped onto the next one and paid our small fare along with half a dozen locals. As our destination was the furthest away we delivered everyone else first, so instead of the promised ten minutes, it was more like twenty minutes, but not a waste of time as we got a tour of Port Vila's suburbs and very friendly chats with all the other passengers.

Finally we arrived at the beach which Beatrice had described so vividly. We walked along the sand until finding some large palm trees, in the shade of which we changed into our bathing suits and enjoyed a delightful swim in the clear, warm water. We continued walking along the beach which was as beautiful as Beatrice's description, and Mélé Island, now Hideaway Island was as she described it. Also was the river running across the beach from a freshwater lagoon where some boys were having a lovely time, running and jumping or somersaulting into the clear water.

Well dried off, we visited a little café/bar, enjoying a couple of beers and some lunch. Our bus driver – Kilmen – had told us to phone him when we were ready to go back to town, and indeed he came at our behest. En route we stopped at a road-side stall and Kilmen bought himself a *'lap-lap'*. This is a local picnic of grated root crop – depending what is available –mixed with local fruit and coconut milk. Add some 'island cabbage' and meat and wrap it in leaves. Cover with hot stones and bake it for around an hour and a half until cooked. This, Kilmen brought back into the car on two huge banana leaves. He offered to share it with us and tucked into his lunch with gusto.

Back at the museum we met up with the elderly Ambong Thompson. He was very interested in my quest for Beatrice. When I told him she had stayed with a Mr B, the missionary at South West Bay, he knew that Mr B was in fact Mr Boyd. He thought that the Reverend Boyd had built his own house and that his wife, Mary, had died and was buried there. He also told us that dynamite fishing still occurred, and that yes, stupid men still lost hands and arms, and even their lives.

He told me there was a lady called Anne Naupa, an English woman who had come to Vanuatu in the 1950s and who married a local man and worked at the library as an archivist, documenting everything she could find of the history of the Vanuatan people. I phoned her later and made a date to meet up.

Girl making Dresses

Port Vila Market

I was keen to see where Beatrice's ship would have docked, so Joyce and I made our way to the waterfront, first of all going to the local market which I don't imagine would have changed much since Beatrice's time, except for the vast selection of imported fabric from which the local women made dresses for sale. Apart from this, there was a plethora of fruit, vegetables and fish to be sold. We noticed that many of the older women had their two front teeth missing. Beatrice discovered that young women, as soon as they were married, having their teeth knocked out by a stone wielded by some of the older women in the tribe, thus insuring that no strange man would find them attractive. A somewhat bizarre substitute for a wedding ring!

We sat at a table in the garden of the Grand Hotel, watching the launches loaded down with overweight, pale-skinned people being ferried back and forth to the shore from an enormous cruise ship. Sometimes a great argument would break out if one of the ferry boats 'queue-barged'. Then there would be shouting and gesticulating which we found quite amusing. A large catamaran arrived and made up to two huge iron bollards. The boat had a wonderful painted gunwale and I got talking to her master. I asked him where he thought boats would have made up in the early 1900s. He said he thought the two iron bollards where he was made up, were brought from the Burns Philp wooden wharves – where the ferries now went from – and that was where ships would have docked.

One day we decided to take a tour round Efate Island, and try a get a feel of where Beatrice stayed when she rode up-country en route to Undine Bay. We were in a mini bus with two rather nice French, two New Zealanders and

Catamaran, made up at the same quay as the Burns Philp steamers.

unfortunately, two very loud Australians, the girl of this twosome could have shattered glass with her raucous laugh.

The road we were on – donated by the USA – goes round the island, while there is almost no way to go across except on tracks. The local houses on this road have no running water, but crossing a bridge over a little river we found a few small boys having a lovely time, jumping into the water.

Our first stop was at the pretty Blue Lagoon. Joyce didn't want to swim, but I did and had the usual scramble getting into my bathing-suit. The lagoon was delightful. Part salt water, part fresh. An overhanging tree had a long rope attached to it where the boys and girls would swing out from the bank and let go to fall into the warm water. It was fun for them doing it, and amusement for us watching.

Continuing on through a village called Eton, with some of the little houses thatched with pandanus leaves; some with corrugated iron roofs, and some patched with plastic since the Tropical Cyclone Pam of 2015 caused so much damage.

The next stop was for those who wanted to go snorkelling – now at Undine Bay. Joyce and I went for a walk to explore a mangrove swamp area – the trees' enormous roots exposed by the low tide. We got talking to an elderly man there with his family, who told us about the Pandanus tree and its properties, and its importance culturally and economically in the Pacific, second only to the coconut palm. These trees grow wild mainly in semi-natural vegetation in littoral habitats throughout the tropical and subtropical Pacific, where they can withstand drought, strong winds, and salt spray. Species growing along beaches have thick 'prop roots' emerging from the stem about a foot above the ground. These serve as anchors in the loose sand, exactly like the tree we were looking at.

Our new friend also told us that the pandanus is used for lots of handicrafts. Men collect the mature leaves from plants in the wild which are sliced in fine strips and sorted for weaving mats, and a specific type of pandanus – 'the screw pine' – is used for thatching.

Round the top of Efate, our road continued now southwards. We pulled onto the verge on the high hills looking down towards Mélé Beach where Joyce

Gentleman telling us about the Pandanus Tree, and its Properties

and I been the previous day, and where Beatrice had remarked as she gazed up to where we sat, 'blue sea, blue sky and blue mountains'.

I never discovered exactly where Beatrice stayed while in Port Vila. It wasn't until 1906 that Vila was declared the national capital and the seat of the newly proclaimed condominium government, so no wonder it was – as Beatrice had discovered in 1905 – a rather seedy town, much favoured by beachcombers, freed convicts from New Caledonia, and the odd trader.

Port Vila domestic airport was total chaos. People queue-barged; some with enormous luggage and colossal packages. We stood for over an hour in one queue while people came from nowhere and stood in front of us. Ten or so people got boarding cards for a different flight. About ten white people and over a hundred locals fought for position. We ended up, each with a fistful of paper pieces, Joyce having one of my boarding cards and I had one of hers – both giving different boarding times and destinations! We couldn't decide whether to laugh or cry. There was a Destinations board, but we noticed that although it gave the correct date, it didn't change all the time we were waiting there.

Eventually we left. What joy; no security or passport control, just hop on board and off we went. Our journey had to go via Luganville on the island of Espiritu Santo, due north of Malekula Island – our destination. We endured three hours in this airport because we were told the plane had had engine trouble. We took it in turns to look after the bags while the other one explored. Joyce – always observant, enjoyed watching the women coming and going, all wearing virtually identical dresses. These are not a Vanuatu-born design. Like many things that have leaked into this culture, and as Beatrice discovered, the modest Mother Hubbard dress was first introduced and encouraged by Victorian missionaries. So there the women were, today, wearing this floral-printed frock, closely resembling a maternity dress. I expect they are really quite comfortable when you've got a good breeze. They were certainly cooler to wear than the tight stays and long heavy skirts in Beatrice's day.

Malekula Island, 1905

Malekula is the second largest of the Vanuatan islands, separated from the islands of Espiritu Santo and Malo by the Bougainville Strait.

After a few weeks stay in Efate, in October 1905, a steamer – the *Tambo* – came into Port Vila and, with Beatrice on board, made for Malekula Island and South West Bay. Although only sixty-five miles as the crow flies, the boat took a very long time getting there, stopping frequently for small requests, calling at countless ports on the smaller islands before 'doing' Malekula with the thoroughness of a Cook's tour.

Malekula Warrior

By then they were in the country of the real heathen, but the stops were so short that it was impossible to see anything:

> It rained Presbyterian babies throughout the whole tour. They lay on saloon sofas sucking bottles, they flopped on smoking-room seats chewing bananas, they toddled up and down perilous unprotected decks, and attempted to commit suicide over precipitous rails ... I like to be accurate, above everything, and therefore I do not care to estimate the probable infant Presbyterian population of the New Hebrides as over four or five thousand; but that is certainly enough to pacify any possible doubts as to the supply of future missionaries, grown on the premises.[60]

Just possibly a non-admirer of babies, Beatrice then tried to work out the number of babies to missionaries, and found that the Presbyterian baby was the principal product of the islands, coffee and copra coming a good way after.

The steamer stopped at tiny Wala Island on the east coast of Malekula, just long enough to visit a *sing-sing* ground. Beatrice discovered that five or six hundred natives slept on Wala every night, the men looking for safety from the fierce bush tribes of the interior, going ashore by the day to attend to their yam plantations. So when she went ashore, there was almost nobody on the island but a few men who had come home early wearing the native dress of Malekula, which simply consisted of a cartridge belt of woven pandanus fibre drawn tightly around the waist, a boar's tusk suspended around the neck, and a pig's tail in each ear. This totally unshockable woman continued to describe another man with a retinue of several wives also coming ashore; the women carrying both babies and heavy yams. She figured out that he must be a rich man to be able to afford so many young wives, each wife costing somewhere between ten and twenty pigs. But Beatrice thought there must be some difficulty with this system as usually a man cannot afford young wives until he is old and ugly. That's all very well, but what happens when some fine young man, with hardly a pig to his name, and an expensive twenty-porker wife takes a fancy to him, and they run away to the bush together? Then everybody would laugh at the old man, and call him a fool. Not at all a happy state of affairs.

Beatrice continued on to the *hamal* the reed house where the men slept and which was strictly taboo for all females. She was tempted to go into it, but for once, refrained, to wait for another time. The *sing-sing* ground she describes as being a nightmarish place. A gloomy alley, about one hundred yards in length, shadowed by dark, overhanging trees. Along one side ran a number of altars for sacrificing pigs – and other things. It was not very often by this time, that the other things – i.e. people – were available; the resident missionary from time to time preventing the holding of a cannibal feast.

60 Grimshaw, *From Fiji to the Cannibal Islands*, pp. 208–9.

As Beatrice wandered back down to the beach on her way back to the steamer, she noticed some of the beautifully carved canoes, amongst which were one or two war canoes, large enough to carry around fifty or sixty men.

The bay on the south-west corner of Malekula was her destination, and a place of evil reputation. Her steamer put in for a short length of time to land cargo – and her – and take up a load of copra. These calls were short and irregular:

> A wide stretch of water, with little shelter for ships; ominous overhanging cliffs and rocks; a beach of black volcanic sand, torn by thunderous rollers. On the shore, assembled the whole white population of the district – the Presbyterian missionary and his wife, one married and one unmarried trader, and a French missionary priest. This was Sou'-West Bay.[61]

Beatrice was warmly welcomed by the Presbyterian missionary, the Reverend Mr B, and invited to stay for as long as she liked, and she and her luggage were taken off to the neat little house above the beach where the family had their home. The steamer left almost immediately – the disappearance of which marked her last link with civilisation.

At the time that Beatrice visited the New Hebrides in 1905–6, very few Europeans knew anything of the islands, and in particular, Malekula. Although only about sixty miles by thirty-five, it was still mostly unexplored, and the missionaries and white settlers, of which there were only a few, tended to live around the coast, leaving the interior unexplored. Beatrice was told that many of the people of Malekula were apt to being rather impulsive by nature, and expert in the use of poisoned arrows. Certainly there was plenty of proof of this hostility, as, from time to time, the men made attacks on the coast, where they burned and destroyed wholesale, retreating to their mountain strongholds, unpursued and unpunished. These hill tribes were just one of the reasons why the island was still virgin ground to the explorer. The other is that the interior was mountainous, irregular, and covered by dense forest, and it would have been extremely costly to try and make anything of the land.

When the crews of the French and English warships – the *Meurthe* and the *Pegasus*, marched eleven miles inland for a retaliatory burning of the village of Bilyas – there and back in a day in October 1905 (just before Beatrice arrived there) – the exertion was so great that many of the men fell exhausted. So, if fit young men would react thus, it would be impossible for an ordinary expedition to be able to cover such a distance without collapsing.

So, with these vicissitudes, it was no wonder that neither the Catholic, nor the Presbyterian missions had had any effect on the local people, both representatives having escaped with their lives on several occasions, so much so that a man o' war had called to take them off the island, but both had decided to stay and chance it.

61 Grimshaw, *From Fiji to the Cannibal Islands*, p. 162.

Off South West Bay, close to the entrance, lay a tiny island. It appeared that the island had been used for target practice from a man o' war so frequently, that it seemed in danger of being completely shot to pieces. The chief who owned the island protested and wanted compensation. The captain of the ship realised that sooner or later there would be trouble over the head of the island unless the problem was settled, and asked the chief for his price. He subsequently bought the island outright for the British Crown for ten sticks of tobacco, and everyone was happy. The place, ever since then, has been called 'Ten Stick Island'.

Behind the Reverend B's house rose the heavily forested, unconquered mountains. Not unusually, Beatrice decided she wanted to go and explore as far as she could, up into the bush. Her host didn't think the Malekulans would kill a white man on sight, but probably only if he was a threat, and reckoned that if suitably introduced, one might venture into his mountain den, and come off unscathed. He gallantly offered to escort Beatrice on her exploration inland, and never before entered into by a white man, let alone a woman.

The missionary thought they should go unarmed and accompanied by a couple of local boys to find the way. According to the bush telephone, there was to be an idol dance in a couple of days, and this they determined to see. So they set off early one morning wearing light clothing, carrying food and drink and accompanied by two young natives. First of all they had to go by boat up a narrow winding arm of the sea dotted with mangrove islands:

> a very home of the fairies ... Spreading a close rampart of glossy pale-green leafage, starred with small white flowers, above the china-blue water of the lagoon – weaving quaint reed-work of interlaced black stems and roots.[62]

They continued on for some time by boat before landing, and then started their walk up towards the mountain village. As a result of the huge annual rainfall the track they were on was very narrow and slippery – and hilly. You were either struggling up such a steep slope that you had to hold on to roots or whatever was available, and then again to stop sliding down the other side. Also, there was very little light, the track being covered by a canopy of trees and undergrowth, making it hot and humid.

Beatrice, her missionary friend and the two boys, continued on up the difficult terrain, until suddenly, in a glade, they came upon about twenty young Malekulans, clothed as usual in their native 'impudence' and making themselves ready for a dance. One had used burnt coconut to give himself dark eyebrows and circles round his eyes, making a very theatrical appearance. Some others had fixed feathers and flowers in their hair, and all were striped about the face with vermillion paint in different patterns.

62 Grimshaw, *From Fiji to the Cannibal Islands*, p. 231.

They almost all wore little pouches hung round the neck, and down their backs, apparently as a protection against murder. A pig's tail in each ear and a boar's tusk worn like a necklace was the finishing touch. All were armed with rifles. From a safe distance the lads regarded the two white people with a sullen curiosity and some fear. They did not smile, or ask the two native boys about them.

Before long, Beatrice and the missionary became hungry, and sat down to eat their picnic, watched by the Malekulans. After a while Beatrice went over to the men to look at their decorations, and to try and converse with them through the two missionary boys with no great success. Then a few women appeared carrying yams, but when they caught sight of Beatrice, they took fright and wouldn't go near her, one woman dropping her loaded basket. Beatrice picked it up and tried its weight on her shoulder finding it amazingly heavy, and though she was nearly a foot taller than the wizened little woman who had been carrying it, decided she could not have carried it very far. The women of Malekula were bent and misshapen with the enormous loads they were obliged to carry, their expressions sadder and more degraded than that of the men. Pleasure of any kind seemed unknown to them:

> I shall never forget the face of a bushwoman who came down to the mission-house some days later, from another village, carrying yams for her husband to sell and I gave her a pink ribbon and tied it round her neck. A sort of sacred joy seemed to overflow her whole countenance, and lift her far above the things of common earth. She seemed to feel ennobled and exalted by this wonderful thing that had happened.[63]

And what was it? Just a simple piece of ribbon. She was all one ecstatic smile as she went away – treading on air.

Unfortunately Beatrice dropped the basket of yams she had been trying to carry, to the enormous delight of the men watching her efforts. When she asked one of the boys why it was so funny, they explained that she would have been no use as a wife, possibly breaking the yams. Luckily none of the yams were destroyed, but nevertheless Beatrice felt severely chastened by the experience.

A little further on, in a clearing, stood a cluster of great drums being beaten loudly by a boy, with the natives running full tilt round and round, singing as they went. The women stood nearby silently shuffling their feet, while the men fled past. Other men, adorned with leaves and trinkets, stood in silent groups watching the dance.

Beatrice began to feel confused, only able to remember vaguely the dances of the two chiefs – Atamat and Fintimbus which took place sometime during the afternoon.

63 Grimshaw, *From Fiji to the Cannibal Islands*, p. 238.

She seemed to remember that Atamat had a face like a devil. He danced silently by himself over a large area of ground. Even his bare feet were noiseless as he flitted about the ground, showing great agility and lightness. Beatrice thought that perhaps he was representing a bird of prey as he glided with outstretched arms before suddenly making a pounce. Then his dance swiftly came to an end, to be joined by Fintimbus. He approached the dancing arena accompanied by loud chanting, and together the two men performed.

Fintimbus was quite a handsome young chief, adorned with cuffs of solid tortoiseshell with the usual boars tusk as a necklace. On his shoulder he carried a live black pig which he offered to Atamat, and flowers were laid at the feet of a little idol. The whole dance probably had a symbolic meaning and Beatrice was annoyed that nobody – then or later – was able to tell her what it was all about. Then later when the men were singing, she thought it was like a Gregorian chant with the same minor cadences. Both she and her companion were amazed at the beautiful sound, and keen to discover more about it.

At the end of the dancing an enormous tusker pig was led in as an addition to the coming feast. Beatrice and the missionary and their two boys were getting restless as they were aware that the white people's presence was not welcome. Just before they left, one of the men came up to Mr B who turned to Beatrice and told her he was the man who had recently killed a Frenchman. *'Yes, I killum alright,'* the man ascertained, watching to see the effect of his words. However, when Beatrice tried to take his photograph, he disappeared.

Some time later, Beatrice was recounting this episode to a British naval officer who asked her why on earth they had not brought the killer back down with them. Her reply to him was somewhat caustic:

> Six miles from anywhere, up in the fighting country, in a town unknown to whites – Mr B, myself, the boat-boys, with a penknife and two hatpins among us for arms, against two or three hundred murderous savages, provided with rifles, and very easy to offend. I am content to acknowledge that I thought the order too large to execute, and think so still.[64]

Beatrice visited one other village at South West Bay on the edge of the lagoon. The approach to the village was by two paths – one for men and one for women. She joined the men's party taking the men's route, trying to emphasise that the white race did not have to conform to native regulations. However, when she tried to get permission to enter a *hamal* or sacred house, there was no way she was going to be allowed in. The missionary though, to Beatrice's disgust, was allowed to enter.

64 Grimshaw, *From Fiji to the Cannibal Islands*, p. 250.

The two of them then entreated the villagers to at least bring out one mummy for Beatrice to see. At first they refused, but with a little more persuasion and a few gifts, one man brought out a Thing which he set up against the wall of the house, warning Mr B not to let Beatrice touch it, or go near it. It just happened to be the stuffed skin of a man. It was attached to two poles which ran up through the legs and body, and out at the shoulders, the fingers dangling like old empty gloves. There was still hair on the head which was represented by a modelled mask made of vegetable fibre. Standing there in the dancing light of the sun through the trees, the creature looked extraordinarily weird and goblin-like. It had a ghostly grin on its face, and its loose rubbery fingers moved in the current of the strong wind. It certainly looked very much alive (exactly what Joyce and I had seen in the Port Vila museum).

Beatrice observed how many of the women of Malekula had egg-shaped heads, rising up to a most extraordinary point, the slope up from the forehead at such a degree that you might think the brain would be affected, which apparently it was not. She eventually learned that this was not a natural phenomenon when a young woman explained how the shape was achieved by first putting a piece of matting on the head of a baby, and then winding strong cord around the head of the child, tightening the coils from time to time. The mother of the baby who was telling Beatrice about this operation, seemed very proud of her baby's head, pointing out the strings to Beatrice with a smile. One would presume it to be very painful.

Beatrice seemed to have a compulsive fascination with cannibalism, and one thing that she coveted very much was a human skull, leaving no stone unturned in order to acquire one. In time, a native of South West Bay found one for her in a temple. When the captain of the steamer she was on, heard about her acquisition, he had to tell her of his experience, when a fellow in a canoe carrying a sack, came up to the ship with 'something' for him. The sailor told the man to come aboard, when out of the sack tumbled a very new head, hair on and eyes in their sockets. The captain went on:

> 'What the, etc. etc., do you mean ... bringing that filthy thing to my ship?'
>
> 'I think you wantum one-fellow head,' says [the native].
>
> 'So I do ,' says I; 'but I don't want a dirty thing of that kind; it's a nice clean skull I want,' says I; 'and what's more, my man,' I says, 'I'd like to know where you got it anyhow, for you're a pack of murderers, the lot of you.'
>
> 'Oh, he all right, he right,' says the fellow in a terrible hurry; 'plenty all right I tell you! Pappa belong me, he go finish yes'erday, and I bring him head; I think you give me big-fellow tobacco!'[65]

65 Grimshaw, *From Fiji to the Cannibal Islands*, p. 260.

The captain told Beatrice that he did get a clean head soon after that, and put it into a basin of carbolic to soak, just in case. But as true as he was standing there, a cockroach the size of a mouse ran out of each eye, and one out of the nose, and there they sat on the top of the skull and grinned at him. Beatrice laughed and laughed at the captain's stories, as usual reporting this conversation with huge humour.

As mentioned before, Beatrice was always curious about native culture, aware she was not qualified to make scientific studies. She felt that it was a pity the missionaries, who had such good opportunities, were unable – or unwilling – to record what they learned about the natives and their culture, their education being strictly specialised, and geared to destroying these customs and beliefs.

She was also interested in the cause of death of many of the native's enemies and sought advice on the properties of the poisoned arrow; the wound from one almost always causing death within around ten days. Most of the white people thought that the arrows were poisoned by being steeped for weeks in a decaying corpse. However, some of the missionaries thought that death was caused by blood-poisoning from a lethal substance pasted on the arrow-tips.

Luckily, one day Beatrice met a man carrying a lot of arrows and she asked a boy to ask him if she might view the arrows. They had long sharp points with no barbs, and covered so thickly with a brown gluey substance that she found it too difficult to see what they were actually made of. These arrows were always carried well wrapped up in leaves to prevent any nasty accident to their owner. On that occasion, Beatrice, feigning innocence, asked the old gentleman what the arrows were for. He giggled a bit and replied *'For killum man'*. When pressed for more information, he chuckled some more and retreated into the bush.

Diana on Malekula Island

Joyce's and my flight from Luganville at last took off for South West Bay. We were in a tiny De Haviland, Twin Engine turbo-prop aeroplane, carrying its full complement of fifteen passengers. I peered down at the thick bush, looking exactly like tight heads of green broccoli; and then the stunning blue and turquoise of the sea. The plane landed safely on a short, grassy runway, within moments of landing, surrounded by the locals. Today the village of Wintua has become a regional centre with an airstrip, telephone, and hospital – but without any doctors.

Having been told, somewhat enigmatically, that we would go from the airport to our

Walkway through the Mangroves

lodging by boat, we were delighted when a friendly big man approached us and asked me if I was Diana, and told us he was phoning Damien. We had no idea who Damien was, but it became apparent that he was our host, and indeed was on his way by boat to the beach to meet us. Gathering up our rucksacks, we followed our guide down a steep, narrow path to the beach from where we could identify the famous Ten Stick Island lying a mile or so offshore. In a few minutes, we were met by Damien with a boatful of happy children. Along with our bags, we were swept up from the beach and off we went to Mahun on the Lagoon.

The lagoon was in through a narrow gut from the sea, and surrounded by mangrove trees. I was very excited, and asked if there was any other mangrove lagoon, as Beatrice started her inland trek through mangrove trees. I was told this was the only one. It was unbelievable that we should be actually staying where I wanted to go. It had to be Beatrice's place.

We called at the nearby village of Lembinwen to get fish for our supper. Then away up the shallow lagoon to where we stopped at a little bamboo jetty. Two girls welcomed us with grass necklaces and coconut to drink. Then up a very steep path to the loveliest little bungalow – Mahun, meaning 'top of the hill'. We were apparently to be the first visitors to stay in this remote spot. Our little house – belonging to Damien, was built on the same lines as the local houses, and was completely made of materials from the forest except for the concrete floor and a modern shower and loo. Solar energy would provide our electrics. Joyce and I were thrilled with it.

Malekula Island, South West Bay, our Accommodation

When we got settled in Damien asked us what two Irish ladies were doing in South West Bay. I then explained to him about my search for Beatrice Grimshaw. Yet again, here was another person fascinated by the woman, when he read a few pages of her book. He then told me he was a retired teacher of geography and history and that he came originally from the Sepik area of Papua New Guinea. Damien was amazed that I had been there – actually on the Sepik River.

This search for Beatrice Grimshaw has been full of pure serendipity.

We discussed our programme for the following days. Damien and his young helper William hoped they would get an elder from a neighbouring village to come with us to try and find the house of the missionary, Robert Boyd, with whom Beatrice had stayed. I thought we would have to persuade people to help, but in fact it was quite the opposite.

The following morning I was woken at 5 a.m. by the cock crowing. Then the trees around us became alive, first with an early light breeze, then with birdsong. I got up and dressed and walked down the steep path to the landing stage, avoiding the myriad crab holes, and watched men in canoes paddling to their gardens further up the lagoon where they grew coconut palms and cocoa bushes as well as root vegetables.

Back at the bungalow, the two girls who were looking after us asked if we had been woken by the fruit bats during the night as they made a lot of noise in a nearby tree. We hadn't, but when I went to look for our soap which I had opened from its packaging the previous night, it had disappeared. Rats, the girls said. WHAT? Oh dear, I wished they hadn't told us, but apparently they are attracted by the sweet scent and would have eaten it all.

We had an unbelievably wonderful day. We did indeed collect the local elder from the village of Elu across the lagoon. A sprightly 72-year-old, called Joley Simeon, immaculately dressed in whitish shorts and T-shirt, and a pair of brand-new sun glasses, still with the price sticker pasted on one of the lenses. He joined me, Joyce, Damien, William, two other young lads and a boy of ten or so. Off we went to find another elder from the village of Wintua, who, they all thought, would know more about the missionary than anybody.

The "Exploration" Team. TenStick Island in the Background

Joyce and our elderly Guides

To begin with, we thought this elder, called Johnsen, seemed a bit dubious about being asked to find Robert Boyd's house. However, having told him about Beatrice, off we went across the grassy runway, and into the bush. We followed a vague path to start with; then the two old men got going with their long knives, slashing the undergrowth and small bushes. It was hot and humid, but there was birdsong, and many of the bushes and plants held colourful and sometimes scented flowers. Our path led upwards, becoming steeper and steeper. Eventually after about twenty minutes, we came upon some graves hidden in the undergrowth. These were all that remained of the burial ground attached to the missionary's church. We passed by them and struggled on upwards, after some minutes arriving at a large gravestone. It was the stone for Mary Boyd, the missionary's wife. We were able to brush off the dry soil and ants to read the text. The wording on the stone was as follows:

Sacred to the Memory of Mary Young Boyd
Who entered into her rest
14th June 1927
Aged 59 Years
IMESBA COHA TLA OHA

Self Explanatory – Rev Boyd's Wife's Grave

The bottom line of the text was in the local Nahava, saying 'She Died for the Sake of Other People'. It was really very moving, and I wondered if any of Mary Boyd's family had ever been to this spot. Beside the grave was another stone, the words very poorly cut but just about legible, for a young Englishman, who was here studying the people's culture. How sad for one so young. The wording on his stone was:

AB DEAKON
Anthropologist
1903–1927

Arthur Bernard Deacon had arrived eighteen months earlier and travelled throughout Malekula studying the habits and customs of the native people, learning their language and even gaining access to cannibal tribes. On his return to the Presbyterian mission after one extensive journey into the interior, he contracted malaria which developed into blackwater fever from which he died.

We started off again, down past the other graves, then turning back uphill. I couldn't understand why we were cutting our way uphill again. Some of our party split up, obviously searching for something. It was now really hard going, clinging on to branches and roots to pull ourselves upwards. Then all was revealed by the old man, Johnsen. We had arrived at the sparse remains of Reverend Robert Boyd's large house. Easily recognisable were the concrete foundations, a flight of steps, and the fireplace. The building was perched on the highest point above the beach, and would have had a wonderful view all around. There would have been none of the trees here a hundred and ten years ago. Instead of trees, the Reverend Boyd grew vegetables and fruit, and had a few sheep and goats, for both milk and meat.

Again, even though this place was only temporarily connected with Beatrice, I found myself picturing her staying here with the family, and enjoying their hospitality. I had stumbled upon far more than I could ever have dreamed of.

Back we went to Wintua to say goodbye and thank-you to Johnsen, and to see the Boyd Memorial Clinic. What a wonderful bequest to the village people. We then returned to Mahun to go over the day's explorations.

Ruins of the Missionary's House

I told Damien about Beatrice's adventure with the Reverend Boyd through the mangroves and up the steep slippery path to see a festival and extraordinary dance by two natives – Atamat and Fintimbus. I gave him the book again to read about this occasion and he tried to figure out who the men were and just where the festival took place. William and the two girls joined us – all very interested in the book. William said he thought that one of the boys who had been with us earlier in Wintua, was the great, great, grandson of Fintimbus. Karina, one of the girls was very interested in my whole venture. She borrowed the book and went off to read it for an hour or so. We all agreed that although the missionaries did some good, they also did a terrible lot of harm, not only bringing disease, but also destroying local customs and traditions.

William - Damien's great Helper

As Karina said to me, 'It's terrible that I am learning about my past through two ladies from Ireland.' Just how sad can that be?

Meanwhile I had plenty of queries for William and Damien. What was the hierarchy in the villages and how did one become chief? Apparently, in Malekula, the chief is voted for by a local council, in other islands it seems to be a hereditary position, as we learned in Tanna.

Also, Damien's young son was undergoing traditional circumcision in Lembinwen with some other boys aged between eight and thirteen years. For a young boy, circumcision was a terribly painful operation performed with a bamboo knife, and Damien was always thinking about him. The operation was performed in a house – a *hulneyo* – which the boys were not allowed to leave until after some days, when by custom, they would have become men. Damien was able to visit at night, but not the lad's mother.

Karina was so curious about Beatrice that she said she thought perhaps it would be possible to find out more about Atamat and Fintimbus from her grandfather. I later discovered from Karina, that Lororah was the name of Fintimbus village, and that Atamat and Fintimbus were cousins, and the get-together was a visit done regularly on family ties. Simply a normal family visit. It didn't sound very simple by Beatrice's account. I wonder would she have been just a tiny bit disappointed.

Each morning I woke almost on the dot of 5 a.m. with the cock crowing. I would lie on my back gazing at the ceiling, looking at the beautifully worked pandanus thatch supported at random intervals by lengths of unfinished timber. One morning I decided to explore the path to Lembinwen which I knew started behind and above the little cook-house. Off I went with high hopes of getting to the village by land, only to find that it was, just as Beatrice stated, either straight up or straight down. The path was almost indistinguishable through the bush, and within a few minutes I gave up, afraid I would get totally lost.

So having discovered all we could about Beatrice's visit to South West Bay, Joyce suggested we might visit Lembinwen village, and hopefully see some village crafts. The first thing we saw was the dryer for making copra. The flesh of dozens of coconuts had been taken out of the shells and put in a big metal tray on top of a furnace fed by enormous logs. Here it would stay for three to four days until dry. This is then put into sacks and sent away by ship where it is weighed and the villagers paid immediately.

Everything that does not grow locally has to be brought in by ship, there being no roads to South West Bay, Lembinwen, or any of the other local villages.

The ship would anchor in the bay and the merchandise brought ashore by launch or dinghy. Karina told me it sometimes could be two months between calls, and frequently commodities such as flour, coming in paper bags, would be full of weevils or cockroaches. Not much had changed since Beatrice's day, I thought. Damien said the village was about 100 years old, maybe just before Beatrice was here 110 years ago.

We walked through the pretty village along a sandy path between flowering plants. It was immaculately clean and tidy with not a scrap of rubbish to be seen. Water pumps stood at corners surrounded by bright lines of drying washing. The piped water system had been brought about 1980, from a river about two hours walk away, into a big tank above the village. Originally, the village water came from wells which are now covered up.

We were taken to watch two ladies weaving large mats using split pandanus leaves. It looked quite complicated to start with, until I watched and got the hang of how they did it, but I certainly didn't have their deft movements, born of years of practice. Both ladies had taught their daughters how to weave as it is an essential of village life, for floor mats, partitions, wall coverings, and various other household uses.

Our next visit was to the village kindergarten. Three or four little children had been following us, holding our hands and giggling. One wee one was getting into all sorts of trouble for being a bit too boisterous, but they were all gorgeous and most endearing. (Beatrice virtually never wrote about children or babies, and when she did, it was mostly derisive). Although Nahava is their native language, the children learn Bislama – a sort of pidgin English, and, I recognised quite like the Tok Pisin in Papua New Guinea where I found I could almost read it. Then, at primary school they learn English.

We discovered that the church in Lembinwen was entitled, The Christian Life Centre, and before catching our flight back to Port Vila we went to see the church in Wintua which was originally built by the Presbyterian Reverend Boyd. He had arrived in South West Bay in 1895, so was already there ten years before Beatrice stayed with him and his family.

Lembinwen Girl Weaving Mats

Our little Home at SW Bay

After our stay at South West Bay, Joyce and I returned to Port Vila for a night before flying south to Tanna. I had a very early text message in the morning from my daughter in the UK, asking if we were alright as there had been an earthquake in the Solomon Islands, and a tsunami was forecast for Vanuatu. I dressed quickly and went down to reception to find out the situation. I was told that the danger was past, and that the tsunami had by-passed Efate. Thank goodness. We would have been fine in our hotel which was situated uphill, but South West Bay and its villages would have been decimated.

We seemed – by very small margins – to have avoided an Earthquake in New Zealand; the centre of a Cyclone in Fiji; and a Tsunami in Vanuatu.

Beatrice in Tanna, 1905

Tanna is the second most southerly island of the Vanuatu archipelago, twenty-five miles long by twelve miles wide. As part of the Pacific's Ring of Fire, Tanna, being volcanic, is the most fertile of the islands, and enjoys a somewhat better climate than Malekula. In 1905 it had no harbour to speak of, and the anchorages were very poor. Beatrice took little notice of this information assuming it would not affect her, until a stormy morning in November 1905 when she found herself standing on the deck of a Burns Philp steamer, surrounded by all her luggage, to be told that she could not possibly land. Her option was to go on to the island of Aneityum, and wait for a boat to take her back to Tanna once the weather cleared.

However, as they watched and waited, she discovered that two other people also wanted to go to Tanna – to Lenakel, the same as Beatrice. They were watching the shore with interest and some excitement. After a time the sea calmed a bit and they hoped a boat might be able to leave the shore and take them from the steamer – as indeed it did:

> the methods of landing passengers that obtain about the islands seem at first a very bad joke, and then a very unpleasant reality. Later, you grow callous; you become used to the dangling rope ladder skipping above the plunging boat, and

the playful billow that drops a ton of cold water in your lap, the unbroken reef that must be literally jumped on the crest of a wave, the narrow passage full of tumbling foam, and edged by coral splinters and pinnacles as sharp as broken glass; the squall that may get up at any inopportune moment, and maroon you for a month where you least desire to stay – and all the other little excitements that attend embarking and disembarking about the 'sunny isles of Eden,' beloved by poets who have never been there.[66]

The three landed safe and sound; Beatrice, a surgeon missionary and his wife, both, she happily discovered from Bangor, County Down in Ireland. The missionary and his wife kindly invited Beatrice to stay with them – there being no hotels or any other kind of accommodation in the islands in those days.

Beatrice thought that the people of Tanna were a remarkable race in spite of their murderous tendencies, having a much better character than the Malekulans. They were a cheerful-looking race and quite devoid of the sulky, hang-dog look that disfigured most other New Hebrideans. Many of the men were taken both legally and illegally to Queensland in Northern Australia to work on the plantations.

A few days after her arrival, Beatrice went, with her host Mr C, to visit the village of Imale. There was, apparently, a lot of fighting here, and Mr C went to try and convert these heathens to Christianity; Beatrice went because she hoped to get a good thigh bone from one of the slain! Beatrice, Mr C, and the village chief were enjoying a conversation which mostly concerned the disposal of an enemy's body, supposed to have been partly eaten by him a few days previously. The pair of whites were keen on prolonging the chat, but the old chief proclaimed he had never heard of cannibalism, the man had not been eaten at all – he wasn't even sure he'd been killed.

What an innocent sounding old man. What a naïve and childlike smile that he put on. Such an attitude of respectability, even dressed as he was in nothing at all:

'Now look here, you know you did!' says the missionary plumply.

The nice old gentleman's smile takes on a different character – becomes, in fact, a giggle, like that of a schoolgirl caught eating surreptitious chocolates.

'Well – I eatum jus' little fellow bit!' he allows.'[67]

However, in the middle of Beatrice having a good irreverent laugh, suddenly fifteen Tannese lifted their rifles and pointed them straight at the trio. The missionary shouted to them in Tannese to stop, and the men, looking rather astonished sat back down again, lowering their guns.

66 Grimshaw, *From Fiji to the Cannibal Islands*, p. 281.

67 Grimshaw, *From Fiji to the Cannibal Islands*, p. 294.

The excuse was that they had seen a strange head immediately behind the trio. That the trio were in the direct line of fire appeared to be of little consequence.

If the tribes could have been disarmed by banning the sale of rifles by unscrupulous traders, all the wanton killing might have ceased. But it had become self perpetuating as a system of 'pay-back'. For every killing, the murderer, or even one of his clan, had also to be killed in retaliation. But the law did not prohibit the sale of arms, and consequently the loss of native lives continued unabated.

One day, Beatrice's medical missionary host, had reason to visit a bush village to see a young woman's injuries after being shot. She was so badly hurt that he decided to take her back to his hospital to try and save her life. She was tied onto a stretcher and carried by the natives some nine miles through the bush, and then twenty miles in an open boat. The following day the doctor decided to operate, and when half way through his surgery, he sent for Beatrice, knowing she had nursing experience. Beatrice made her way to the little hospital and into the tiny operating theatre. There she found the young, attractive woman, her chloroformed breathing audible, and her arms and small hands hanging limp and lifeless over the edge of the table. Beatrice was appalled at the terrible wound in the girl's side. The shell had ruptured her liver and broken three ribs, the splinters from which had penetrated her lungs. Gangrene was evident around the wound. The girl had already survived ten days in this appalling mess, so Beatrice thought she might live, but the missionary held very little hope for her. As she walked despondently back to the house, all Beatrice could think of was the sound of the girl's laboured breathing. The country so badly needed the hand of a strong government who might disarm the natives by force.

Having stayed a week or so in Lenakel, Beatrice rode across the island on a rough and hilly track, to Whitesands, on the east coast some twenty miles away. She brought with her a native, Simoni, as a translator. Sometimes she had to dismount and lead her horse as they scrambled up and down the slippery path. At around 1,000 feet, they stopped for lunch at a windy but wonderful viewpoint, with the whole of Tanna lying at their feet, and the great live volcano, Yasur, rumbling and smoking away on their right-hand side. A little way down the east side of the mountain, Simoni started to giggle:

> 'You savvy that-fellow place you eat 'um dinner?' he asks chuckling.
>
> 'Yes; what about it?' [Beatrice replied].
>
> 'All same place, Tannaman he eat woman, leg you got in one-fellow box; two, three, four week!' Simoni cackles explosively.'[68]

This required an explanation. Some time before, a native woman had been eaten by the tribe above Lenakel, the missionary, retrieving some of the relics of the victim,

68 Grimshaw, *From Fiji to the Cannibal Islands*, p. 310.

had given Beatrice the thigh bone – a rather grizzly souvenir she admitted. The bone she had put into her box for safe-keeping, and Simoni knew this, and it was he who had chosen the picnic place. For all their terrorism, the natives were not without a spot of humour.

All things come to an end, and after a hot and wearisome journey across Tanna from sea to sea, Beatrice seriously writes:

> I and my guide (it is not grammar, but racial pride is above grammar any day – and the guide was black) arrived at the hospitable mission station in Whitesands Bay, where I had been asked to stay a week or two.[69]

Mission stations filled much the same position as monasteries in the Middle Ages, and were almost the only centres of learning in the midst of ignorance. Like the monasteries, they were safe and comfortable, full of cheer and some of the simple pleasures so badly missed by the traveller. The missionary at Whitesands made Beatrice welcome. The house was large and very comfortable with a long veranda facing east across a lawn and then the sea. There was handsome furniture; a shower and good food – a veritable oasis in the midst of the heat, and the constant possible danger.

Yasur could be heard clearly as its thunderous eruptions echoed over the land. At night it was most dramatic, the hot, burning lava being thrown high into the air, gleamed a burning red against the night sky. Although very seldom visited, Beatrice of course, was anxious to have a look into the crater. All things considered, it was surprising that her kind host let her venture off to visit the volcano with just a couple of pidgin-speaking native guides, particularly as most Tannamen had a deadly horror of the place.

They set off late one afternoon as Beatrice wanted to see the 'fireworks' in the dark. From Whitesands it took them only an hour and a half easy walking to reach the volcano and get to the top. Although a good walker herself, she admired how the boys loped along with an easy stride, unhampered as they were from far too much clothing. She frequently had to ask them to stop and wait for her.

Gradually the thick bush became thinner. The trees ended, and suddenly the trio were walking across an old lava field, then a flat plain of black ash which led them to the cone towering another 800 feet above them. Gradually they attained the summit and were able to look down into the fiery crater.

She thought it a little disappointing at first. Having expected a livid sea of fire, all that could be seen was a black hole traversed by a bright red crack across the middle and a modest fountain of fire jetting up small globules of burning lava and pieces of red-hot rock.

69 Grimshaw, *From Fiji to the Cannibal Islands*, p. 314.

But suddenly the dozing fire fountain jumped a hundred feet higher into the air, the crater bellowing right into the faces of the trio standing nearby, turning their spines to jelly. Beatrice found herself running helter-skelter back down the ash slope hand-in-hand with the two terrified natives. It wasn't courage that made her stop a few yards from the crater lip. Oh no – white people must not be frightened in front of blacks. So, with a great deal of bravado, Miss Grimshaw climbed back up to the crater, where, by and by it erupted a second time, the ground shaking beneath her feet, and the noise primeval. It was impossible for her not to feel that there was something alive and powerful, and extremely wicked down there.

Ashfield below Yasur Volcano

For more than an hour Beatrice stayed on the summit watching with a fascinated terror. Her two boys came and went depending upon how brave they felt. One of them, looking down exclaimed that it looked *'all same hell'*. As the sun went down the whole crater became lit up, the air above it reflected red while far above hung the dark blue heaven, calm and silent, studded with a billion stars, unimaginable distances away. Now it was as she had imagined it. Now it looked alive.

It was February 1906, and a few days later, lying off Tanna Island, Beatrice could see the crimson cloud hovering high above the black cone, blotting out the crystal stars. She was on the SS *Malaita*, en route for Sydney, via the islands of Erromanga and Aneityum.

For a few hours, Beatrice's ship put in at Norfolk Island. It seems probable she did not go ashore, but she was well informed about the island which was first settled by East Polynesians. It had served as a convict penal settlement from March 1788 until May 1855.

Beatrice was disappointed not to have visited the island, as evidently she missed the exciting spectacle of huge whale boats tearing through the sea with the speed of an Atlantic liner, in the chase for a whale. The hunt was a dangerous one, but those who had done it said there was nothing more exciting in the world of sport. Few tourists visited Norfolk Island, just an occasional wanderer. But Beatrice had heard that visitors were made welcome by the bare-footed, uneducated but quite self-possessed ex-mutineers of the Bounty and their descendants:

'Here, (she says) the tale of my wanderings closes; not because the story is ended.'[70]

In the two years, between arriving in Tahiti in Feb 1904, and leaving Sydney for the UK in Feb 1906, Beatrice managed to visit the Cook Islands, New Zealand, the Friendly Islands, Sydney, Fiji, and the New Hebrides (Vanuatu), and almost never mentioned any dates of arrivals or departures.

Diana on Tanna Island

Before leaving Port Vila and Efate, Joyce and I were joined by Joyce's two sisters, Jill and Jay from New Zealand. They were keen to come to Tanna Island with us to visit the volcano, Yasur. So off we trooped once again, enjoying the mad domestic airport with no security/passport-control/immigration strictures. I loved the little twin-engined Otter aeroplanes flying so low that one could see the wonderful colours of the lagoons and coral reefs, the mountainous islands, and the various shades of green tropical bush.

70 Grimshaw, *From Fiji to the Cannibal Islands*, p. 353.

Yet again I had had one of those serendipitous meetings before leaving Ireland, when I had met Barbara Mayne. In her book, *A Remarkable Man* (2006), she had put together a collection of her surgeon/missionary grandfather's letters from Tanna to his mother in Ireland, and one letter caught my eye. It is dated November 3rd 1905, and describes James Campbell Nicholson's arrival back to Tanna after sailing round some of the other islands:

> We have a Belfast lady journalist on board and she is coming to Tanna to stay for five weeks. Her name is Miss Grimshaw and her people live now in Portrush. She is a manly big woman of about 13 or 14 stone weight and keen on yarns. She is going to write a book. At present she contributes to some of the magazines.[71]

We were driven south from Tanna Airport, by Harry Nikiau Iawia to our hotel – Tanna Lodge – near the village of Lenakel. When we were planning this trip, Joyce and I chose to book in at Tanna Lodge, being near to Lenakel where Beatrice had stayed with the surgeon James Nicholson, whose book of letters we were supposed to be leaving at the church. Indeed when we arrived there, it was exactly what we wanted, with two separate little thatched 'villas', surrounded by beautiful gardens and literally a stone's throw from the sea. Joyce and I were delighted by our choice. It also turned out that our local driver, Harry, knew everyone and everything about the island, and offered his services for anywhere we wanted to go, including the volcano.

At dinner that evening, our host and owner of the hotel, Hugh Lowe, came and asked why we were there. I again had to regale him with stories of Beatrice Grimshaw, and lent him her book for a night. He, in turn regaled us with stories of Tanna Lodge, and some of the tales of the island.

We arranged for Harry to take us up the road that Beatrice rode along to get to Whitesands on the other – east side – of the island where we might be able to find the missionary's house where she stayed before visiting the volcano.

We set off up the unmade road until reaching a large clearing surrounded by three or four enormous Banyan trees. The Banyan trees are where the *nanamas* live. These are special spirits that the chiefs only may speak with, and so consequently the trees are spiritual.

Having arrived at the *kastom* (traditional) village of Yakul, I was aware of a small, thin, seemingly naked man, sitting alone on a wooden bench. Harry approached to ask if it would be alright for us to talk with him. I could see that when the man stood up his penis was covered by a small bunch of leaves, tied on round his waist. Other than this he was completely naked. Many years ago this village had refused to become Christianized by the missionaries who were afraid of the villagers. These folk live mainly off what grows naturally, but also cultivate yams, bananas and other vegetables.

71 Barbara Mayne, *A Remarkable Man* (Bloomington: Trafford Publishing, 2006), p. 90.

Head Man and two others in the village of Yakul

I gathered that the children did not go to school in the past, but some nowadays do. They believe in spirits, so when they want a good yam year, they perform the yam dance, and when they want rain, they do the rain dance and so on. However, everything they explained eventually comes from the skies. (Don't we *all*, to some extent believe this, regardless of our chosen religion?) There is also here, initiation for boys when they are circumcised as in Malekula. A bride can come from any other village but will come here, to her husband's village, to live. Here, on Tanna, the chiefs are hereditary.

We hung around for a bit in the silent arena. Gradually more naked men wandered around, while a young boy beat out a rhythm on the huge tree-trunk drum. Within a few minutes, out of the surrounding forest, on noiseless bare feet, appeared other children, and women who laid down mats with some artefacts for us to buy. The men were all adorned with the same little bunch of leaves while the women wore long grass skirts under naked breasts. The skin of the older men was very dry and rough. The children mostly looked quite healthy but had horrible snotty noses.

We all bought some small item. I was exceptionally pleased with a boar's tusk, as, according to Beatrice all the chiefs wore one round their necks. It was a bit mucky and had no cord attached to hang round my neck, so I said I would pay a little less than the asking price if the vendor would make, and attach the prerequisite cord. This she did, while I watched her deft fingers entwining the long bits of grass into a piece of string and attach it to the tusk, and off I went with my trophy.

By then, the village had begun the Taro Dance. The men in the middle stamped and shouted and sang, and the women and children ran and skipped round the periphery laughing and shouting also. It was all excellent fun. Yakul may not be Christian, nor join in the mores of today, but they are not averse

Tribal Dance, asking for a good Taro Harvest

to putting on a show for tourists and making a little cash by selling their beads and necklaces.

Back into the car and we continued our drive eastwards along an earth road full of lumps and bumps, up and downhill, towards Whitesands. Harry was certain there was a school named after Beatrice that I thought was a very long shot indeed. Why would there be? Twice Harry stopped to ask about this school, eventually finding a man who said he knew of an old missionary house with a school, but it was much further down towards Whitesands.

On we went, off the main road and down a narrow, high-banked lane where we found a village elder. While Harry was talking to him, they both became very animated and I thought this looks good. Sure enough, the elder knew the school and the missionary's house. First of all we came to the school called 'Petros Memorial School'. I still wondered why on earth there would be a school named after Beatrice – even if indeed, in the local dialect, Beatrice was mistaken for Petros.

The elder introduced himself to me as Caleb as we walked on down a grassy hill to a church, built much more recently than 1905. But inside, hanging lopsided on one of the walls was a photograph of Thomson Macmillan, who had been the missionary in Whitesands from 1895–1935. What a find. It would have been he with whom Beatrice had stayed in 1905. Then Caleb brought me through a neglected, one time beautiful garden, and, as in South West Bay, to the concrete foundations of a large house. As well as the foundations, it was easy to make out the huge fireplace at the back of the house. This area had been destroyed in one of the cyclones that plague these islands. James Nicholson, in his book, mentions a bad one in 1910, but the present occupiers didn't know when it had occurred.

Picture of Thompson McMillan, Minister at Whitesands

Old Minister's House where Beatrice stayed

However, part of the house still stood – a sad, dilapidated relic of past glory – and in it lived today's native pastor who came to meet us with his wife. I explained why we were there, and again they were amazed at where Beatrice had travelled, and where I had travelled also – shadowing her. The front of the house still had the remains of a long low veranda and a level piece of grassy ground which would surely have been a manicured lawn. I nearly wept. It was almost as Beatrice had described it. We wandered on over the 'lawn' and a field to where a high cliff fell down to the sea. It was so beautiful, and must have been even more so in the palmy days of the past. We were carrying a copy of Barbara Mayne's grandfather's book to refer to from time to time, but Caleb became very interested in it and asked if he could keep it. This put us in a bit of a quandary as we were supposed to give the books to the church in Lenakel. However, as we still had two remaining, and Caleb had been so helpful saying he would share it with the pastor, that we thought they would give it a good home.

Harry also told us that his great grandfather, Iawia was the person who was responsible for the upkeep of the Petros Church and school. He wasn't certain of the exact date, but it was for a long time and most definitely he would have been looking after the area when Beatrice was there.

A couple of days later, Harry reported a meeting he had had with a man from the UK who was an NGO to do with the local schools. He remarked to Harry that all but one of the schools were named after a biblical character – and that one, was Petros.

Harry was able to tell him that he thought it was named after a woman called Beatrice, an Irish woman who had visited here.

Beatrice said she walked from the missionary's house to Yasur with two young men in about an hour. She was some cookie if this is correct. Of course she was only thirty-five after all. It took us over an hour driving to this frequently visited volcano. Yasur has been more or less active since Captain Cook first observed ash eruptions in 1774.

Jill, Jay and Diana at Yasur Volcano

Probably we went by a more circuitous route than Beatrice; across a large ash field where we stopped to take photos of the field and the volcano belching smoke, and rumbling away in the distance, every now and then emitting a thunderous roar. Our road, winding gradually upwards, took us through a forest where Joyce spied a pleasant little restaurant where she said she would wait for us. I was surprised when she said she was frightened of Yasur. We left Joyce at her refuge for the evening while we continued on to the Volcano Reserve. Having gained permission from the local chief, whose land the volcano was on, off we went in a pick-up, attended by an official Volcano Guide, along a clay track to where we were disgorged at the foot of a long, steep flight of concrete steps, up and up, to the crater rim.

It was an extraordinary experience. We must have stayed up there for an hour and a half as the sun set and gradually dusk fell. I think it was mostly the sound which was so eerie. The swishing sound, as of waves in a cave, but was in fact, the molten magma rolling around beneath our feet, slopping and gurgling against the crater walls. Then, every so often, the pressure would build up and there would be a thunderous roar which permeated one's entire being, thumping through my chest and head. This elemental noise accompanied an eruption of smoke, gas and steam while red-hot pieces of magma were hurled high into the air.

Even while it was still daylight I could see a red burning vent below us, shimmering in the vapour from the colossal heat. Then gradually, as dusk fell the red fire below was reflected in the cloud above, while each eruption became the world's most terrifying and extravagant firework display. Below us, in her pretty restaurant, Joyce was delighted to tell us she also was able to view the fireworks, and the wonderful fiery rockets soaring into the night sky.

There were no safety precautions 110 years before, and no final concrete steps up to the rim. But Beatrice was never daunted by danger – except from sharks – and even though the first eruption thoroughly frightened her and her two boys, she went back for more. No wonder she was enthralled by this view into the heart of the world.

As we still had two of the Nicholson books waiting to be donated to the church at Lenakel, we asked Harry if he would take us to the Tannese chief – Peter Marshall. However, apparently Peter was not in Tanna, but he said he had been in touch with Peter's younger brother who would be pleased to meet us.

We arrived at Iavis' home on the outskirts of Lenakel. He was an elder of the church and extremely religious. He and his wife and family lived in a delightful house-cum-restaurant right on Joy Beach. We met his family who wanted to sing a hymn for us. 'Lead Us Oh Thou Great Jehova' was their choice, and I have to say their harmonious rendering was superb. However, no matter how much I asked about Beatrice, it was the missionaries that Iavis wanted to talk about.

We discovered that this Iavis' grandfather was also called Iavis, and it was he whom Beatrice would have met.

Eventually we persuaded Iavis 'the younger' to take us to see the church and hopefully the house that James Campbell Nicholson lived in, and therefore the house which Beatrice had stayed in for some weeks in November 1905.

Barbara Mayne's book is extremely interesting in many ways, being a first hand account of a missionary's life in Tanna. There are many of Nicholson's references to the Reverend McMillen – whose photo we had seen in the church at Whitesands – as being 'a grand man'. The Nicholsons and McMillens became close friends, particularly the two wives. He also describes his own house in Lenakel as being 250 or 300 feet above the sea. So we knew exactly where to find it as we climbed up the steep path to

Where Beatrice would have stayed at Lenakel in Tanna

Higher than the Mosquitos!

where the house now lies in ruins. It would have been a delightful place, high enough to catch the breeze, and with wonderful views all around. Here is where Beatrice would have lived during her stay in Lenakel.

Iavis also took us to where the original church had been, and also the old hospital – both now in ruins, but replaced by newer buildings. James Nicholson had, at that time, a splendid right-hand-man called Lomai, a converted native who learned to speak excellent English, and who also learned to assist the doctor. A book was written about him by Frank H. L. Patton BD, for six years resident missionary on the west coast of Tanna. The book is called *'Lomai of Lenakel'* and was published in 1903 by Hodder and Stoughton.

When it was time to leave Tanna, our host, Hugh, drove us to the airport. We talked at length about 'pay-back' which I knew still existed in Papua New Guinea. According to Hugh it was still carried out – of course illegally – in Tanna. Mostly the victim is not shot but either bludgeoned to death or the throat cut, and mostly over land disputes.

Whatever the political/legal situation on Vanuatu, Joyce and I had loved our visit there; mostly, of course, because of my successful search for Beatrice Grimshaw. We had discovered from the locals so much interest in this Irish woman and her travels. Her descriptions of the islands brought it all to life, and fascinated everyone I spoke to. Their consequent involvement and assistance in finding out more about her was astonishing, and a joy.

Our onward journeys would take Joyce back to New Zealand, and me via New Zealand and Sydney, to Adelaide. We would both be spending Christmas 2016 with our families.

Chapter 12: England and Ireland

Like everything about Beatrice, there is very little personal information, so whether she already knew of her mother's death in November 1905 she doesn't say. Her mother must have been staying with Beatrice's elder sister, Maud and husband Dr Howard Sinclair, at their home in Warrenpoint Co Down, when she suffered a cerebral haemorrhage from which she died, intestate, shortly after on November 6th. On the 1st December, her widower, Nicholas Grimshaw, renounced all rights, title and interest in the personal estate of his deceased wife. Their daughter, Maud Sinclair was granted letters of administration, with an estate value of £71 in cash, which, after funeral expenses left £51. When Beatrice arrived in Sydney at the end of February 1906, she would surely have known the sad news by then.

In any event, she sailed from Sydney to London on March 14th. *The Evening News*, Sydney, of 13th March 1906, reported that the magnificent P and O liner, *Mooltan*, would leave Circular Quay at noon, for London. Miss Beatrice Grimshaw was on the list of passengers.

The ship, having called at Hobart, Melbourne, Freemantle, Colombo, Aden, and Marseilles, did not arrive in London until the 28th April 1906. Here Beatrice had three books published: *In the Strange South Seas, From Fiji to the Cannibal Islands* – which she dedicated to her father, and also *Vaiti of the Islands*. The three books were all published in 1907 along with several factual pamphlets, including *Islands of the Blest* and *Three Wonderful Nations: Tonga, Samoa, Fiji*, for the Union Steamship Company

As well as going west, as she had done, from Liverpool to the US, and onwards across the Pacific to Australia, Beatrice knew it was possible to travel from Tilbury and go south to the Mediterranean and then east via the Suez Canal and India to Australia. So consequently she opens *From Fiji to the Cannibal Islands* with an 'invented' first few paragraphs – describing a journey as though she was actually going east around the world starting at Tilbury in order to give the two books a different beginning. Quite clever, but initially for the researcher, extremely confusing.

Later that same year, almost as soon as she arrived in Papua, Beatrice was bold enough to register her impressions with – *The Real Papua*, for *The Sydney Morning Herald*.

For some time Beatrice had been interested in Papua New Guinea, and, like everybody else thought it belonged to England. While in London, she visited the reference library, discovering, to her great surprise, that England did not own Papua New Guinea. The Netherlands had a large half of it, and Germany a quarter leaving a portion to Britain, almost twice the size of England.

But what really drew her attention to Papua was the death by suicide in 1904 of the Chief Judicial Officer, Christopher Robinson, who was temporarily in charge of the country.

Early in 1904 Robinson, a young Brisbane solicitor had been appointed acting Administrator and Judicial Officer of British New Guinea, pending the implementation of legislation formalising the Territory of Papua under Australian control. En route by ship to his new post early in 1904, some local natives approached the *Merrie England*, firing arrows from their canoes. This was, apparently, in retaliation for the arrest of kinsmen, believed to have taken part in the killing of two missionaries on Goaribari three years earlier. Robinson and the crew of the *Merrie England* appear to have acted in haste and fired shots from the ship killing several of the natives. Perhaps, with no prior experience of New Guinea, he had simply panicked and imagined himself massacred like the missionaries in 1901.

The incident resulted in a Royal Commission of Enquiry under Judge Hubert Murray. However, shortly before the enquiry commenced, Christopher Robinson, sure his reputation was at stake, went to Government House in Port Moresby, stood at the foot of the flagstaff and shot himself.

Beatrice also discovered through her research that the scenery of Papua New Guinea was fabulous; the bird and insect life fascinating; and for the rest, the books told of cannibals and crocodiles, fevers, snakes and swamps. There were unexplored rivers and unnamed mountains. It all sounded totally fascinating to Beatrice.

Although not mentioned, one has to presume that Beatrice went to see her family in Ireland during the year she was back in Britain. After all, her mother had died and her widowed father was very ill, suffering from Bright's disease. He still lived at Skerry Bahn in Portrush. But on 16th March 1907, Nicholas Grimshaw also died, leaving an estate of £30. His son, Osborne was present at his death. Nicholas was buried next to his wife at Clonallon graveyard near Warrenpoint. Maybe Beatrice was there, with some of her family, for her father's funeral.

We know that Beatrice did not stay long after, sailing away on 27th March from Tilbury to Sydney on board the *SS Mongolia*, arriving in Sydney on 6th May 1907. Here she stayed with friends for some time before setting off for Papua.

The articles in this copy of *An Illustrated Weekly Magazine* - 18th Aug 1906 - had different titles, but were all derived from Beatrice Grimshaw's book *"Vaiti of the Islands"*, promoting Beatrice's forthcoming book, published in 1907

Chapter 13: Papua New Guinea

It wasn't until November 1907 that Beatrice finally ventured to Papua New Guinea, the governing of which had been taken over by the Australian Government, under the title 'The Territory of Papua'. She set off from an obscure Sydney wharf on board the Australian Steamship Company's steamer, *Arawatta* – her luggage labelled, 'Port Moresby'.

There followed ten days of absolute bliss as the steamer ploughed her way up the coast of Queensland. There, on the comfortable steamer, warm breezes blew in off the sea with a bright sun dancing each morning on the calm waters that lie inside the Great Barrier Reef. Beatrice revelled in the lazy days, lying on her deck chair, occasionally looking up to see the purple hills, rising away in the distance behind a coast of creamy gold. Day by day they arrived at the hot little towns of Port Macquarrie and Townsville and the already large town of Brisbane. At Cairns – a town of some importance – everyone went ashore to a hotel for the night. Here, Beatrice saw a stuffed cassowary. Up until then she had thought they only lived in Timbuktu, amusing herself by remembering the rhyme:

If I were a Cassowary,
On the plains of Timbuktu,
I would eat a missionary,
Cassock, bands, and hymn-book too.[72]

72 Attributed to Samuel Wilberforce, (1805–1873), Bishop of Oxford, FRS.

In fact the cassowary is a fearsome looking creature. He is about five feet tall with a huge red and blue skin-covered 'casque' on his head, which grows up to seven inches with age. His legs, with large, three-toed feet, carry him along at a good pace. The inner toe has a dagger-like claw five inches long. Normally very shy, when disturbed, the adult cassowary is capable of disembowelling a man.

Eventually Beatrice's ship docked at Cooktown, well north on the coast, and where the steamer would go no further. There was a main street lined with shops and several hotels, and a statue of Captain Cook who arrived here, naming the town after himself. It was from here one would take a ship of the Burns Philp line, to continue on to Papua; in Beatrice's case it was the SS *Mokambo*. BP's boats never went anywhere that was settled, and her captain and officers – almost to a man, had lived lives of adventure. Perhaps because of this they were rather blasé and not at all interested in anything mundane. Burns Philp was a keen trader. The ships leaving port were usually laden down with such romantic cargoes as pearls and pearl-shell, sandalwood and cedar, beche-de-mer, and coconut, ivory-nuts and tortoiseshell. There was usually plenty of local colour on board also – an odd explorer or two, a gold prospector, and native peoples who would do war-dances on the after deck in the moonlight.

Beatrice and the friends she had made, had by then a fund of information on Papua New Guinea, and especially Port Moresby where they would land. She herself wondered at the fact that by 1907 most of Africa and South America were well known, and Central Asia and Central Africa were well explored. But not Papua. Why? She was keen to find out.

From her research Beatrice discovered that the first known Europeans to sight New Guinea were probably the Portuguese and Spanish navigators sailing in the South Pacific in the early part of the 16th century. In 1526–1527 the Portuguese explorer Jorge de Menezes accidentally came upon the principal island and is credited with naming it 'Papua', after a Malay word for the frizzled quality of Melanesian people's hair. The Spaniard Yñigo Ortiz de Retez applied the term 'New Guinea' to the island in 1545 because of a perceived resemblance between the islands' inhabitants and those found on the African Guinea coast.

Although European navigators visited the islands and explored their coastlines thereafter, little was known of the inhabitants until the 1870s. Then, the Russian anthropologist Nicholai Miklukho-Maklai made a number of expeditions to New Guinea, spending several years living among native tribes, and describing their way of life in a comprehensive treatise. In 1873, the English Captain Moresby annexed some of the islands at the eastern end of the country, which was disapproved by the British government. The capital Port Moresby was named after him.

In 1883, the Colony of Queensland had tried to annex the southern half of eastern New Guinea, but the British government again did not approve. However, when Germany began settlements in the north, a British protectorate was proclaimed in 1884 over the southern coast of New Guinea and its adjacent islands. The protectorate, called British New Guinea, was annexed outright on 4th September 1888. The possession was placed under the authority of the Commonwealth of Australia in 1902. Then, following the passage of the Papua Act in 1905, British New Guinea became the Territory of Papua, and formal Australian administration began in 1906.

The Lieutenant-Governor, soon after Beatrice arrived in Papua New Guinea, was His Excellency John Hubert Plunket Murray. This doughty gentleman had had a notable career at the New South Wales Bar, and had served with distinction in the Boer War, being honoured by the British government with the rank of major.

As they approached Papua, the impatient voyagers should have been able to see some of the higher mountains of the Owen Stanley Range, but they were disappointingly almost invisible beneath low clouds. Beatrice could hardly contain her excitement.

Before long the steamer rounded a green headland, and the *Makambo* dropped anchor in Port Moresby Bay. There was no mistaking the pioneering town without roads and just one or two large buildings – government offices, the residence of the London Missionary Society, and a score or two of houses, all painted white, surrounded by deep verandas and perched on top of piles, eight or nine feet high. Beatrice learned later that this was not because the ground was marshy, but in order to avoid ants, snakes, iguanas and sundry other livestock eager to make their homes, in the wet season, with the residents.

There were three or four long wooden piers, but the steamer discharged her passengers and cargo by tender, landing on the central pier. Beatrice and her new friends walked up the path into the town, assailed by the scent of sandalwood from a huge pile of rough logs beside the track. As a well-educated and interesting Irish Catholic; a noted sportswoman; an advocate of commercial enterprise for tropical countries, and having much in common with the Lieutenant-Governor, Hubert Murray, Beatrice was lucky in having been invited to stay at Government House. Murray described her in a letter to his brother, Gilbert – a famous Greek scholar – as an extremely nice woman and not a bit superior.

Accompanied by his wife, Murray had arrived in Port Moresby in September 1904. Although married, his wife Sybil disliked Papua, and before long returned to her less primitive home in Sydney. Over the next thirty-five years Murray was rarely to have both wife and children in his official residence.

The only trained lawyer in British New Guinea, Murray heard all cases coming before the Central Court and he was soon travelling on the government boat to take cases in outer administrative divisions, constantly resisting the special pleading of white settlers, and maintaining the English-Australian legal system. His court procedure was simple – in English, and therefore often dependent on interpreters, and at sentencing he took native customs into account. His strongly worded instructions of 1909, telling officers that they were never justified in firing on natives by way of punishment, and warning them that self-defence would not always protect them from charges of manslaughter. These orders were issued when punitive expeditions were still common in German New Guinea, and in northern Australia.

Murray read current anthropology, and created the post of government anthropologist. Most of his opinions derived from wider humane studies and his own shrewd observations. His views were more liberal than those of nearly all white residents in Papua.

His one champion, however, was Beatrice Grimshaw. Impressed with Murray's work, she found in Papua ample scope for her ability as a publicist, and was interested in helping Murray attract settlers. During 1908 she wrote letters to the Prime Minister of Australia, Alfred Deakin, praising Murray, and assuring him of the native Papuan's respect for him. She was outspoken to Deakin in her attitude to the missionaries. Although more or less a supporter of the missions, she deplored their tendency to usurp the functions of government, and to retain as much power as possible for themselves.

Diana in Papua New Guinea

In 1995, I wrote a diary during my trip to Papua New Guinea with my sister and her son. I was about to follow in the footsteps of Beatrice Grimshaw without realising it.

We too arrived in Port Moresby via Cairns, and a visit to Cooktown, but by air rather than the more exciting sea journey. Having arrived at Port Moresby, we didn't hang about too long as we had been warned about the 'rascals', a euphemism for pick-pockets and thieves. We had decided to start our holiday with a couple of restful days on an island resort off Madang, then join Andrew Storey and his wife Darcy in the highlands at Mount Hagen, before going on to the Sepik River.

The town of Madang on Papua New Guinea's north coast is rather pretty with lots of green areas and big trees. In some of the trees there were hundreds of huge fruit bats, hanging like breadfruit from the branches. They chittered and squawked and defecated like mad so that passing anywhere near was a real assault on the senses. The people also chewed betel nut, so there were long squirts of bright red spit here and there and all over and around trashcans.

We went off to shop in the market for provisions for Kranket Island, our little hideaway for the following few days. All that we needed was available in the supermarket, and the open market, which was filled with fruit and veggies all just a few *toea* (local currency, with 100 *toea* to a *kina*.) All prices were fixed so there was no haggling. Some people spoke a little English but mostly it was Tok Pisin, one of the official and most widely spoken languages, derived from *pidgin* English.

The snorkelling off Kranket was wonderful. Our little lodge was at the furthest end of the island, a coral atoll – horseshoe shaped so the middle is a lagoon. You could swim from both sides of our peninsula where the corals and variety of fish were amazing. Trish and I were up in good time the first morning, in bright sunshine, and as nobody was about, had a marvellous skinny-dip and snorkel in the calm sunlit sea.

We Arrive at Krauket Island

We had several resident birds and many beautiful butterflies at the lodge. Some birds had the most melodious warbling song but there was a type of crow which had a raucous call which sounded as though he was a witch laughing and jeering at us. He was very funny, and kept us in fits of laughter – except first thing in the morning!

In the cool, quiet of the evenings we would take a walk through the tropical bush. It was as though we were the only people in the world. Our lodge had cold running water, and electricity for lighting from a generator from 6 a.m.–9 p.m., after which we had torches and a lamp. There was an almost full moon so when the lights suddenly went out it was still quite light outside and the grotesque branches of a dead tree were sharply silhouetted against the moonlit sea.

One morning we went to Madang in a little boat with an outboard engine we had been lent. It poured while we were on our way back to the island, the wind blowing up quite hard making way-on horribly rough and bumpy. We found a spot where we could tie up to a tree-stump and tried to get some shelter under the trees, but still we were soaked when we arrived back at the lodge. To our horror, the wind had blown the rain through the mosquito-screens onto where we sat and everything was sopping wet.

The native village, about forty-five minutes walk away, was well kept, and barring the betel spit, the streets were clean and tidy. But it was the beautiful gardens that struck us most; full of flowers and tidy rows of vegetables. It was dusk when we arrived back at the lodge, finding that David was covered with bites that Trish and I had so far escaped.

A Local Canoe Builder'

We didn't know if they were mosquito, some other insect, or some sort of grass that we had brushed against on our walk.

The local folk went fishing from minute craft. They would sit on a box perched on top of a small, hollowed-out log, in turn attached to a bamboo outrigger. It all looked so small and fragile, and yet they would go some distance offshore, trailing a line. There were two large Korean fish factory ships in Medang Harbour. They had helicopters on board which would go and search for big shoals of tuna and then send for the ships when the fish were located. This was very big time fishing, scouring the seabed and discarding a terrible lot of by-catch. Not at all eco-friendly.

The mainland opposite us was very mountainous – the clouds seeming to rise up like smoke, between the ridges. On the occasions when it was clear and sunny you could see just how extremely rugged and heavily forested it was. We hoped we would be able to get to Mount Hagen in the next few days. Situated in the middle of the mountains, and in this very changeable weather, we were afraid it might not be possible.

Mount Hagen Market

Diana Up-Country, Mount Hagen, 1995

Mount Hagen did not exist while Beatrice lived in Papua New Guinea. It was not until 1933 that two brothers, Mick and Dan Leahy, and government officer Jim Taylor were conducting an aerial reconnaissance of the highlands when they discovered the huge and heavily populated Wahgi Valley. Some time later they walked there with a well supplied patrol and became the first westerners to come into contact with the tribes that are now in the location of Mount Hagen. The town is, today, the third largest in the country.

We found all the locals to be very friendly; they shook your hand and said *apernoon* –good afternoon. Tok Pisin is such a logical language, for instance something that is broken is *im buggerap*, I would like to buy is, *mi laik bai-im*.

Papa New Gunea: Mud Men & Women from Asaro, Central Highlands. April 1995

While staying at Mount Hagen, we went to visit the Mud Men of Asaro, near the village of Goroka. It was an amusing and edifying experience.

We arrived at the village and were shown down a very steep wet, red clay track to a clearing. We would have been better with either bare feet or walking books as we slipped and slithered down to where there were laid out the preparations for a large celebratory party. Many pigs had already been fattened for the feast, and were lying, slaughtered, in a circle round the rest of the meal. The guests would enjoy whole roasted pigs, chicken and fish, plenty of sweet potatoes, yams, taro and tapioca flavoured with coconut milk, ginger and garlic, and a variety of local greens and tropical fruit - much of it cooked in a *mumu*, or earthen oven. The wedding garden was decorated with tropical flowers of Impatiens (Busy Lizzy), bougainvillea, frangipani and, bromeliads collected and arranged by friends. It all looked spectacular. We continued on to a large clearing where the mud men's performance would take place.

Legend has it that many years before, the clan was attacked by an enemy tribe, and some of the men were forced to hide in the Asaro River, waiting until dusk before attempting to escape. The enemy saw them rise from the muddy banks covered in pale-coloured mud and thought they were spirits, so the enemy fled in fright, and the Asaro men escaped. They arrived back at their village not knowing that some of the enemy were still there. They too, were so terrified that they ran back to their own village and held a ceremony to ward off spirits. As it was believed that the mud from the Asaro River was poisonous, instead of covering their faces with the mud, they made terrifying-looking masks, and used them to frighten away enemies.

We had a wonderful display of the mud men and women, and indeed wearing fantastic, grotesque, masks. Some looked very uncomfortable and rather vague about what they were doing. It was all very amateurish, and all the better for that. We gave them a resounding ovation.

We were not yet quite ready for our big adventure on the Sepik River.

September 1908, Beatrice back in Papua New Guinea

Beatrice returned to Australia from Papua for a few weeks, hoping for a meeting with Prime Minister Deakin. She returned to Papua via a brief visit to the Solomon Islands.

When Beatrice's ship to the Solomon islands arrived in Tulagi – the port with the same name as the island – the few inhabitants normally came on board as soon as she docked, expecting a great spree of unlimited whisky. But Beatrice with a few other abstainers had organised to go on an illegal dynamite fishing party. They all left the ship in their bathing suits and rowed to a spot where fish should be found. The leader cut the fuse as short as possible, keeping hold of the plug of dynamite until a shoal of fish appeared. Then he lit the fuse and, waiting till the last moment, threw it into the shoal. Everyone knew it was a dangerous moment by waiting too long before getting rid of the lethal weapon. As agreed, everyone jumped into the water, regardless of the sharks. Not one fish did they catch, but the sharks had a good dinner, and at least there were no accidents.

Beatrice returned to Papua with a commission from Deakin and the Australian Government to publicise Papua's need for settlers, and capital. This contract included, as well as pay, free government transport to, and throughout Papua. She would need to write up the country's facts and figures on the practicalities of planting, to produce rubber, copra, hardwood, coffee and hemp. In order to gather material for her reports she would have to search out the company of schooner-men, planters and gold-miners, and take every opportunity to travel anywhere and everywhere.

She wrote pamphlets extolling the possibilities of becoming a planter in Papua, and sent them to the main London clubs, shipping companies, and magazines, as well as to 800 names from Whitaker's Peerage.

Following her initial stay at Government House, Beatrice had several addresses in the Port Moresby area. First was the Top Pub – one of two pubs and a somewhat unlikely residence for Miss Grimshaw.

Beatrice would frequently walk through a pretty native village, not far from the Port, giving her a good idea of how the people lived. They knew the value of money to some extent, though most of them preferred tobacco to coin. They liked Western clothes, but only to wear for going into town, normally wearing a waist cloth or voluminous grass skirt – depending on sex. They mostly knew a little pidgin English, and would work as servants or in the fields, and were on good terms with the white population. Although some of them had become Christians, they mostly believed in magic and sorcery.

One day Beatrice was invited to visit the village of Elavara approached by a rickety bridge stretching out over the water some 100 yards or so. It was a nightmare. Fine if you happened to be small, light, almost naked, and barefoot. But for one wearing too many clothes and shod with heavy walking shoes, it was a great relief to get to the other side. The town was old and crumbling, but the locals kept mending the houses as they fell apart – partly from habit, and partly because of the coolness to be found at sea. Beatrice's thoughts were interesting:

> We of the superior races are very fond of laughing at native conservatism, but there are glass panes in our own houses for all that. Why is it that in such a hot climate it has never occurred to any of the people who have built, and are building, houses in Port Moresby, that a European house can be set out on piles in the sea just as well as a native one, and that this style would certainly be more healthy than the present plan, not to speak of the difference in temperature?

Local Village

> Mosquitoes would be less troublesome ... the full benefit of every breeze would be enjoyed, and ... there would be the clean, fresh, cool water of the sea, ebbing and flowing with the tide.[73]

Keen to see something of the country, especially up into the mountainous interior, Beatrice decided to go hiking into the Astrolabe Mountains, south-east of Port Moresby.She had another lady and a gentleman for company, and several native boys to guide them. Once again kitted out with porters, horses, and *swags*, (canvas sacks) for their belongings, Beatrice and her friends set off early one morning, bound for the Sogeri country, some thirty-six miles away. They were all aware that there would be no roads or bridges, nor hotels – nothing in fact, but themselves and their horses, and were to take three days to accomplish everything they wanted to see.

To begin with a bridle path took them across open grassy plains, then, quite suddenly they were faced with a steep down-slope into dark forest. Knowing how difficult that sort of country could be, Beatrice wondered to herself – short of flying – just how it was to be done.

The party did, of course make it through the forest, ending the day's ride on the banks of the Laloki River, where there was – in the middle of nowhere – a jail. The head jailer, a native who spoke good English, received them as though they had arrived at his grand mansion, with all the jolly-looking prisoners running around looking after the horses, and collecting fruit and vegetables as though for a grand feast. When Beatrice asked what the prisoners' crimes were, she was told, mostly for murder, though some of them were sorcerers.

Beatrice had heard of several murders, one of which she described as so hugely humorous that one could only laugh, as follows:

> A young man killed his father. No cause apparent. The strong arm of the British Government took hold of him, and he was asked if he could 'assign any reason for the rash act' before the passing of sentence. The native interpreter of the High Court replied, after putting the question to the prisoner (who did not seem to feel his position at all acutely): 'He says, Sir, that the old man was not much good to anybody.'[74]

In all the cases, the murderers were imprisoned for several years.

Anywhere else in the world, it would have seemed totally bizarre for two white women and a white man spending the night in a jail. But in Papua New Guinea, nothing was too unusual. Beatrice's first night in jail proved peaceful enough in spite

73 Beatrice Grimshaw, *The New New Guinea*. Illustrated edition (Philadelphia: J. B. Lippincott; London: Hutchinson, 1911), pp. 42–3.

74 Grimshaw, *The New New Guinea*, pp. 89–90.

of the whirring of a myriad crickets, and the croaking of regiments of frogs. Her cell was part of the head jailer's house and was built of slabs of uneven wood which only met intermittently. The floor was made likewise, enabling the 'prisoner' to see the rats, lizards, and other wildlife running about below.

The trio spent the whole of the following day in and around the jail, visiting the government nursery – about half an hour's walk from the jail. Beyond the jail gardens, along a cool pathway through the bush, Beatrice and her friends came to the government nursery. It was from here that the planters got their seeds, cuttings and young plants; also advice on planting.

The following morning the cavalcade set off again, several well-mannered assassins seeing them on their way. Beatrice enjoyed the intense silence of the forest; experiencing a frisson of fear mixed with excitement, engendered by the solitude of her surroundings. Their path took them up along the side of a very beautiful river valley, at least one thousand feet deep, closed in by high ramparts of black basalt. White cockatoos flew about – discernible against the dark purple ranges in the distance. Gradually the path became steeper, making it difficult for the horses and necessitating the riders dismounting. At the top came the reward. They were in sight of the beautiful Rhona Falls, tumbling in a magnificent cascade into a clear, pale grey lake.

The party continued on towards their camping ground. No one wanted to talk, each person lost in their own reverie. But what did interest them all was how, eventually, they would have to cross the river which, after a lot of rain, was in spate. The track became very slippery as they descended to the fording place. The force of the river was indeed tremendous, the animals staggering against the rush of water. The whole party was elated having survived the crossing, and scrambled up the bank on the other side.

The camp when they reached it – by then in the dark – was a welcome sight. There was a good fire blazing, and a Papuan was tending a delicious-smelling pot. After eating, the two ladies slept in a small surveyors' tent, while the gentleman made use of a thatched, but un-walled edifice. The horses were set free, but hobbled, and with bells round their necks so that one might know where they were in the morning.

By this time the group were high up at around 2,000ft, in coffee country. The climate was completely changed from the coast, with still hot, but not oppressive days, and quite chilly at night. There were no mosquitoes at this height, and consequently no malaria. The sparse villages were – like Fiji – mostly situated high up on the peaks of hills, enabling the inhabitants to see their enemies coming. But the natives here appeared not hostile.

On the third day, en route home, the group visited a plantation in the heart of the Astrolabe Mountains. The tiny house was situated on a little hill, with a growth of giant feathery bamboo behind, serving as a background to its prettiness:

> It was a mere three-roomed, one-storied bungalow, almost all deep veranda and overhanging eaves, with a flight of rustic steps leading up to its little brown door, and a high, deep, palm-thatch roof set low down on its walls of woven bamboo, like a shady hat pulled over a planter's sun-browned face. It looked absolutely harmonious, and as much a part of the place as a bird's nest built in a tree ... all were perfectly fitted to their end and perfectly satisfying to the eye. And the view![75]

The party arrived at an area of level ground just large enough to bear the house and surrounding wonderful plants. Indoors, the furniture was made from the forest, all of which you would have been proud to have in your own home.

Beatrice and her friend settled down to stay here for a couple of weeks, their escort and the horses returning to Port Moresby. There they were, two white women among a heathen population. The natives in the hills had never seen a white woman, as witness the many parties that came down to stare shyly at the ladies during the course of the next few days. Although the house was open to all, they felt perfectly safe.

The two ladies passed their days in the little house very pleasantly, usually walking and exploring in the mornings, or swimming in a crocodile-free river; reading or writing in the afternoons when it poured with rain, the deep thatched roof of the house spilling a continuous waterfall. They would then enjoy a cup or two of the wonderful Astrolabe coffee before the rain cleared just before sunset. Then the friends would sit on the veranda and enjoy the beautiful display of jewel colours, after which the valley would be submerged in a sort of veil of translucent green for some time, before darkening into night.

One of the chief events of every afternoon was to see what their nearest, and generous, white neighbour's 'shooting boy' would bring them. The big Papuan would arrive at the veranda, shaking the rain from his huge mop of hair and set out his booty of parrots, pigeons, hornbills, maybe a wallaby or the hind quarter of wild pig. The choice would be made and given to the native cook to prepare for supper.

Quite soon after this visit, the beautiful Gaura Pigeon, all the birds of paradise, and one or two other species were placed under legal protection. Although at that time these birds were plentiful, and their harsh call was frequently heard, they were in fact quite elusive. It must have been tantalising for the ladies to know that so many beautiful birds were close to them in the bush, yet never seeing one.

75 Grimshaw, *The New New Guinea*, pp. 80–1.

One evening Beatrice heard the jingle of horse bells, and knew that their escort had arrived to take them back to Port Moresby.

It was a nightmare journey, the red clay road disintegrating into a cross between a path and a river. They had to lead the horses a good part of the time the going was so slippery. It took them all day and well into the evening before reaching their destination – as usual, dirty, wet, and hungry. The following day there was more of the terrible track downhill. They had been slipping and sliding for the best part of the day, when a messenger arrived from a copper mine, inviting them to come up and have lunch.

As they say 'never give away high ground,' but the travellers could hardly refuse. So once again, they turned and battled back uphill until arriving at a little hut, and the mine. This was Beatrice's first visit to a mine, and here she met two young, well-educated, ex-government officials, both well-mannered despite their rough miner's clothing. The hut was clean and tidy, and their native boy served lunch as though they were at the Savoy. The party didn't see much of the mine as they were anxious to get going. After this, their way down ended on a real carriage road and an exciting race. The horses, realising they were on the homeward stretch, took hold of their bits – and bolted. Quite astonishing considering how much they had already done. Obviously the New Guinea horse, like many things in this extraordinary country, was a good deal better than he looked.

Having already seen something of plantation life, Beatrice was interested in finding out more about the labour question, for it was always a topic of conversation as to whether the supply of native labourers would be sufficient to keep the plantations going.

There was not a problem about numbers, the native population being around three-quarters of a million. However, not all the natives were interested in working for wages. This was a new idea for most of them, not understanding the nature of money. Then there were those whites who thought that the 'primitive native' should be left in his natural state, and not change his way of living. In any case, Beatrice decided that she needed to see for herself the attitude of the natives from the more remote areas.

She was invited by the Lieutenant-Governor to join an official group to visit some of the little-known villages on the Purari River, west of Port Moresby, from where it was hoped there would be men willing to train as plantation workers. The party travelled for the sea journey on board the *Merrie England*, but as nobody knew the depth of the river, they towed a smaller boat, the *Kia Ora* onto which they transferred at the mouth of the Purari. At the date of Beatrice's journey – early 1908 – only one hundred and forty miles of the river were known, and the delta (about five hundred square miles) almost not at all. The number of islands and waterways, and the population of mostly cannibals were a matter of guesswork.

Purari Canoe, Labour Recruiting

The Purari River trip started badly. They didn't know the depth of the bar, but those on board simply hoped the *Kia Ora* would be able to cross it. Incredibly, they engaged in this experiment on an ebb tide, and almost at low water, and of course the *Kia Ora* went aground – stuck there for most of the day.

The heat was terrible, and the scenery boring. Mile upon mile of yellowish-brown water from the outpouring river, from which half submerged trees and branches came hurtling towards the marooned boat, often crashing into her. She banged and bumped on the seabed, rolling around to such an extent that most of the passengers were sea-sick. Very gradually, as the tide turned, the banging on the bottom ceased, and hurray, the little boat regained her freedom and they were able to think again of starting up the river. The banks began closing in and one of the tributaries opened up. Beatrice was ecstatically happy as she contemplated how in life there are moments of pure delight that stand out through all the years:

> It is hard to say why the Purari – as one enters the lower reaches of the main channel, to forge slowly upwards against the tearing current, through a fever-smitten solitude, that is deathly in more senses than one – should be such a wonderful sight. An immense tea-coloured flood, fully half a mile wide, dotted with downward-skimming logs, on which the tall white cranes perch fearlessly ... bordered by stretch after stretch of the melancholy, drooping, lovely Nipa palm, which stands with its root in the water and the mud, lifting a splendid crown of tall green plumes to the heavy, heat-brooding sky – this is what one sees – no more.
>
> It is, perhaps, the inner rather than the outward eye that sees the wonder of the place ... More, there is, in some fashion hard to explain, but easy to feel, something of the spirit of every great river in every other.[76]

They laboured on upriver until someone noticed coconut palms and suggested they must be somewhere near a village. Almost immediately, around a bend in the river appeared three large canoes, each containing about twenty men, paddling furiously towards the Kia Ora. The men paddled standing up, their timing perfect, the sweep of the paddles making the water boil, and leaving a line of foam in their wake. The men were naked but wore the most elaborate and brilliantly coloured head-dresses of Bird of Paradise and Cassowary feathers. They wore necklaces of teeth and armlets of white shells.

76 Grimshaw, *The New New Guinea*, pp. 124–5.

The whole picture appeared to be aggressive but, although there were spears in the boats, there didn't seem to be firearms. The canoes soon caught up with the steamer and the men caught hold of the little ship, pleased to get a lift upstream to the village of Maipua.

Dancing Masks: Gulf of Papua

The sight of Maipua came as quite a shock. The men's houses stood prominently beside the river, the largest of which was fully ninety feet in height, and four hundred in length. The gable end ran up into a great horn – or cone – the sides being swept away indicating some real architectural skills. Smaller houses, in the same style, stood along the bank, all of them standing high up on piles in the river, protecting them against crocodiles and high water levels.

A stroke of very bad luck had knocked Beatrice over with a fever, and disappointed, she was unable to go ashore with the rest of the party. As she lay on a lounger on deck, and now in silence, Beatrice became aware of a distant native chant coming closer and closer to the boat, at last passing under the *Kia Ora's* bows producing a sight worth seeing.

Two great canoes had been lashed together, and were decorated with a mass of foliage so that the whole structure looked like a floating garden. In the middle of the boats lay a trophy, which later she was told was a slaughtered pig. She had no reason to doubt this, but with her interest in cannibals, was sure that it wouldn't always be as innocent as a pig. Maipua had already been visited by other white men in the past, but those reports told that they were not happily received.

In order to recruit some of the unmarried men, once ashore, the captain had a system. First of all, he would have to have an interpreter. Then he would sit down and have a smoke, asking one of the boys if he had any tobacco. When the boy answered no, he would tell him that the boys on the plantations had plenty of tobacco. Then he would ask did he have any fish hooks, and when the answer again was no, he would say about the plantation workers having plenty of hooks. So when he finally asked did he have a wife, and the boy, now almost in tears would say he couldn't afford a wife, the captain, as though he had just thought of a good idea said:

> you come away with me and go to work for a year on a white man's plantation. You plant coconut, you cut down tree, all the same as you do here.

> You get plenty-plenty tucker, meal all the days, biscuit, rice, tea, plenty tobacco. By and by you go back Maipua, you take calico, fish-hooks, tomahawks, beads, knives; you big man; you buy wife.[77]

Money was not mentioned as the native hardly understood the value of coins. The prospect worked, and quite a number of young men were interested. The following day the captain went ashore again, returning with about twenty-five boys, half scared, half excited, but keen to go with the white man. When the boys would arrive in Port Moresby, they could not be employed until they had been signed-on by a magistrate, with strict laws preventing injustice between employer and employee. The native had to understand all the terms of his employment, and no employer was allowed to hit his worker – except in self-defence.

With everyone else back on the *Kia Ora*, they steamed away from Maipua, hoping to go to Kairu. But again, nobody had any idea of this tangle of rivers and islands as they butted their way upstream for a dozen miles or so. They zig-zagged up and down tributaries, the leadsman continually taking the depth which varied a lot. The *Kia Ora* continued on all day – eventually finding Kairu, more by good luck than good guidance.

Here, the captain found some more recruits for the plantations before proceeding now downstream. But again they became lost, frequently finding themselves in narrow and very fast-running streams, where the little steamer was at the will of the current.

Native Canoe

77 Grimshaw, *The New New Guinea*, p. 133.

On these occasions, everyone had to go below in order to avoid the overhanging trees shedding copious quantities of branches, and with them a myriad unknown insects, including various ants, grasshoppers, stick insects and praying mantises.

That night, they again went aground far from the bank, remaining there for some time hoping that a flood tide would free them. After dinner, when the steward was serving coffee, somebody nervously remarked that they were in a very lonely place. But there wasn't much the crew and passengers could do if they were attacked. They couldn't move; they had virtually no firearms; and it would have been ridiculous to imagine that the few recruits would take their side. So, instead of worrying about an attack, they finished their coffee, and discussed the possibility of the rain stopping before morning.

By the morning the boat was free and they set off again with no idea where they were. They banged into banks, and branches banged into them. Then, suddenly, with no warning, they found themselves back in the Coral Sea. What a joy, as with no further disasters, they made their way back to Port Moresby.

It soon became apparent that the indigenous workers from the Purari region were perfectly satisfactory employees in the various plantations. Many of the men went back year after year, but difficulties arose when they inevitably found a girl to wed and then the married men naturally missed their wives. To this end, some of the planters began to build married quarters, and to offer light work to the women.

Beatrice also made it her business to find out what she could about mining in Papua. It was known that the miners had done a great deal of exploratory work, discovering that the country was certainly rich in valuable minerals including gold and copper. The mining industry, however, was lacking in capital, and at all the mining centres she visited, she heard the same story – excellent possibilities, but no money to attain them. So it seemed that the mineral wealth of Papua offered good opportunities to anyone who had a thousand pounds to spend, but otherwise Beatrice could not recommend mining to the same level as planting.

Back in the capital, the social round continued unabated. Beatrice found that there were mostly four subjects that the local white folk gossiped about; crocodiles, sorcery, the comings and goings of the steamer *Merrie England* – and scandal.

One of the troubles with life in the Pacific came when the men lived on the islands earning a living, while their wives stayed at home – preferring the cooler climates of Sydney or Melbourne. Naturally enough, tongues would wag over the slightest suggestion of 'goings-on' between these men and any other women.

There was another aspect of social life in Papua. As Beatrice discusses the rare times when white men and women would be involved with the natives:

> Brown men, violent and unrestrained of feeling, like all savages, are separated, sometimes for years, from their homes and families, and go to work in the houses

> of white people, where the women are constantly left alone for the greater part of the day, sometimes for weeks, in the absence of husbands and fathers. Tropical houses lack privacy; the heat makes people who would otherwise be careful, somewhat careless in dress and demeanour. There is gunpowder here, and at times it has been known to explode.[78]

Thursday Island

Beatrice was once again invited to join the Governor and his entourage, this time for a visit to the Torres Straits and the Australian-owned, Thursday Island. It was important as the centre of the pearling industry, and for all its size held a town and barracks, and a good-sized fleet of pearlers constantly at work. Most of the work was done by the Japanese, who had more or less taken over the island. Beatrice's description of the Japanese man is beyond recounting, but she tells of the women in kimono and obi, with puffed and oiled black hair, walking in and out of the shops, with their quaint little slant-eyed children.

As it proved to be impossible for Beatrice to see the pearling fleet at work, the next best thing was to take a trip on a sloop. This, for once, was owned by a white man and his wife, who very kindly offered to take Beatrice, and see how the diving was done, even offering to lend her the diving dress in order to try a dive herself. She was keen to have a go at this, but thought that someone might accompany her; but apparently that was too dangerous as often the lines became entangled, so she would have to go by herself.

Now, the Torres Straits, as everyone in Queensland knows, is full of sharks, and also alligators, devil-fish, sting-ray, and various other unpleasant creatures. Beatrice could not help thinking about them a little as they began to prepare her diving gear. It was considered rather bad form, and really very silly to make a fuss about sharks and alligators in the countries where they abound. Nevertheless, the normally unafraid traveller was somewhat apprehensive:

> If by any chance you should see a shark, don't be the least bit alarmed; just pull up the cuff of your jumper a little so as to let out a few bubbles of air, and he'll be frightened off. Don't pull the cord till he is well away; you're all right on the bottom, but they have been known to make a grab at a man when he was being pulled up – as they do at a fish on your line, you know – and bite his boots off.[79]

The men prepared everything for Beatrice, putting the lines ready, and the ladder in the easiest place for her to get over the side, so that it was impossible to be scared, so

78 Grimshaw, *Isles of Adventure*, pp. 18–19.

79 Grimshaw, *The New New Guinea*, pp. 211–212.

of course she was not. Nevertheless she didn't feel one bit like herself – and no, she was not scared.

Down below, Beatrice was helped into the thick woollen jersey and tights by her hostess, and then the diving suit itself – an all over garment, with legs, feet, and sleeves all made of stiff, thick, rubber cloth, into which she had to crawl, feet foremost, through the neck!

It was done at last, and two panting creatures climbed out on deck, one in a cool white dress and hat, the other in a shapeless, shambling sort of costume that made her look like a toad with a tendency to apoplexy. Then there was a pair of boots with lead soles to put on. They got a wrench, pulled up the metal yoke of the dress tight round the neck, and screwed it down by means of nuts. Then a mass of copper and iron, which seemed a fair load for a horse, and clapped it over Beatrice's head. This was the helmet which was screwed down on to the metal yoke. Then they told her to try and walk.

Her host was busy going over the air pumps, looking over everything, and seeing that the machinery was in good order, assuring Beatrice – rather too emphatically, she thought – that he meant to take charge of the pump himself, and let the tenders merely watch the line which she would pull to let them know she was ready to surface. The use of the line and valves were all explained to her. A rope fastened round her waist for letting her down and pulling her up, and another line to be kept in her hand for a varying amount of signals, the only important one she could remember was the one for 'pull me up'. She kept on repeating to herself that she was not afraid:

> They lifted my feet for me and put them down singly on the ladder. They helped me a step or two down into the water. They took that horrible lead necklace and laid it gently, almost caressingly, round my copper and iron neck. And then they said 'Goodbye,' and put the glass window in, and screwed down the coffin – I mean the helmet. Their faces were faint through the glass, but they smiled and signalled (for I could hear no longer), and I knew that they were asking 'Are you ready?'
>
> It was at this point that my fiction broke up, and I realised that I was extremely afraid.
>
> I hated the plunge to the bottom – scarcely thirty feet, but might have been a thousand – that followed when I carefully slid those gigantic boots off the ladder. I was disgusted when I landed – as all beginners do – on my head, and had to struggle to get right. ... my hands were bare and sharks could nip them off ... I had no knife as a diver should have, and ... there might be 'something' in every black cavern of the dead coral over which I found myself walking. But I got interested in the surroundings by and by ...

> After all, it was worth some trouble and discomfort to find oneself walking on the bottom of Torres Straits, down where the divers had been at work.[80]

The water was a bit murky – the light from above dim and green, but there was a little dead coral to be seen, pearly white along the weedy bottom. Beatrice found the walking with strange soft steps an odd sensation. Everything was muffled, her breath, her sight and hearing. She was not quite sure that she was, in fact, alive. Her nose and ears hurt, but as she walked along, shoals of pretty coral-fish swam past quite unafraid, sometimes coming close up and peering at her with cold glassy eyes, through the window of her helmet. She was always looking out for the swoop and rush and scythe-shaped tail of the monster she most feared, but there was no sign of it.

Then she decided that it would be very pleasant to see the light of day again. She was able to stoop down slowly and gather up a bit of weed and a fragment of coral for a souvenir, and then pulled the cord. No sensation of movement followed, and for a moment her heart stood still. Had the tender forgotten to tend after all? But in another second she noticed that the air bubbles were rushing in a long stream past the window of her prison. The rungs of the ladder appeared. The light suddenly brightened – she was up. What a relief to be back, and in the first rush of warm air breaking upon one's cold, perspiring face.

The undressing that followed was just as trying as the dressing, but Beatrice was so glad to be alive that she did not care.

They only had time for a quick visit to Thursday Island, for the *Merrie England* had work to do all along the coast. Their next stop was at Goaribari Island where the two missionaries had been murdered and cannibalised.

Collecting the Bones of the Murdered Missionaries

Goaribari

Goaribari Island is located within the Gulf of Papua. Its highest point is only about 3ft above sea level, and consists mostly of mud, so that during very high tides and storms, parts of the mangrove-covered island become inundated.

Because Beatrice had been so interested in the deaths of two missionaries in 1901, and the consequent suicide of the then

80 Grimshaw, *The New New Guinea*, pp. 216–17.

Chief Justice, Christopher Robinson in 1904, she was very keen to see the natives of this island whose reputation was one of the worst as being treacherous and cruel. This visit, hopefully, was to be peaceful.

Nothing happened for an hour or so after the party's arrival, then, tentatively a couple of canoes paddled towards Beatrice's boat. An interpreter spoke, offering calico and tobacco, but the natives hesitated, paddling around and talking. They seemed nervous and excited. All day and night the steamer lay at anchor, waiting to see what would happen.

Beatrice was woken at daybreak by a clinking noise, and, opening her eyes, saw a long dirty brown arm coming through her porthole, trying to snatch her water bottle. When she shouted, the arm disappeared, clutching her bottle. Beatrice jumped out of bed and slammed and screwed shut her ports. Later, every closed porthole on the ship showed a mosaic of painted faces and bobbing feathers. The Goaribarians, had obviously decided the white men were going to be friendly, and were as naturally curious about them as the whites were about the black men.

Before long the Lieutenant-Governor and several armed constabulary started off in small boats for the shore. Beatrice was allowed to accompany the party in the second boat, also with some policemen and a couple of missionaries. It was the first time anyone had made a peaceful visit to Goaribari since the affair of the murdered missionaries. This friendly call by the *Merrie England* was a new event.

The party landed and walked in the black mud, up among the houses, the men of the village watching with excitement and indecision, giggling and grinning. The wild nervousness of their demeanour was very much emphasised by the style of their dress. This consisted solely of ornaments – nearly all of a fluttering and trembling kind – of grasses and feathers ingeniously mounted on a stem that quivered with every movement, surmounted by haloes of long shaking white and yellow parrot quills fastened round the head with tight bands.

Meanwhile the Lieutenant-Governor was making a speech to the villagers through the interpreter. He told them they were to stop eating each other, as it was disapproved of by the government. Also, if they persisted in eating the young people, soon the village would die out. They were not to bury their corpses under the houses, or hang them up in the trees. They were, in particular, not to kill any white men, but to receive them civilly if they came to visit. The government wanted to be friends with them, and would protect them from their enemies if they behaved.

The speech was received very seriously, and the distribution of calico and tobacco took place among the chiefs. The man who was distributing the largesse offered two lots of calico to one of the older chiefs, saying it was for his other wife, assuming he had more than one:

'No!' cried the old man unexpectedly.

> 'Why not?' asked the dispenser of favours, rather surprised at such a reaction from a chief.
>
> 'Because,' yelled the old man, dancing with excitement and feeling, 'one is enough – quite, quite enough!'[81]

The next day, the ice now having been broken, the Lieutenant-Governor went ashore again, and succeeded in getting possession of the bones of the murdered Chalmers and Tompkins. These were easily identified by means of certain peculiarities. The *Merrie England* took them to the London Mission Station, nearby at Daru, where the representative of the Mission saw to their decent burial.

Samarai

> It is half-past five o'clock. I sit up on my mattress, dressing-gown clad, and look round. On the bridge-deck above, the sheeted dead seem to be lying in heaps, limbs cast abroad, heads thrown back to the lightening sky. It is only the Government officials and the ship's officers wrapped in the quilts that they have pulled up as the chill of dawn began, but it certainly suggests a battlefield in the dead stillness of this early hour while the *Merrie England* is yet asleep.[82]

Exploring eastwards now, still on board the *Merrie England*, Beatrice and the onboard party were anchored off the beautiful tiny island of Samarai, cut off from the Papuan mainland and Sariba Island, by the China Straits. This is a navigable strait in the Milne Bay Province of Papua New Guinea, connecting the Solomon Sea with the Coral Sea. Samarai was the region's most important port, with ships travelling from Tokyo, Shanghai and Brisbane passing through its deep-water harbour. It had been a rough night, with the boat behaving badly. Beatrice, remembering the Irish accent, described it as like *'the way the divil wint through Atlone – in shtandin' leps'*.[83]

There were other small islands, with native canoes plying constantly up and down between the islets. The tribes who lived on the mainland were all on good terms with the white people. The town had several large wooden hotels, several stores and a whole street of tin-roofed bungalows and offices. It was neat and tidy with cut grass and pretty gardens.

The government officials were en route to find some Japanese luggers which were causing suspicion, taking Papuans without licence, off to the pearling grounds on Thursday Island. However, it proved to be an elusive quarry, able to take their shallow

81 Grimshaw, *The New New Guinea*, p. 235.
82 Grimshaw, *The New New Guinea*, p. 257.
83 Grimshaw, *The New New Guinea*, p. 261.

draft luggers in to tiny hidden coves. Indeed, they did not find the Japanese, without even catching a glimpse of their sails.

However, the investigations made by the crew of the *Merrie England*, took them to several other places off the map.

One interesting island was Rossel. It had a reputation of being the mildest and quietest of all the surrounding islands. However – quiet maybe, but mild and harmless, apparently not. Beatrice thoroughly enjoyed the story of the 326 shipwrecked Chinamen in 1858, as told by a pair of young Australian traders who had lived on Rossel for a couple of years.

The Rossel islander was a small meek-looking man who carried no arms. Yet he was among the most expert murderers in the world. The people of the island killed each other for a variety of reasons. If a chief died – someone was killed. If you were caught stealing – you were also killed. So how was it done? In one way only. It seemed the Rossel islanders were expert at smothering! Once a victim was ear-marked, he would be jumped upon and brought to the ground. Then one man would hold his mouth and nose, while the others would sit upon his chest. It would be over quickly, and no bloodshed. If an islander did not want to eat his victim at once, he would be caught, taken to another island where his arms and legs would be broken so that he could not run – or swim – away. They would bring him food – just enough to keep him alive until his Day of Judgment.

So, the story goes, this is exactly what happened to the Chinamen who had been shipwrecked on their way to Australia. The officers escaped in a small boat and were never heard of again. The others were captured and brought to a deserted island where they were kept fed and watered and from time to time, one or two would be carried away to be eaten. Eventually there was just one old man left. He somehow, managed to get away and told his story which, of course, was met with total disbelief. However, it was apparently true, as proudly verified by the sons of the 'quiet and gentle' perpetrators. Moreover, some of the neighbouring islanders verified the tale, saying that during this time, the Chinamen were often taken by boat to some of the near islands to be sold – like pigs – for consumption.

Other surprising things were that these silent, but lethal murderers, spoke a recognisable English. They were also very fine gardeners, growing all manner of plants – not just vegetables – but a kaleidoscope of coloured flowers. They also kept cats as pets, apparently never thinking of eating them.

After leaving Rossel Island, the *Merrie England* turned west, back in the direction of civilisation and Port Moresby. Time now was of the essence, and the *Merrie England* had to keep going, just having time for a quick visit to the Trobriand Islands. The Trobriand natives were good-looking – more Polynesian than Papuan. They had straight hair, and were never cannibalistic.

Author Returning to Australia from Papua

On 1st November, 1910, Beatrice set sail once more from Papua New Guinea to Sydney, having with her the results of the research she had been doing for Alfred Deakin, plus the manuscripts for two more books – one fiction and one non-fiction.

While she was in Sydney she stayed with friends, and gave several interviews to the newspapers, many of which were syndicated around the world.

Beatrice gets a mention in the *Hull Daily Mail's* Social Record column:

> We are gradually narrowing down the places which we may select for our next year's holiday. To-day we crossed Trobriand, New Guinea, off the list on reading in Miss Beatrice Grimshaw's book on that spot that 'the Trobriand people find much enjoyment in the study of poisons. One, taken from the gall-bladder of a fish, is so deadly that a banana pierced with a thorn which has been dipped in the poison will kill the man who eats it within a very few hours. They can also poison coconuts without opening them visibly.[84]

84 *Hull Daily Mail*, 7th November 1910, p. 4.

In Sydney, Australian's were also reading about Beatrice:

> 'I don't come of a family of explorers' said Miss Beatrice Grimshaw, 'although to judge by my brothers and sisters, scattered in the four corners of the earth, you might think so. Way back in the past there may have been some rovers in the family, but as far as my own parents were concerned they were mid-Victorian, and stayed where fate had placed them. I believe my mother may have had some of the wandering spirit in her; for it has come out so largely in all her children; but when one is mid-Victorian and the mother of 11 – well, one just makes up one's mind that anything different is impossible, and stays at home.'[85]

(Eleven children is incorrect; Beatrice was one of eight, two of whom died before their first birthdays.)

> The longing to roam was certainly finding full outlet in Miss Beatrice Grimshaw and her brothers and sisters, for while one sister was trekking in South Africa, one brother in South America, and another in China, Miss Grimshaw as we know, has been wandering through the wilds of Papua into places where no white woman ever went before: 'They had never seen a white woman before, those little Papuan women, but there was the same quick summing up of me as there would be in a Sydney drawing room.'[86]

Beatrice goes on to describe the difference in dress and behaviour between the unmarried women and the married women, and compares those women of the west to the eastern ladies:

> Amongst many of the tribes the women are always hidden at the approach of strangers, and a man who had journeyed into the far parts of the country told me that he came across one tribe whose women were veiled to the eyes. You may find that hard to believe, but after you have lived in Papua for two years you will find nothing hard to believe, for it is a land where the impossible happens every day. Sorcery is practised every day, and I believe it is the only country in the world where the sea-serpent has been seen by an Archbishop.[87]

She continues:

> On the whole, I do not think Papua is as interesting as the South Sea Islands. There is not the same romance about it. But its newness and strangeness have a very strong attraction for me, and I intend to go back again very soon.[88]

85 'A Woman Traveller', [interview] *The Sydney Morning Herald*, 16th November 1910, p. 5. Published in the paper's weekly 'Page for Women' series.

86 'A Woman Traveller', [interview] *The Sydney Morning Herald*, 16th November 1910, p. 5.

87 'A Woman Traveller', [interview] *The Sydney Morning Herald*, 16th November 1910, p. 5.

88 'A Woman Traveller', [interview] *The Sydney Morning Herald*, 16th November 1910, p. 5.

Both Beatrice's books were published in 1911, *The New New Guinea* and the novel, *Where the Red Gods Call*. The books were enthusiastically and widely reviewed. *The New New Guinea* became the standard authority for those considering a life in Papua New Guinea.

Beatrice spent the remainder of 1911, and all of 1912 in Papua, taking her fiction writing very seriously.

By 1912, she had been lodging for some time in the half-built upper storey of what should have been a hotel, but which had been abandoned. There had been a caretaker who collected a few rents for himself, but unfortunately he was drowned, and nobody came to take his place. The other inhabitants of this strange place drifted away, leaving Beatrice there on her own. Since she had nowhere else to go, she stayed on – rent-free, happy and solitary, until the miners of the Lakekamu gold rush made an appearance. They would arrive clad in ragged clothing and politely ask Beatrice if they could stay. Eventually she abandoned trying to make an explanation, and gave the permission asked for. At least a hundred miners camped all over the place. In the evenings they lit fires, cooked a meal and told stories. She lived amongst these rough men in the half-built hotel for weeks, but they were as quiet and well behaved as a Sunday School on a prolonged Sunday Treat. She heard afterwards that they regarded her as the owner, and had agreed among themselves that she was not to be annoyed, and anyone who wished to get drunk would have to go elsewhere.

It was the season for heavy rain and high winds, sometimes the huge crazy building standing on its stilt legs rocked so violently that most of its inhabitants would leave and go into the open for fear it might collapse. But it never did. Gradually the miners drifted away to seek work elsewhere – and Beatrice with them.

She moved house to a place on the beach. A visiting clergyman from Australia described it in the press, after visiting Port Moresby in March 1912. The Reverend Canon Frederick Bevan was born from a family of landed gentry in County Limerick, Ireland, and as Beatrice was also from Ireland, and somewhat of a heroine, he was anxious to meet her. He writes:

> When we returned from the village the Governor very kindly proposed coming with me to Miss Beatrice Grimshaw, the well-known novelist and authoress of works and articles on Papua, all of which are of abiding interest … Her magnum opus, *The New New Guinea* will remain for years a standard authority, while her vivid articles, written expressly for the great Australian dailies, have done more to advertise the Territory than all the Government reports published. Miss Grimshaw lives about a mile from Government House, and on the way His Excellency gave me some interesting details of the wonderful progress of Papua in the last few years. In that short time, the white population had almost doubled, while native labour had more than quadrupled …

> 'Miss Grimshaw's home!' It was the Governor who spoke, and, following the direction in which he pointed, I peered over the edge of the narrow road on which we were walking, and saw what is perhaps the most original residence of any authoress in the world. It was a kind of houseboat, and the prevailing colour was green. It was moored close to land, and, the tide being out, the greater part lay high and dry on the shingle. We scrambled down the cutting, and presently were able to view this original structure at close quarters. The foundation was supplied by two enormous native canoes, without outriggers, placed side by side, and about six feet apart. On these a platform about 30 feet long and 12 feet broad had been nailed securely, and this platform formed the floor of the authoress's house, one room only of which I was privileged to see, but there were others beyond the pretty cretonne curtains at the end, through which Miss Grimshaw occasionally passed during our visit, and one could readily imagine that a quieter and more comfortable home could not possibly be devised, or one more calculated to suit the profession of the talented lady who resided there quite alone, except for her black servant, who did her messages to town and such light manual work as might be required. Miss Grimshaw is absolutely fearless, and on several occasions has been alone in native villages where the people were avowed head-hunters and cannibals, but wherever she has been through New Guinea, she assured me that she had never received anything but the most courteous consideration from the blacks, for whose characters she expressed genuine admiration.[89]

However, in an interview by the *West Gippsland Gazette* on 19th November 1912, as well as discussing the research for her latest novel, *'Guinea Gold'*, recently published, Beatrice tells a hair-raising story about living on the houseboat. Apparently some alligators one night had a terrific fight at the stern of her home, bellowing like bulls, and emitting a horrible musky smell. One other night, an alligator cruising around got right underneath the boat, in the water directly under her bed. The musky smell was so strong that Beatrice had to get up and move to another part of the houseboat. On very dark nights they would haunt the shore she had to cross, so she always carried a lantern to keep them off. In the end, she said, she had to leave that place as it was becoming too trying for her nerves.[90]

Thoughts of Timor

Beatrice was keen to get travelling again. She hoped, this time to visit Dutch Timor, part of an island at the southern end of Maritime South East Asia, north of the Timor Sea. The island had been politically divided in two parts for centuries.

89 'Fact and Fiction from the Far North', Rev. Canon Bevan, Albury, in *Albury Banner and Waldonga Press*, 3rd May 1912, p. 40.

90 'Woman Among Alligators', *West Gippsland Gazette*, 19th November 1912, p. 3.

The Dutch and Portuguese fought for control of the island until it was divided in 1859, but they still did not formally resolve the matter of the boundary until 1912. Because of its history, and because of its mix of very different native peoples, it appealed to Beatrice.

However, she decided that before going to Timor she wanted to buy some smart new clothes. She set off from Port Moresby in May 1913 on board the SS *Van Waerwick* – her final destination, the fleshpots of Sydney. En route, the ship arrived two days later in Townsville, Queensland. Here Beatrice was interviewed by *The Townsville Daily Bulletin*, and described by the reporter as: 'a tall, graceful woman of fine handsome build' and who is 'a native of Ireland with all that nation's love of humour, and has a very attractive personality.' The report goes on to laud her writing and her love of hard travel: 'Indeed it was very hard to realise that the graceful smiling woman, in correct evening garb had ever scrambled through scrub and over rocks attended only by a long string of uncivilised natives.'[91]

They departed for Sydney, arriving in the capital on Saturday night, 17th May. *The Sydney Morning Herald* reported the *Van Waerwick's* arrival, with Miss Beatrice Grimshaw on board.[92] She would be staying at the Hotel Metropole – intending to be in Sydney for some weeks. Again she gave an interview with the paper, and when asked why she had been away so long in Papua, she replied laughingly, that Papua had just got hold of her, and had the charm of the unknown. She revelled in her exploring trips, and counted her sojourn in Papua as the most enjoyable experience in her life.

Beatrice's intention had been that she would leave Papua, and stay in Sydney for a few weeks before taking a ship to Timor. However, she met up with her old friends, Lieutenant-Governor and Mrs Murray, who persuaded her to return with them as their guest in the new Government House in Port Moresby. This she did, abandoning her plans to go to Timor, arriving back in Papua in July. In August, Beatrice reported to *The Brisbane Courier* – by the new fangled radio, that contrary to rumours, there had not been an outbreak of smallpox in Port Moresby and that the Governor was now recovering from a fever![93]

But Beatrice was never in one place for long, and her ideas of visiting Timor almost came to fruition with an odyssey round some of the Indonesian Islands.

91 'Adventurous Authoress. Miss Grimshaw in New Guinea', *Townsville Daily Bulletin*, 14th May 1913, p. 10.

92 There are a couple of articles in *The Sydney Morning Herald* in May (19th and 21st) about Miss Grimshaw's return.

93 'Report from New Guinea', *The Brisbane Courier*, 4th August 1913, p. 7.

Chapter 14: Malaysia & Indonesia

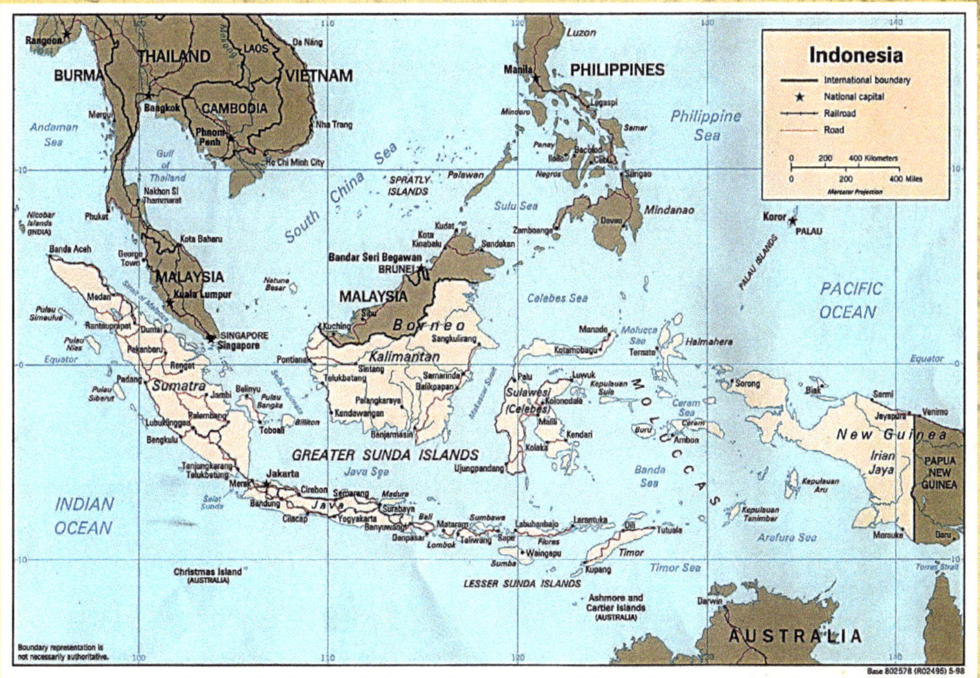

Around the end of August 1913 Beatrice set off on a KPM (the Dutch shipping line – Koninklijke Paketvaart-Maatschappij) steamer – the SS *Tasman* – to explore round the Indonesian Islands. She wrote up her experiences for *The Sydney Morning Herald* after she returned to Papua. The series was called 'Sarong and Spice', and ran in the paper from February to May 1914. In her opening gambit she was certainly enjoying herself:

> To lie in a lounge chair, on the hurricane deck of an eight thousand ton liner, watch the pale blue satin sea of the tropics slip past beneath the edge of the cool, overshadowing awning, and eat the passion fruit ices brought round at 11 o'clock by members of a brown and subservient race – is not this perfect?[94]

The ship was, by then, about two weeks from Sydney, with everybody on board loving the luxury and relaxed atmosphere of the liner. Many of the passengers were interested in, and frequently looked at the ship's maps and charts. Most of them knew nothing of the Wallace Line, and were fascinated to learn about it.

94 'Sarong and Spice', *The Sydney Morning Herald*, February 1914.

Now well known, the Wallace Line is a faunal boundary line drawn in 1859 by the British naturalist Alfred Wallace. It separates the eco-zones of Asia and Wallacea, a transitional zone between Asia and Australia. West of the line are found organisms related to Asiatic species; to the east, a mixture of species of Asian and Australian origin is present. The line runs through Indonesia, between Borneo and Celebes (today's Sulawesi), and through the Lombok Strait – the twenty-two miles between Bali and Lombok. Groups of plants and animals show differing patterns, but the overall pattern is striking and reasonably consistent, with human characteristics also, to a great extent, following the line.

While looking at the maps, the passengers also saw England's possessions marked in red. But it came as quite a shock to see that there was another colonial empire – Holland's 'Insulindia', including practically the whole island world from the Straits of Malacca over to New Guinea and down the coast of Australia. And it was prosperous land, full of rubber and coconuts, spices and precious stones, coal and oil.

For days the ship sailed along since leaving the port of Darwin until one morning, there appeared a misty blue line on the horizon. It was the island of Timor, signalling the beginning of Malaysia. The ship took just a couple of hours passing, leaving it to the south. Other small islands followed, until Beatrice woke one morning aware that the ship had stopped. They had arrived in Macassar, on the south-west corner of the island of Celebes situated some distance east of Borneo. The intoxicating scents of sandalwood and spices came through the portholes before anyone had risen from their beds.

Ashore, Macassar was fascinating with its high-tiled roofs, and stone-pillared verandas. The town was three hundred years old, and two dominant white races, Portuguese and Dutch, had left their mark, plus variations of Chinese, Arabic, Indian and Javanese, all leaving some legacy of their cultures. All around was a massive cross-section of nationalities – German, Italian, Dutch, and a few Australians, mixing with the natives; hawk-faced Arabs, timid looking Punjabis, and literally the 'wild men from Borneo' with amazingly little clothing, swaggering hand on hip looking with contempt at the tame people of the town. It was surely a melting pot of races.

Beatrice and some of the passengers stayed in a local hotel. Almost everyone disappeared to their bedrooms for the afternoon after a gargantuan lunch, and were horrified when Beatrice went exploring. She was told by some of the Dutch ladies that it was very bad for her health and she might die going out in the afternoon. But Beatrice would have none of it, saying it was much more likely that she might die if she stayed in her room. She enjoyed wandering through the Arab and Chinese quarters, and exploring the seventeenth century Dutch fort.

While she was on board the ship, one or two people talked about the Chinese Temple in Macassar, but nobody seemed to be particularly interested in it, so when a kindly Dutch official offered to take her on a tour of the site, Beatrice was rather unenthusiastic about it, but agreed to go.

Well... everyone knew that the Chinese made china – or porcelain – but nothing prepared her for the astounding building she went to see. The lower part was amazing enough with carved doors and gilded Chinese lettering, but the whole top of the temple was made of porcelain, vividly coloured and glittering as though it had just come out of the furnace. There were moulded fruits, flowers, animals, goblins, spirits and foliage. On the very top of the roof, unsupported by anything at all, two shining grass-green centipedes about four feet long, stood on their heads, waving their tails against the blue sky. Inside the temple there were beautifully carved screens mainly of insects and fish.

Leading away from the temple was an interesting circular gate in the stone wall. It was a 'moon gate', and something Beatrice had never seen before. It was then explained to her that it was a traditional architectural element in a Chinese garden. Moon Gates have many different spiritual meanings, and were originally only found in the gardens of wealthy Chinese nobles. Beatrice was entranced by the gate, and wondered why the superior races of the Western world had to be taught this simple and lovely device by artists from the east.

Beatrice also became suitably impressed by the intellect and artistry she saw all around her. She was amazed at the ability of a Chinese tailor to run up a gentleman's suit or a lady's dress in half a day; the artistry of a carpenter to create modern European furniture while she watched, and jewellers who could make a copy of your own pieces in a few days.

As Beatrice was interested in horses, she always noticed the breeds that came from different countries. There was, in Macassar, the usual small donkey-sized beast used to pull the *karetta* or little hired carriage, but occasionally she would catch sight of something entirely different. Pony-sized, it would come spanking along with the speed of a small hurricane. Fire and spirit; this little horse seemed to almost hurl itself through the air, the smart carriage flying along behind it.

From Macassar to Borneo, Beatrice had changed ships to the SS *Van Eyck*. There was a full complement of passengers on board, both white and half-caste. Beatrice – not surprisingly – was amazed to see the latter, and how the Dutch treated everyone as equals. The Dutch men frequently married Malay half-caste women. Nor was it even frowned upon for a government official to marry a half-caste. Often the Dutch would dress in like clothing to the Malays – even in the towns. Well, Beatrice thought, as you dress, so you think. She did not like this business of the coloureds and the whites not being sharply marked off; it was a bit of a shock seeing one overflowing into t'other.

And so the ship with its multi-cultural passengers, arrived at Balikpapan on the east coast of Borneo. At that time, Borneo was more or less divided between the British and the Dutch. After many changes, today it is divided into four unequal parts. The largest south-east area is Kalimantan. The far north is Sabah. The west side is Sarawak, with tiny Brunei tucked into the northern part of Sarawak.

Borneo lived up to its reputation for being hot, but Beatrice, undaunted, decided to go ashore, hoping it would be cooler walking around. Along the street full of endless ranks of oil containers were a few offices and houses perched like the native houses – or *kampongs* – on high piles. There were electric light poles along the street with fat, pink Dutch officials riding up and down on bicycles. Over it all was the nauseating reek of the thick, oily petroleum which ran down alongside the road and into the sea, glittering in the sun as it lay – poisonously – on top of the water. There were notices and fire alarms everywhere forbidding smoking. The very thought of fire breaking out was too terrible to contemplate.

Only a few miles at the back of this mayhem lay the wild Borneo of huge forests; home to marvellous tigers, rhinos, orangutans and elephants living together with the proboscis monkey, sun bear and clouded leopard. Here, also, was the fearsome Dyak country where it was reputed that no girl would think of marrying a man who had not captured at least one enemy's head.

The *Van Eyck* had been refuelled, at the same time disgorging a cargo of bellowing buffaloes brought from Macassar. But at last the ship was ready to go, and off they went north up the coast of Borneo, the sky heavy and dark with thunder, and lightening flashing over the deep, dark forest. Night came and the *Van Eyck* now headed north-east, back up the coast of Celebes. A gentle day was spent passing beautiful scenery on the starboard side. Round the corner at the north-west end of Celebes they sailed, and east to where the Peleleh gold mine was. As everyone else on board went to see the mines, so did the recalcitrant Beatrice, only because:

> I had not the courage to say that I did not want to see the mines in the least, and would much rather lie on deck with a book and an ice. It was hotter than Balikpapan; a fact that beggared description![95]

The group set off up steep hills with the sun overhead at midday. They arrived at the mine gasping, and aimed for one of the machinery sheds hoping for a little shade rather than a huge interest in mining mechanics. But their guide – the manager – loved the machines, describing them with great delight. They went on past different parts of the working mine until they came to a little bake-house where the enthusiastic manager said they would actually see some gold. These were like little round pale-coloured buns. They did not look like gold, but they did feel like it, each one worth fifteen hundred guilders – about £120 (at that time). Back out into the sunlight, and everyone looked longingly at the sea and the ship. But it was not to

95 *The Sydney Morning Herald*, 14th February 1914.

be. They were told by the sparkling manager, that they did their own smelting, and they were about to visit the furnaces. A child began to cry, and at last one of the men plucked up enough courage to start breaking up the party, with everyone heading gently back down the hill to the machinery shed. Here, someone mentioned in a loud voice that the pathway to the beach lay on the right. Immediately a chorus of 'thank-yous' rang out, with everyone assuring the little man just what a wonderful tour he had given them. Back on board, the ship weighed anchor, blew her whistle, and went off round the most northerly point of the island.

Beatrice was now bound for Amboyna and Banda, two small islands of the Maluccas Spice Islands group. The large and luxurious ships of the Dutch Packet Company did not go in the direction she wanted, so she had to make do with the *Van Cloon*, a smaller steamer of the North German Lloyd Company.

The captain had alerted her to be ready to board at a specific hour, and so she went to collect her bags which were in a left-luggage room in the hotel where she was staying. The manager was at reception and Beatrice paid her bill, and asked for her bags. The manager was very polite but told Beatrice it was not possible for her to have her bags, that his partner had the key and his partner was out and no one knew when he might return. He then relapsed into silence, gazing calmly out of the window in an attitude of bored resignation. Beatrice told him that she must have her bags before the ship left in fifteen minutes. The manager shaking his head repeated that he was very sorry that his partner was out. He then rose from his seat and bowed as if to say 'This interview is over' and walked away.

Beatrice was incandescent – shouting to his departing figure that she would break down the door. One of the hotel staff was very sympathetic and tried to break down the door by putting a shoulder to it, but the man was small and slight and the door did not budge. Beatrice then spied a long metal rod leaning against the wall and by putting one end of it under the door, they managed to break the lock and Beatrice was able to find her bags. The boys threw everything onto a handcart and they ran down the street and on to the steamer.

It was a calm three-day run from Celebes, past some smaller islands, to Amboyna; the weather still being very kind:

> The ship floated in a hollow sphere of silver, without a tinge of any other colour, save where the rusting keel made shadows of deep blue. From the bows, across the unrippled surface of the wide sea plate, ran back two slanting satin folds of water, and the flying fish, rising by hundreds in this cloudy calm, drew sharp lines of black, like pen strokes on the silver grey.[96]

96 *The Sydney Morning Herald*, 7th March 1914.

Amboyna, when they arrived there, looked exactly as one had expected a spice island to look, and smell. From the deck of the ship one could see the locals carrying trays of drinks and fruits down to the dock, singing as they came. Life was easy here; a man was able to keep his family almost without having to work at all.

Many years back, Portugal had taken possession of these islands, and had discovered, through some chance of position or climate, the very best spices in the world. Both the Portuguese and later the Dutch, were together shameful in exploiting the natives, enslaving them and dispossessing them of their lands and possessions, forcing them to work without pay in the plantations of spice-bearing trees. It was decided to keep Amboyna exclusively for cloves, and Banda for nutmeg, at the same time destroying all the clove and nutmeg bearing trees in every other island of the East Indies.

Gradually, however, other nations wanted a share of these riches, and 'slips' and seedlings were stolen from the two islands and began to be planted in other parts of the world. Sometimes these pirates were caught and put to death, but even that did not deter the thieves of these valuable products.

Amboyna was the chief port of the Moluccas, and so was comparatively busy. Beatrice was told by the natives that there were several hundred whites living there. However, being 'white' included anyone with even just a touch of white blood. Again, the Dutch treated everyone as equals – the Germans treating everyone with a certain distain.

They steamed away towards Banda in the late afternoon, taking with them a few natives. Banda was enchanted – of course! Where else would a boat come into a port that was the crater of a volcano, walled with green cliffs and floored by a turquoise sea? The water was so deep that the ship was able to tie up as close to the land as the length of a carriage. But the town had shadows cast across the buildings by volcanoes belching fire and smoke. It all seemed extraordinary and very dangerous to Beatrice. But instead of the inhabitants being terrified all the time they appeared to be totally relaxed. It was sixty-two years since the last eruption of Goonong-Api, so why worry about it? Nothing much seemed to matter in Banda; the warm air was always full of the heady perfume of the spice forests; the days were long and there was little work to do.

Ashore, Beatrice wandered along, coming upon an avenue of enormous canary trees. She followed the avenue in the dying sun, quite alone but for one solitary man who drifted past her and disappeared down a little side road. Curious as ever, Beatrice followed him and saw, there in the setting sun, a fort, complete with drawbridge, castellated arch, and gate. The exterior of the castle was in good order, looking as though it might still be lived in. Darkness was coming quickly but Beatrice was just able to make out some figures cut in high relief above the door – 'Anno 1517'. She left the fort while there was still enough light to find her way through the tangle of greenery and back to the *Van Cloon*.

The following morning Beatrice went ashore again and found herself in a nutmeg forest. At first the sheer height of the trees astonished her. Then she discovered that these huge trees had been planted as shade for the young spice trees:

> They were canary trees. A huge and splendid forest, spreading out umbrella-wise towards the summit, so as to make a canopy of delightful coolness and shade. Beneath them stood the nutmegs, slender, rather spindly trees with light foliage rising to 20 feet in height. They were loaded with dainty-looking fruit. On the ground lay drifts of the fruits, split open, and showing the jet black kernel, beautifully laced over with the splendid scarlet network of the mace...and smelling sweetly and strongly of the spice within.[97]

They were beautiful, as was everything connected with this dying industry; both the blossoms and the dark, dreamy natives who wandered about collecting the fruit. Beatrice met a few of the young men in yellow or red tunics and loose white jackets, and girls dressed in pretty sarongs, each carrying a long bamboo with a forked end to remove the fruits from the trees. In one place there were a few men stripping the mace from the nuts and spreading it out to dry in the sun. Nobody was in any hurry.

In the dusk, the North German Lloyder sailed north round the west tip of the large island of Ceram (now Maluku), continuing on through the Halmaheira Sea.

97 *The Sydney Morning Herald*, 21st March 1914.

Chapter 15: German New Guinea

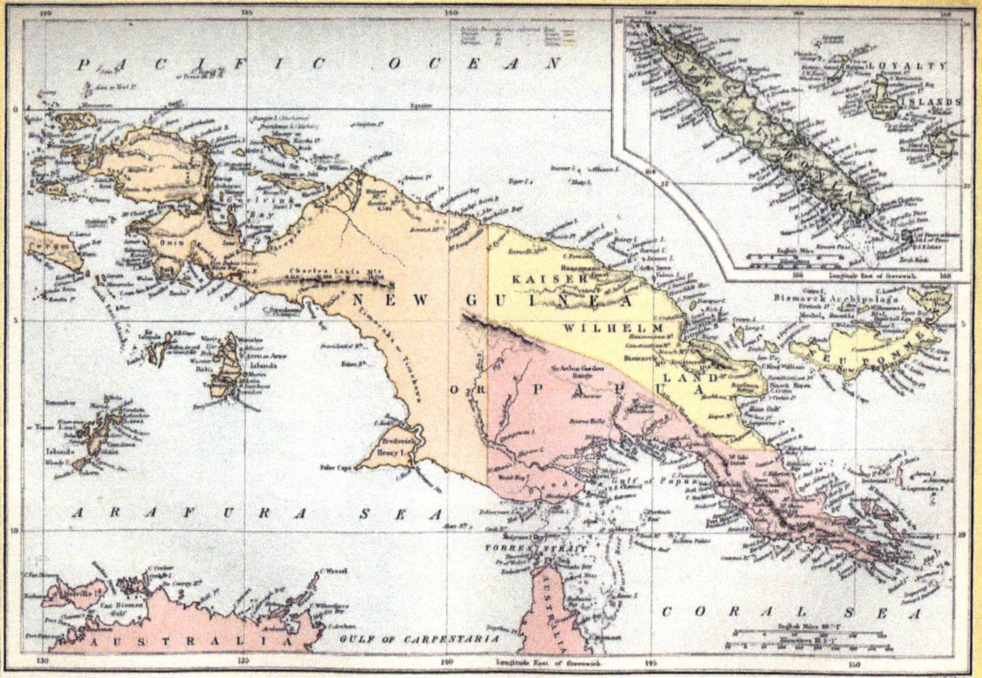

Map pre 1914

Next morning they had left Malaysia behind as the steamer sailed across the Dampier Strait between the island of Waigeo and mainland Papua, having crossed the invisible line between the straight-haired natives for the frizzy-haired, the crowded islands for the remoteness of Papua and her islands, and from the sweet-smelling spice islands to the wet, heavy jungle scents. By the evening they had left behind the calm waters of the west and into the swell of the wide Pacific. The dead calm of weeks of travel was over.

One day, as the *Van Cloon* was sailing along, the beautiful blue sea turned into a brassy-yellow colour, and full of huge broken trees and logs. They were crossing the mouth of the Lorentz River (today's Memberamo River) the largest river in Dutch New Guinea. The following day Beatrice and her shipmates were beyond Dutch territory and had entered the German division of New Guinea. (German New Guinea was a protectorate from 1884 until 1914, when it fell to Australian forces following the outbreak of the First World War).

They arrived at last at Eitape and anchored in the wide and beautiful bay. The officers' boat manned by native police came out to meet the ship. Here it was possible to see the effects of German drill upon the natives. It all seemed well organised, but Beatrice thought that the native's uniforms were less well adapted to the hot climate than the British; and the British, she discovered, caught many more criminals than the Germans.

This of course was not surprising as Britain had three centuries of colonial work behind them, whereas Germany had only one generation.

By this time Beatrice and her ship were eleven days out and now beginning the long run down the German New Guinea coast, passing the mouth of the Kaiserin Augusta River (today's Sepik). They then began passing the Schouten Islands, a collection of vicious-looking volcanoes, two of them unmistakably active, pouring forth tongues of fire so bright that the sailors on board said they could read at night by the light of it.

The ship soon arrived at Freidrich-Wilhelmshafen (today's Madang), the oldest settlement in German New Guinea. In 1884 the German New Guinea Company had arrived here and tried to establish a base, raising the German flag in 1885. But they were continually beaten by malaria.

As the *Van Cloon* glided into the port of Wilhelmshafen, Beatrice could see some well-built bungalows and a large store near the wharf. These, and all the land around belonged to the German New Guinea Company. She disembarked and, as usual, went exploring. She walked on along the dirt road until she had passed some smaller houses, and sat on a stone to rest, the only sounds just the patter of the palms and the distant breathing of the sea. Suddenly a crab came scuttling towards her:

> no larger than a tea-biscuit, very red, very black-eyed, and charged at me across the road. I never saw anything so small and so wicked and exceedingly bold. Mostly crabs are timorous as spiders but this creature had no timidity in its composition, it attacked with a deadly earnestness that was incomparably absurd...I could almost hear it gritting its teeth as it went straight for my stockings... I let the crab get a good grip of my umbrella and then flung it many yards away into the long grass. A faint clicking as I walked away suggested that it was talking dumb swears to itself. I am not yet clear to whom the honours of war should fairly have been given, for it would have certainly charged again as soon as it got out.[98]

For several days they continued down the coast, past unknown and uninhabited country. Past mangrove swamps and sago marshes, with never even a solitary fishing canoe to be seen. One afternoon there was massive thunder and lightening, sometimes lighting up the hinterland of huge mountain ranges disappearing into the distance. The wind that blew from the land was strangely cold after the heat of recent days.

They had turned the corner at Finschafen, and were arriving at Morobe only about forty miles north of the border with British New Guinea.

This little town with its sheltered bay and its splendid mass of overhanging mountains was beautiful enough to excite the most jaded traveller. The peaks were adorned with light and shadow and wreaths of sunlit mists. Four emaciated Australian miners were

98 *The Sydney Morning Herald*, 11th April 1914.

waiting for the SS *Van Cloon*. They had been prospecting but had had very little luck, finding just small amounts of gold.

One of the Australians, however, had taken out a licence to shoot birds of paradise and had a good cache of a few hundred birds to take to Rabaul for sale. The question of shooting these beautiful birds was one of great interest all over Australasia, as almost everybody knew that the bird was only found on New Guinea and some of the surrounding islands. For many years past the birds' exotic plumes had been adorning the fashionable hats of Europe, and consequently the bird had been remorselessly hunted.

British New Guinea – under its Australian mandate – had been the first to pass laws for protecting the birds, and German New Guinea had also prohibited shooting them. Up until Beatrice's trip, Dutch New Guinea had remained open ground but there were rumours that they, too, would prohibit the shooting of the valuable birds. If so, the value of plumage would escalate, doubtless leading to massive poaching, in itself a big problem. But all agreed that it would be an appalling tragedy if these splendid birds were to be lost for ever.

As they set off for Rabaul, at the far north tip of Nieu Pommern island (today's New Britain) everyone was handed a paper to fill in, answering a multitude of questions including name, age, place of birth, etc, etc. Assuming you passed muster, could you actually stay in Rabaul?

No, there weren't any hotels. Supposing you were insane enough to want to stay – what then?

After questioning everybody, Beatrice gave up in despair, and was advised to go and visit the Governor with her peculiar request.

The Governor seemed extremely kind, as he handed her the address of a house where she might stay. However, he was also keen for Beatrice to know that as there was no hotel, no one could stay who wasn't wanted. She was flabbergasted.

Nobody was friendly towards Beatrice, or even civil, until gradually the reason became clear. The Germans were building a naval station at Rabaul which was bound in secrecy, one having to pretend that the wharves being built did not exist. But this was the summer of 1913, and already there were rumblings of war. Australia was concerned about this initiative, only two days sailing from her own shores.

Beatrice found she was being followed everywhere, and then she discovered that suddenly, for some unknown reason, her camera didn't work. It was all rather frightening and she wanted to leave.

Luckily, she was able to get passage on a ketch to Ulu Island, just off the coast from Rabaul, continuing on to the very wild island of Neu-Mecklenburg (today's New

Ireland) where she stayed for some weeks with a native missionary, and went camping beside the sea with a woman from Samoa.

Determined not to be beaten, and back in Nieu Pommern, Beatrice had at last been able to find lodgings at a small, friendly hotel. In the face of the knowledge that she was probably surrounded by native cannibals, Beatrice slept surprisingly well, alone in her bungalow, in a room with an open door and windows. Luckily the local natives happened to respect the owner of the hotel who knew them well. Nobody, she hoped, would dare to attack this undefended collection of little houses.

Instead of being attacked, one moonlit night when she was in bed, Beatrice was awoken by some wonderful singing. The air was very still, and far away could be heard one high voice, shaking and yodelling, pausing to listen for a reply before yodelling again. After a while, a chorus, singing in harmony, answered it. The chorus seemed to come closer and then very close to the hotel, before drifting away again into the distance. Meanwhile the far-away yodeller continued to sing, with what sounded like another group of singers starting. Beatrice listened; delighted beyond words, until the thin, high, chanting was silent.

Christmas Day 1913, was spent in Nieu Pommern, very much as Beatrice would have spent it back in Ireland. The natives' Christmas was the following day. They wore a combination of European clothes with massive native war helmets as they performed singing and dancing in wild and exuberant Papuan style.

On 14th January 1914 the steamer – SS *Coblenz* – was expected, and Beatrice set off. As there was no direct travel between the German and British territories, she had to sail to Brisbane first, and thence on the *Morinda* back to Papua. *The Brisbane Courier* reported that Miss Grimshaw had been on a six month tour collecting material for her next book.

When she arrived in Port Moresby, she discovered that the town now had three hotels, and the cinematograph had appeared as well as the installation of wireless telegraph. She stayed with friends and concentrated on writing during 1914.

The infamous First World War broke out in September, with Australia immediately invading, and taking over German New Guinea, so Beatrice was lucky to have visited the previous year. By living in Papua, she of course, avoided the immediate horrors of the war. She was also possibly unaware of the under-current of rebellion in Ireland between the republicans and the British, leading to the Easter Rising of 1916.

For the next few years Beatrice, changed houses again, and, using her experiences of the South Sea Islands as a backdrop to her novels, wrote constantly.

Chapter 16: Sariba, Papua New Guinea

In 1915, Beatrice left Port Moresby to live on the island of Sariba, near Samarai in the area of Milne Bay. She planned the house herself, on a high promontory, and a white man with a team of natives put the house together for her in a few weeks. It was built almost totally from the local bush, with a deep roof of sago-leaf thatch. The floors were tough, split, black palm. The house had shutters which could be open or shut depending on the direction of the wind. The sitting room, which had a marvellous view over the sea, was decorated with a frieze of pearl-shell which sparkled in the sunshine against the soft browns of the walls and ceiling. She, very appropriately, called the house 'Coralsands'.

Beatrice lived here on her own for about two years, doing a great deal of writing. She had a cutter and crew, and was able to sail back and forth to Samarai.

Drying Vanilla

While living here, in August 1916, she entertained a party of Australians to tea. The Australians loved her little house, and were full of questions for Beatrice. She told them that she had recently started a vanilla plantation, and looked forward to reaping good harvests.

Later that year, in October, Beatrice took part in a bazaar in Samarai, known as 'Our Day'. This was an annual get-together of the local white people to raise money for the Red Cross. The money was raised by holding various events and competitions. A wonderful whaleboat race also took place, raising many laughs as some of the boats steered rather erratic courses. At the bazaar Beatrice raffled an elegant Blanchard lamp. The winner of this re-auctioned it, making £27 towards the fund. The jolly day ended with dancing until the small hours. The bazaar took £103, and the total for the whole day – a mammoth £562 – was the most ever raised for the charity.

Building a Planter's House

Before long Beatrice sold her lovely little house on Sariba to a local missionary society, and started to build another house on the Papuan mainland across the China Straits from Samarai.

This new house, however, was situated in three hundred acres of forest and was called 'Marana' – meaning daylight. Here Beatrice lived while she cleared much of her forested land. She enjoyed the clearing and burning off, seeing her own timber fall, and planting new timber:

> If I were asked what I have most enjoyed, in all my life, I think I should say the clearing of that forest – my forest. No one who has not done clearing can imagine the delights of it. You have obtained from the Government so many acres of forest, paying nothing for it but a few shillings for your ninety-nine years' lease; you know that you will have no rent to pay for ten years, and after that only a few pence per acre. The place is yours to dispose of for a century.[99]

She revelled in the power and the authority:

> You return, after a day of absence ... and see ahead of you, a break of light that was not there yesterday. For the first time in centuries, the sun has touched the earth of those dusk acres ... And you have done it ... Power?[100]

Beatrice loved watching her boys leaving the house early in the morning. The day would start with the 'slashers', cutting the undergrowth with their long knives to make it possible for the 'axmen' to follow and cut down the trees. Then there was the planting of pineapples, potatoes, maize and tomatoes. And the timber, the rope and the roofing, worth more than the imported sheets of iron bought in Samarai. Tree planting in the tropics was a delight. The soil was good and the results swift. Then there were also eggs from the chickens fed from her land.

There was, of course a down side to this endeavour – falling timber, snake bites, fever, and unruly labourers. There was also loneliness. The mornings were a new day and always busy, but the evenings and nights could indeed be very lonely, and it was this that eventually made Beatrice move on. But she had not been slacking. Not only was she involved with her land, but by now she had written and published more than nine books and several serialisations in periodicals.

In January 1920, the loneliness and seclusion of Beatrice's life at 'Marana' was due to be disturbed. *The Sunday Times* (Sydney), reported that Miss Constantia Beresford was in Sydney. Daughter of the late Major-General Beresford of Craig-Dhu Varren, and Portrush, Miss Beresford was en route to Samarai where her marriage with Mr Osborne Grimshaw – a government officer – would take place.

99 Isles of Adventure, pp. 199–200.

100 *Isles of Adventure*, p. 201.

(She was stuck in Sydney for a month due to a strike; making her way to Papua by the first available ship arriving there in February.) The wedding was held in Beatrice's home.

In June 1921, a film, *Thunder Island* was made, from Beatrice's story, *My Lady of the Island.*

The following interview is about the most personal piece of writing I have found. In it Beatrice tells about her troubles choosing a career:

> There came an interlude of a year at Bedford College, when the family conclave decided my career for me – classical lecturer in some one of the women's colleges. I, being seventeen, naturally knew everything. I explained, as patiently as I could, that colleges were cramping to the higher development of the ego, and that I meant to be a sporting journalist. After which I went home – to Belfast – and put in a year of classical study at Queen's, just to show something that I have forgotten. There followed a year or two of social duties – the good and useful period of conscription that everyone ought to serve. All that time I was trying to break athletic records, and finding that they took some breaking. I have always been fond of riding, though not up to the old high standard in that way. The family have been outdoor folk from time immemorial – big and muscular, undistinguished, straight-living, straight-riding folk. And I kept looking for the something that was lost. I did not find it up the Lagan River, ahead or behind my pulling boat, nor yet within the range of a bicycle.[101]

She went on to tell about being 'The Revolting Daughter' and going to work in Dublin; learning the art of writing while editing two periodicals, and going to dances, the races, and the theatre. She was most indignant at being asked to join a well-known circus and perform in its arena! She talked about her travels. Papua, she said, had been her home for a good many years, living amongst the cannibals. She never missed an opportunity to talk about the cannibals, naturally enough a big draw to Europeans. She finishes by saying that there was one thing that she had done of which she was proud, and that was to have helped in the settlement of the tropics, and in making these places better known and understood. For that little scrap of pioneering work she was grateful.

In November 1921, Beatrice left 'Marana' and her plantation, visiting Port Moresby before travelling on board the SS *Morinda* to Sydney. Here she spent three months visiting the Blue Mountains and Mount Koscivsko – a mountain located on the Main Range of the Snowy Mountains, part of the Australian Alps, and at 7,310 ft the tallest mountain in Australia, and a stiff climb to the top. With Beatrice now in her early fifties, history does not reveal whether she conquered the summit – or not.

101 'About Myself', *The Register* (Adelaide), 17th September 1921, p. 4.

Chapter 17: To England, via Indonesia

Beatrice departed from Sydney on board the SS *Roggeveen* on the 8th February 1922 for a short visit to England via Singapore and Java. It is unclear if she visited Java on this voyage, or on her return to Papua. On balance it seems more likely that it was en route west as it took her three months travelling to England. Furthermore, she states it was 'the wet season' (October – April) when she was in Java.

Always the explorer, and well informed, Beatrice was interested in visiting Boro Budur, in the south of the island. Batavia (today's Jakarta) was the capital city and port of the Dutch East Indies, lying on the north coast of Java in a sheltered bay. The city originally had a monopoly on nutmeg, cloves and cinnamon, later augmented by non-indigenous cash crops like coffee, tea, tobacco, rubber, sugar and opium.

From Batavia, Beatrice travelled by train to Bandoeng, fascinated, as ever, by her surroundings:

> There are coolies, and Chinese, and Javanese, fancy-dressed. There is growing rice, in thousands of acres, verdigris green; there are volcanoes, sharp and conical, patchworked with agriculture right up to the top. At the end of the day comes swift dark, and a station, and a drive in the warm, windy wet through streets imperfectly seen, to a careless, magnificent hotel.[102]

The following morning, still in the dark, she left Bandoeng in the same train. Travelling south-east, another long day of marvellous scenery greeted her in the daylight, while an army of inquisitive overweight Dutch stared at her relentlessly, and allowed their children – whom she hated – to annoy her. She arrived eventually at Djokjakarta, on the south coast, a junction where she alighted – alone – for her final destination of Boro Budur.

The station was seething with people, pushing one another and shouting in a dozen different dialects.

102 *Isles of Adventure*, p. 227.

She was busy fending off some pushy taxi drivers, when she was lucky enough to find a couple of kind folk who spoke both French and English, and from whom she was able to get information. They shepherded Beatrice to a delightful little steam tram which ran north to within about four miles of Boro Budur.

The other passengers were charmingly mannered, exquisite Javanese, and also a Chinese princess – or duchess – travelling with her maid, and wearing pale-green taffeta, with Parisian shoes and a great deal of beautiful jewellery. It was extremely hot, but the princess sat bolt upright all the time, never moving an inch until, at one stop, she unbent enough to order a pink drink with a large ice-cream sitting in the middle of the glass, being determined to finish it all before the tram got going again. As the tram's whistle sounded, she tilted her jewel-encrusted head back, and slid the icy concoction down her throat. Speechless, she threw the empty glass to the running vendor. As Beatrice watched this entertainment, she reflected that she was glad she had not missed it all by taking the taxi. At Magelang she left the tram and at last took a drive the four miles further, to a quiet little inn a few hundred yards from Boro Budur:

> And the next morning comes that unusual delight – the sole possession, unguided, uncompanioned, untouristed, and generally unbedevilled, of a great and famous place.
>
> Boro Budur, a monument to defunct Buddhism and Hindu days in Java ...[103]

Boro Budur is a ninth-century Mahayana Buddhist temple, and one of the greatest Buddhist monuments in the world. It consists of nine stacked platforms, six square and three circular, topped by a central dome. The monument is both a shrine to the Buddha and a place for Buddhist pilgrimage.

The temple is decorated with 2,672 relief panels of fruit and flowers, and 504 Buddha statues. Further up there are fewer carvings, until at the topmost stupa it is quite plain. Evidence suggests Boro Budur was abandoned following the fourteenth-century decline of Hindu kingdoms. It was never completed and was discovered by the Dutch in the early 1800s when they came upon a mass of ruins choked by the forest. You cannot enter it as it is a casing of solid stone on the core of a natural hill.

Beatrice spent three wonderful days wandering round the ruins, mostly in pouring rain and consequently alone, finding the silence of the ruins quiet and spiritual, flowing like a warm river through the blue, empty air.

On her eventual arrival in Plymouth on May 5th, Beatrice was presented with a beautiful bouquet of flowers from an anonymous admirer. She held a reception of press representatives in the music-room of the liner, readily answering questions with

103 *Isles of Adventure*, p. 230.

which she was bombarded. At times she interrupted to express her pleasure at seeing England and her friends and family again, but assuring all present that this was no longer her home, as Papua was where she now considered home.

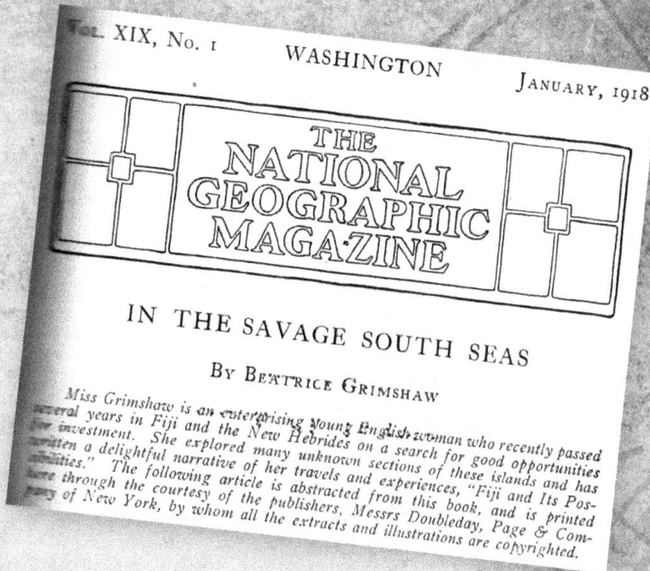
VOL. XIX, NO. 1 WASHINGTON JANUARY, 1918

THE NATIONAL GEOGRAPHIC MAGAZINE

IN THE SAVAGE SOUTH SEAS

BY BEATRICE GRIMSHAW

Miss Grimshaw is an enterprising young English woman who recently passed several years in Fiji and the New Hebrides on a search for good opportunities for investment. She explored many unknown sections of these islands and has written a delightful narrative of her travels and experiences, "Fiji and Its Possibilities." The following article is abstracted from this book, and is printed here through the courtesy of the publishers, Messrs Doubleday, Page & Company of New York, by whom all the extracts and illustrations are copyrighted.

She continued on along the south coast to Dartmouth where she stayed with her sister at her home 'Fernbank', before going to London.

Her return to England after fifteen years abroad, was covered by a large number of newspapers, all with slightly different versions, but all starting their paragraphs with... 'Miss Beatrice Grimshaw, the famous adventurous Irish novelist, after spending fifteen years among the cannibals'... and all greatly lauding her novels. One tribute to her writing was from Francis D Grierson, a well-known, Dublin-based journalist and broadcaster in the 1920s, who said about her new book, '*Conn of the Coral Seas*' – published by Hurst and Blacket at 7s 6d, as 'unusually descriptive writing ... its quality lifting it above the level of the ordinary'.[104] And H. J. C. Grierson – a Scot (they don't seem to be related) – in *The Bookfellow*, was conscious that there was a quality in the book which he suddenly realised was her extraordinary understanding. 'When she writes of men, she writes as though she were a man herself; when she writes of women, you appreciate her femininity.' And yet more accolades, assuring the reader that 'when Miss Grimshaw is back in her palm-shaded house, she will take up her pen again, and that presently there will come to us new story of those islands of sun and shadow.'[105]

The Northern Whig and Belfast Post of Tuesday 9th May, proudly featured a long column entitled 'Belfast Girl's Life Among the Savages'. It was a review of her early life in Ireland as well as her foreign travel:

> New Guinea ... a great deal of it has never been explored by white people ... there are stretches in which cannibal tribes live to themselves. Many, however, have been induced to work on the plantations, and the cannibals are certainly the finest native workers because of their physical development and their demeanour. But cannibalism flourishes, and the people who practice it do not regard it as wrong. One gets so accustomed to this ... that it is accepted as a matter of course. I know the cookery recipes now as to the best methods of preparing human

104 Francis D. Grierson.

105 H. J. C. Grierson, *The Bookfellow*.

> food … The inhabitants of one village torture terribly, and then roast the body alive in the traditional three-legged cauldron … the cannibals are extremely well mannered and in all other respects are the best workers you can find.

She goes on to discuss sorcery and the role of women in native society:

> The position of women is deplorable. They are in effect slaves…they do all the heavy work and their husbands kill them at will. The men get into a rage and smash the heads of their wives and sometimes eat them afterwards. Marriage is by purchase, and is dependent on the number of pigs that can be offered by the bridegroom to the bride's parents. The pig, in fact, is thought to be of very much more value than the wife…When death occurs there is an extraordinary procedure at the cemetery. The widow, if her husband has died, is supposed to go to the graveyard and live there six months. A little leaf house is set upon the grave, and here she stays until her official mourning is over. However, it is not always so dreary a task as it seems, for, as a widower may be living in the same graveyard in memory of his departed wife, there may be opportunities for companionship.[106]

Beatrice was entertained to dinner in May, at the Lyceum Club in London. Among other guests were Sir John Foster Frazer and Mr de Vere Stacpoole. She was also asked to give a talk in June, to the Royal Colonial Institute at their meeting in the Victoria Hotel. She spoke about all the Pacific Islands as well as Papua. However, her association with cannibals was always her selling point.

A selection of Beatrice's books

The Irish Society and Social Review stated:

> Miss Beatrice Grimshaw, the well-known novelist, who has recently returned to Ireland after having spent some fifteen years among cannibals, had her first literary experiences in contributing to The Social Revue, almost twenty years earlier.[107]

106 'Belfast Girl's Life Among the Savages', *The Northern Whig and Belfast Post*, 9th May (1922).

107 *The Irish Society and Social Review*, 2nd September 1922, p. 1.

Chapter 18: Papua New Guinea

Beatrice departed from London on 21st October 1922, as a passenger on board the SS *Caernarvonshire*, leaving her ship, probably in Singapore. It took her six months, until April 1923, before arriving back in Port Moresby, during which time she did a bit more exploring.

The next we know about her travels, she is departing from Ternate, one of the small islands situated off the north-east end of Papua.

As nothing was dated, it became reasonably apparent from newspaper cuttings and various deductions, that on this trip she eventually visited the Dutch part of Papua – and the Sepik River.

> One stormy wet-season afternoon the steamer that comes once in many weeks left Ternate for North New Guinea with myself on board as a passenger.[108]

Beatrice gloried in the wild weather, watching from the ship – in fleeting sunshine interspersed with squalls of wind and rain – tall volcanoes, some of them sending out on the wind, long plumes of grey smoke. The light was so variable; sometimes blanking out everything, then suddenly a splash of brilliant sunlight enlivened her world again. She had, of course, already sailed down this coast, nine years previously, not stopping until reaching German New Guinea, by 1923 no longer in existence.

This time Beatrice was visiting the Dutch East Indies port of Hollandia, (Jayapura since 1962) on the shore of Humboldt Bay. The town had a first-class, sheltered anchorage, boasting one long street with half a dozen stores, and was the centre of the, now illegal, Bird of Paradise trade. When Beatrice arrived here, almost nobody would talk about the trade in birds, which the Malays were still hunting in early 1923, but now had to venture far into the bush where the wild natives lived, who, the previous year, had killed twenty-eight hunters. The Chinese traders never ventured away from the coast. Beatrice, who wanted to go up-country was unable to do so – partly because of the cannibals, and partly because of the flooding which swept through Hollandia, demolishing many of the little houses.

Although the weather stopped her from exploring up-country, it did not prevent Beatrice from seeing the sea villages of Humboldt's Bay – the houses all standing on very long piles. She was taken to the largest house, landing from the boat onto a stage of open poles. Indoors, men and women, all adorned with carved shell jewellery, sat and lay around on beautiful mats surrounded by hand-crafted spears, baskets, canoe paddles, and great jars containing sago.

108 *Isles of Adventure*, p. 146.

Through the slatted floor shone a pale-green light, reflected up from the sea. It was cool and quiet. Beatrice thought of London on that February day with its winter hunger and cold, and reflected on just how comparatively rich these native people actually were.

A few days later she went by whale boat to the village of Tabati, arranging to stay the night there as it was half a day's journey away. Six young natives paddled the boat at an astonishing speed:

> Once in a way they broke into wild, sea-windy songs, things that were the very essence of savagery, and the sound of waves, and something more – something that lies in the heart of savage life, and that no man, learned or unlearned, has ever yet succeeded in defining.
>
> … The youths took it up from one another, tossed it about, sang it with a strange, impersonal smile upon their lips …[109]

Within a few hundred yards of the village, the boys stopped paddling and produced a small piece of looking glass. This, they passed around adorning themselves with paint and flowers. They were all so excited by having the loan of a boat, and bringing this strange white woman into a village for the night.

Tabati's houses were similar to those Beatrice had seen before. But the water was deeper, never less than fifteen feet. There was a main promenade railed in on both sides, but apart from this, you got about on a sort of tightrope with a few boards across it here and there, but with no handrail.

Her refuge for the night had the luxury of two rooms, one of which Beatrice commandeered, hanging her mosquito net and laying out her bedding in the effort of finding some privacy. However, it seemed that all the small boys of the district also came and went from the house, not leaving her alone for a minute. Beatrice found this torture common to all native towns, and that short of murdering the children, nothing could be done to mitigate it.

During the night her camp bed sagged and creaked on the sapling floor through which she could see the surging water. She did wonder if it would hold up for the night, and if not, what were her chances of surviving, enmeshed in a collapsed bed and a mosquito net. However, in the morning, she was still in bed and the poles of the floor were still where they should be.

For breakfast, she had brought with her bread and butter, and while eating, she was being watched by everyone else in the house, the chief looking longingly at this repast. He was overjoyed when she gave him a left-over loaf, which he cut in delicate, slices

109 *Isles of Adventure*, p. 154.

and offering it to some of his favourites. After this, the chief took Beatrice on a tour of the village, and told her she might see the interior of the *laki-laki* house. This was a huge compliment. As Beatrice knew, the *laki-laki* was a men-only club, and to be invited in was a great tribute to her. The young men of the village spent a lot of time here, learning from the older men the traditions and rules of the tribe. As usual, the women were never allowed in, the penalty being death.

After Hollandia Beatrice had no means of transport further east except by canoe, and the weather was not favourable for these little boats. Nor could she hire or even buy a boat of any kind, for the good reason that there were none. However, she was extremely fortunate in the eventual call of a mission launch which was en route eastwards down the coast, and was willing to take her along.

The Sepik River

> I was the first white woman to ascend the Fly and Sepik, those wonderful and mysterious rivers, still little known; and only two or three white men had been before me. On the Sepik, I had my narrowest escape when a body of head-hunters urged me to come and see their village, all by myself, because their women wanted to look at me. I ventured to leave the men of my party – two only, but well armed – as I wanted greatly to see something that no one else had seen, because the head-hunters, when they had brought out two or three old and terrified women as a bait, began to bar me into the house, while the women, hurriedly, disappeared – an unmistakable sign of trouble.[110]
>
> Heads, heads, heads – there was no getting away from them on the Middle Sepik, that March and April of 1923.[111]

It was most likely the same steamer from the Divine Word Mission that rescued her from Hollandia, which took Beatrice up the Sepik.

The Sepik River originates in the Victor Emanuel Range in the central highlands of Papua New Guinea, and is wider, longer and deeper than most of the great European rivers. From its mountain headwaters near Telefomin, it travels north-west flowing briefly into today's Indonesian West Papua, before turning back north-east for the majority of its journey following the Great Depression. Along its course it receives numerous tributaries from the mountains to the north and the Central Range to the south. The Sepik's watershed is over 30,000 square miles.

For most of the river's length it meanders like the Amazon River, to the Bismarck Sea off northern Papua New Guinea. Unlike many other large rivers, the Sepik has no delta,

110 Beatrice Grimshaw, 'How I Found Adventure', *Blue Book* (April 1939).

111 *Isles of Adventure*, p. 33.

but flows straight into the sea about sixty miles from the town of today's Wewak. This enables large ships to travel up the first sixty miles, and smaller boats drawing ten to fifteen feet would find enough water for another hundred miles or so. There are around 1,500 oxbow and other lakes on the floodplain, the largest of which are the Chambri Lakes.

The Sepik was untouched by Europeans until 1885 when Germans began to explore its region. Local villagers have used the Sepik River since ancient times for water, fishing, and transportation.

When Beatrice was writing, the greater part of the river ran through the Mandated Territory of New Guinea (formerly Kaiser Wilhelm's Land) and back through Dutch New Guinea, but, she declared, 'the best stretches were all in our land'. No regular steamers ran along the coast to the river mouth, but a few recruiting schooners had gone up the river from time to time.

Beatrice travelled about two hundred nautical miles from the river mouth. Unfortunately she did not – or could not – name the villages she visited or passed. But there was one which she said sounded like 'come on a bit', which might possibly have been Kamindimbit, followed by Kanganaman, famous for the oldest *haus tambaran* on the Sepik. She almost certainly got as far as the Chambri Lakes. Ambunti, a little further on, is almost exactly 200 nautical miles from the mouth.

The heat was overpowering, and getting hotter with every mile passed, and with it the mosquitoes increased. It was mangrove palm along the river bank at first, and then sago, the main food of the local people.

After forty miles, the boat stopped for the night at the little mission station managed by one missionary father, and one brother – both of them German. The people who inhabited this part of the river were cannibals, and although supposedly Christian, they mostly remained completely 'savage'. A few years before Beatrice was there, some of them plotted to wipe out the mission. The story went however, that some friendly natives warned the missionaries, but insisted that although they would protect them, if by chance someone was killed, the natives hoped the missionaries would permit them to eat the dead man!

A couple of days later, the launch continued on upstream, the river still a mile or so wide, and now in the country of the renowned Sepik head-hunters. The difference between head-hunting and cannibalism was that head-hunting was done for 'spiritual' purposes and was mainly confined to the Sepik River system and in the Gulf of Papua, whereas a cannibal ate people for the calories contained in human flesh and was practised throughout the coastal areas and offshore islands. Head-hunting was done more ritualistically after battle and certain parts of the body like testicles, brains and livers as well as being nutritious, were believed to impart special powers to the people who ate them.

These people of the Middle Sepik were bigger and stronger than the other natives. They had a good idea of art, and their houses were better built. The villages of some thousands were kept in good order; all of those visited by Beatrice had a display of heads in the men's communal house – here called *a haus tambaran*. What they knew of white people was very little.

Some of the labourers they were carrying were becoming reluctant to go ashore as their village drew nearer. They had been away some three years and they were worried about how the tribe would receive them. However, the following day, while all those on board watched anxiously, all seemed to go well. The villagers seemed excited to see their men returned, and, wanting to hear about their adventures, whisked them off into the forest.

Some men from a village renowned for its friendliness, invited Beatrice to leave the white men on the bank, and go with them to visit the women of the tribe. It was always well known that if there seemed to be any danger, the men would keep their women hidden. Nothing daunted, Beatrice accepted the invitation, shortly arriving at the village. Then, out of the door of the women's house a few small brown faces appeared. The men beckoned to them to come on down and see the white woman, and very timidly they came. Most of them would not approach Beatrice until their men laughingly dragged them up to her. They were quite attractive and it appeared that they were rather better treated than some of the other miserable women Beatrice had seen.

There then started lots of dancing about, loud chatter and offers of weapons, feathers and heads, probably for the price of a few knives. As nobody could understand the other, not much bartering was done and Beatrice returned to the bank escorted by the men but none of the women. As the Catholic Fathers had concluded their own business – which as mission work Beatrice thought pretty hopeless – they all went back on board and left:

> It was a typical Sepik River afternoon; over huge open lagoons, steely and livid, under a sky that was black with terrible heat, the launch panted on her way; through narrower reaches, less than half a mile in width, where the silent dark green trees on either bank stirred not a leaf, but stood like gloomy soldiers, stiff at attention ... And with every mile of our advance up the river, the mosquitoes and the heat increased.[112]

Some of the villages possessed ornamented pottery. Some of the cooking pots were enormous, graduating down to saucepan-size, all beautifully decorated in various patterns of raised waving lines and fanciful representations of human faces. Beatrice wanted to know where they were made, but no one seemed to know – even Father

112 *Isles of Adventure*, p. 37.

Kirchbaum, who knew more about the river and its people than anyone else – admitted that he had been defeated in his attempts at finding this mysterious village.

Continuing on upriver, Beatrice became aware of a feeling that there was an uneasiness in the native's attitude. They were always uneasy and fierce, but there was something more, she thought, in their demeanour. Even the missionary Fathers, usually such complete dare-devils, took some precautions, and at night did not tie up to the bank but anchored some way out in the stream.

The following day the party passed by the village which Beatrice thought sounded like 'come on a bit' but possibly was Kamindimbit. Soon they arrived at the next village, its warriors sitting around chewing betelnut. Here, Beatrice felt even more strongly that there was something afoot.

A young muscular man, oiled and painted, came forward, watching the party and smiling to himself. He was joined by an older man who seemed nervous, his face full of fury. However, they stood about quietly enough as the white folk looked at the curios in the men's houses. Then the young warrior, who had been watching her, asked Beatrice if she would come with him to let the women see her.

Although not at all happy about it, but as they say, 'the Lord hates a coward', Beatrice followed him to where the houses stood, but there were no women. Eventually one woman came into sight and Beatrice was beckoned into the women's house. But by now losing her nerve, she said she was tired and wanted to return to the boat. Soon there were more men and the women had disappeared, which always meant bad news to Beatrice. She was no coward, but having decided that discretion was the better part of valour, thought grimly to herself, she was the only one there with a long-haired head!

The next day the secret was out. Some friendly Tok Pisin speaking natives had told the missionaries that three days earlier the villagers had invaded another village, killing fifteen natives and capturing a young boy. What were they going to do with the boy? Would they also kill him and add his head to their collection?

Along the bank stood the village men – a young boy amongst them. He was unconfined but being closely watched. It all seemed so innocent. Beatrice and the Fathers landed and talked to an old man who explained that he had merely adopted the boy and would bring him up as his own, and the boy would say it was true. But when the lad was asked if he would run away, he looked up at the white men, his eyes looking desperate. Still the missionaries played for time.

Suddenly the old man started screaming and yelling and turning somersaults over a log with an agility worthy of the Russian Ballet. This performance continued for some time, the missionaries seeing there was no chance of talking reasonably. They took the boy by the arms and hustled him into the pinnace where Beatrice already sat watching the bank. Only when she saw one of the Father's boys jump for a gun, and the other one leaping into the engine room, did she realise there was trouble. On the land the old man flung something down with which she presumed he had been trying to kill the Father. At this, the other native men stopped and – incredibly – burst into hysterical laughter.

The villagers, quieter now, paddled to the steamer wanting the boy back. Whether they wanted to kill and eat him, or they genuinely wanted to adopt him, the missionaries had no intention of letting him go. Finally the villagers had to eat humble pie when the steamer charged her engines and started off upriver again.

The poor child was miserable. Nobody could speak his language and he just crouched in a corner refusing to eat. His parents had been killed and beheaded before his eyes, and his friends slaughtered. It was the gift of a blue loin-cloth that first made him smile. With a gesture of total scorn, he flung away his little bark loin-cloth and tied on the new one. It was a while before he plucked up the courage to eat what was given him. The other boys laughed at him and showed him how delicious bread and jam was. He soon learned, picking up all the scraps before the others and secreting them under Beatrice's chair.

It took some time to win his confidence, but gradually with feeding and by little strokes and pats, Monkey – as he had been named – learned that the white woman at least meant him no harm. He would creep under Beatrice's chair and look up at her, still with the same stunned expression. But when she, very unexpectedly, caressed him, tears came to his eyes. One day the Fathers took him ashore to see some of his own people who had escaped from the raid. There must have been some enlightening talk with his own people, as when he returned to the boat the despair had gone from his eyes. He discovered he was going to live with good people when finally he was landed at the mission where he would stay until he was an adult. Beatrice watched him following a crowd of farm boys up to the house, an excited, curious, real boy again.

Continuing upriver, the party arrived at a large village on the banks of a great lagoon:

> Even on the lovely Sepik we had seen nothing more beautiful than this secluded, exquisite spot, with its park-like shores, wide stretches of deep grass, dotted with trees, its beds of rustling, bright green sugar-cane out in the water, its palms stooping, mirrored, over the lake surface, its fairy inlets bridged with leafy liana, its sharp, out-running points where the stately egret – tall, white as sea-foam – stood or walked, and gazed at us with fearless eyes.[113]

The village was 'all right' and the missionary Fathers were able to conduct their business without harassment. There was a very large *haus tambaran* in the village, full of treasures which were difficult to see owing to the poor light.

113 *Isles of Adventure*, p. 51. This may well have been the Chambri Lakes.

Beatrice wrote about the difficulties of photography on the Sepik. I also discovered years later, the same problems. The people were dark brown in colour, and one normally saw them under the shade of trees. A gleam of sun in a clearing was the only chance of getting a good photograph, and that was more than likely around midday when the sun was overhead, and facial features were lost in the shade of huge mops of hair. Beatrice, of course, in the 1920s, also had to contend with film, plates, paper, and chemicals, all of which went bad in the damp heat of the river forests. Furthermore, many of the natives were frightened of spirits being inside the camera, and would avoid being photographed if they could. On one occasion, everyone was most obliging and helped take into a sunny clearing, some good pieces of pottery; one of the big sago jars, and a cooking pot. Three heads had been oiled, cleaned, and fitted with masks of sculptured clay, each displaying a different expression. At last Beatrice was able to get a good picture of the artefacts.

She was invited to stay the night in one friendly village. The chief was very pressing, saying it would be a great honour. His house was well built and pretty, and, like so many other houses, covered with green flowering creepers and orchids, and verandas adorned with ornamental lattice work. The boat was spending the night at anchor in the river, and she could have accepted the invitation, but she didn't, and was sorry afterwards. The reason was that some of the family were suffering from some horrible skin complaint, and the thought that she might have to share some bedding with the afflicted people, was too much for her.

When it came time to leave, all the villagers came to see them off, with hugs and good-will wishes. One canoe came alongside with three totally naked old gentlemen, pressing gifts of yams and sago cake upon Beatrice, rubbing their tummies indicating it was all good to eat. She was sad to be leaving such merry, hospitable people.

On the way back down the Sepik to the river mouth Beatrice learned a lot more about the Sepik and its natives. They had on board by now, about sixty young men bound for the plantations, and some of them already had a smattering of pidgin English, learned from visiting missionaries. Among other traditions, she found out about the scar tattooing.

This tattooing was a real ordeal. When a boy became of age, as part of his initiation into manhood, it was a prerequisite that he was tattooed, something he would have been dreading for years.

A day would come when one of the elders would decide it was time for two or three boys to be tattooed. Each would be spread-eagled on the ground, with four hefty men sitting on their arms and legs. Then the operators would take sharpened bamboo knives, and set to work. It was a bloody operation, and with the shrieks of the boys, the fierce beating of village drums and the taunts of the on-lookers it was all mayhem. When the cutting was finished, the boys would be flung into the river and then the sap of a certain tree would be rubbed into the wounds as an antiseptic. After a few days, red clay would be rubbed into the cuts and for many days the youths were closed up in seclusion, lying on their faces and hardly able to move. Gradually the cuts healed, the final result displaying small raised 'keloid' scars in a design all over the 'patient's' back and shoulders.

Artifacts collected by Beatrice

The river flowed on, but underneath its beauty it teemed with mystery and secrecy. The biggest mystery of all was spiritism or devil worship. Almost all Papuans were involved in one way or another. Then there was the famous hidden pottery town already spoken about, but there were also hidden fighting towns that the government knew nothing about. The head-hunters knew a lot more than they would ever disclose.

The party arrived eventually at the river mouth; with every mile it had became a little cooler, the mosquitoes a little less vicious. Beatrice foresaw the day when big ships would sail up the Sepik, and the head-hunters would be civilised and wear shirts and trousers, and drive motor cars and mend broken-down launches. She declared she was glad she would not be there. She liked her wicked, artistic, sometimes hospitable head-hunters just as they were.

Diana's Trip Up The Sepik, 1995

Our transport for the Sepik River

From the small coastal town of Wewak on Papua New Guinea's north coast, to Ambunti on the Sepik River, our flight in a tiny six-seater aeroplane, was magic. We landed safely, and there at the water's edge was our canoe with two local men, waiting to take us off into the unknown.

With Moses and Dion in the canoe, Trish, David and I set off up the Middle Sepik River – further upstream than Beatrice's trip – through low hanging trees,

Sepik River trip

until quite suddenly we emerged into the Wasui Lagoons. It was so beautifully calm and sunlit, but such shallow water that we couldn't use the engine and just poled ourselves along with accompanying sounds of frogs and crickets. The mountains all around were reflected in the glassy water with not a breath of wind. We pushed through a lot of small white water lilies until the vegetation became thicker and thicker and we discovered we had come the wrong way. We tried to retrace our passage but it was just a maze of water plants, so thick there was very little trace of where we had come. It was all a bit unnerving, and behind us now, the sky looked dark and ominous.

As luck would have it, we came across two boys fishing and they directed us to our overnight stopping place at Wagu village. By then it was almost dark. Nothing had been organised in advance, but we met the village elders who decided that we could stay the night in a borrowed house.

With no ladder in sight, we had to scramble up two poles tied together, leaning against our house on stilts. Here we were all together for the night. Even inside it was humid and sticky. We had sweet potato, sago, and steak and onion from a tin for dinner – put together by Moses. We were ravenously hungry having eaten practically nothing all day. Of course there was no electricity here, nor, indeed candles nor lamps. Luckily I had a little torch, just enough to light us to bed. Trish and I seemed almost private under one mosquito net and David under another. The house was full of men talking quietly and coughing. They smoked home-grown, air-dried tobacco wrapped up in news print. I wondered did they all have TB or lung cancer? Well, there we were, it was all so amazing and different – and exciting.

We knew, of course that the Bird of Paradise was indigenous to Papua New Guinea, and had asked Moses and Dion about the chance of seeing them. That first morning, we got up at 5 a.m. and went off to try and find these beautiful birds, as one of the men had told Moses he thought he knew of a display tree. Everything was dripping wet as we scrambled up a muddy mountain stream with Moses and the local guide.

And there, magically, in two tall trees – birds of paradise, displaying for us. There were two large yellow and brown birds, the males having dark emerald green faces and throats, two very long tail wires and large white ornamental side plumes. We discovered on our return home they were Emperor of Germany's birds of paradise. They were absolutely superb. They would throw their tail feathers over their backs and quiver. What a thrill. The females were quite dull in comparison to the males, with no ornamental plumes. Their call varied from a soft warbling, to fluting, building up to a sound like a crow. Sadly, the Emperor of Germany's Bird of Paradise is now a threatened species, so how very lucky we were to have seen them.

We watched for about two neck-breaking hours before returning back down. En route we found a gorgeous waterfall where we were able to have a long, sweet drink, and a good wash – standing there under the falls.

As we continued our way back downhill, we were aware of a lovely lemony smell, and there beside us was a huge tree of wild lemons, draped with long racemes of white orchids. We gathered lots of the fruit which we took back to the long-house where I made lemonade, sweetened by the local sugar cane.

After breakfast we set off once again in the canoe. It was dull but dry so far. To my amazement we saw a terrific shoal of flying fish skittering across the water and even landing in the boat. Until then, I thought that flying fish were only found at sea. On we went back into the main swirling river, creating whirlpools and eddies. There were some young people fishing from tiny canoes. They had little charcoal fires in the stern of the canoe, set on a bed of clay so it wouldn't burn the boat, where the fish were smoked as soon as they were caught. Then our motor wouldn't start, so we floated off downstream without any power. I wondered where we would end up.

Trish departs from the night's dwelling place

Moses friend Iwa

After ten or fifteen minutes Moses got us going again. Apparently it was a spark plug.

Soon it became sunny and we draped our wet and dirty things over the sides of the canoe. We took off our shoes and trailed them in the water getting rid of the clinging mud. The river was around half a mile wide, but we were able to take short cuts through *barats* which are channels cut across the meanders in the river, so avoiding a long laborious journey. The high grass lining the banks had long seed heads blowing in the breeze, shining like silver pennants in the sun.

We passed the village of Swagup, at that time mostly underwater due to the height of the river. This was the home of the quite isolated insect cult people who have their own language, and a ferocious reputation of hunting the many crocodiles in the swamps nearby.

In the early afternoon we tied up to a fallen log and had our normal gourmet lunch of a dry cracker, a slice of spam and more orange squash. It was so hot. When we were motoring upstream it was remarkably cooler, but stationary it was hot and sweaty. I had never in my life before been so covered up from the sun. We all wore long thin trousers and long sleeved shirts, against both the sun and the mossies. David had terrible looking feet and ankles, red and swollen and very hot and itchy. I have been taking off my shoes while in the boat, and rolling up my trousers to the knee and dangling my lower legs in the river to keep them cool.

It had been another magical day. By then we were in the Nixa River – part of the April River, a main tributary of the Sepik – and approaching the village of Woukomas. Moses' friend Iwa lived here. He was a boat-builder and was making a new canoe for Moses. We discovered we would stay over night in his long-house. As it was all so flooded we had to disembark from the canoe on to a little landing platform and up three or four steps in to the house which was still only about a couple of feet above the water. The first thing Trish and I needed was a pee! So along comes, Iwa's daughter, Bao, in the tiniest canoe you have ever seen, and off we paddled into the trees. She stopped the boat and waited, and we waited, and eventually we looked enquiringly at her and she gestured to the water! Well, try taking down your trousers in a foot wide canoe, balancing on the side and peeing over the edge. It was hysterical.

While one of us was performing, the other had to counter-balance by sitting on the opposite side of the boat. Even Bao could see the joke, and shyly giggled along with us.

Iwa, his two wives and all their children lived in the long-house. It was about 45ft x 20ft and totally made of wood. Because the river was in high flood, we could see the rushing river between the bamboos which made the floor. Every joint was connected by strips of sago palm bark. Everything was beautifully and painstakingly handmade from the forest, and absolute works of art. It was completely open-plan, with both families having their own area and fireplace, yet there appeared to be total harmony all round. Just how Iwa allocated his favours was anyone's guess. We were given an area to live in for the night and here we had our own paraffin stove and ate our 'Western' dinner.

There was a baby and one or two older children being breast fed, and another family member making baskets by a window in the fading evening light. I hunkered down and watched her for a while, her deft movements creating an intricate piece of weaving. The women were small and quiet – even the babies were quiet. Everything was calm and unhurried, and such a difference to our crazy Western world. There was again no light except daylight, so it was dark inside very early in the evening. In any case everyone went to bed as soon as it was dusk.

I slept on the floor again remarkably well. There was total silence during the night until 5 a.m. when the first cock crowed. People started moving quietly around going about the business of the day. During the morning we saw some artefacts, and heard about local traditions and 'pay-back' killings, which although now outlawed, still continued. Some of the older men showed us their initiation keloid scars, (which Beatrice had learned about). Iwa put a carved shell through his nose totally changing his appearance. We gave him a present of a bag of salt which was hard to get on the river.

Iwa came with us as our guide that day and took us through lots of short cuts through quiet green leafy tunnels of ferns, orchids and lianas – a botanists dream. There were screaming parrots and a beautiful large white cockatoo appeared above us hanging upside down from the canopy. We were now on the Wogamush River – only about 100 feet wide at this point. The scenery was quite hilly as we were that much further upstream. We noticed with concern that there was quite a lot of logging going on here.

And then the heavens opened. It was like suddenly having dozens of buckets of water turned upside down at the same moment. We struggled into our thin, disposable plastic capes – but were soaked before we got them on; and immediately we got them on, the rain 'switched' off and out came the sun again. While we were going through this pantomime, we had arrived at Sio village. I had never seen so many butterflies, blue, green, brown, yellow. Soon a clatter of smiling children arrived on the scene, and a comical-looking cassowary chick appeared, wet and bedraggled.

Our Fasionable Waterproofs

We were escorted ashore and made welcome in this very remote village which keeps a lot of its traditions and initiation cults. There was however, to our surprise, a normal loo, a school, and a Seventh Day Adventist Church, although what good any of it could do for the young people here, I couldn't imagine, so far removed from what we call civilisation. The children we saw were very cheerful and appeared healthy but had dreadful snotty noses, and dry peeling skin from a common fungal infection called 'grille' (*Tinea embricata*). They also had appallingly rotten teeth. I wondered where they got the sweet stuff from – and then realised it was from sucking the wild sugar cane. One very young child cried bitterly when it saw us, thinking we were bad spirits. This time it really was the first time he had ever seen scary white faces. We noticed there was a drum, beating a low echoing call which we were told was to guide a man back home who was lost over on the other side of the river. That night we slept on the church floor.

In the morning we explored around the village, starting our downstream journey about midday. Gliding gently along, I dozed off in the pleasant cool of the morning. Sometime in the afternoon we left Iwa off at his home. This time as we reached Swagup, we went to see what was going on. Although it had appeared that everybody had left the village, there was in fact, lots going on. We watched the sago being washed and beaten to a pulp. Sago comes from a giant palm that is covered in very sharp spines. Once the palm flowers, it is ready to harvest. The tree is felled and then all the bark is cut away and the pith is chipped and pounded out, producing what looks like fibrous sawdust. Next the women kneed the pith in a bark funnel with a rough filter, draining water through the pith to dissolve the starch. The starch-laden water is then collected, and the starch settles in a glutinous mass. It is basically pure starch, but in a land where it is often too swampy to grow much else it is vitally important. The dried sago is usually mixed with water and fried into a rubbery pancake.

Mixed with coconut it becomes quite palatable and supplemented with bananas, fish or vegetables it will keep you going. Some men were boat-building. Hollowing out a long log is a time consuming occupation but most of the canoes are beautifully made and, of course, are indispensable for living along the river.

Again, one of the spark plugs went phut, and we continued drifting downstream, arriving about five pm at the village of Yessan. We were offered a rather dilapidated house belonging to a doctor who, we were told rather enigmatically, had run away. Bits of the house kept collapsing which was rather unnerving as, yet again we were right over the swirling river. However, it was good to have some sort of roof over our heads as Trish and I stayed up till late watching an electric storm not far off across the river. It sounded as though a lot of furniture was being hurled about in the sky with flashing and crashing all around us. It was soon to be accompanied by a downpour preceded by a vast host of mosquitoes. So far Trish and I seemed to have avoided being bitten, but David's body was covered by the red, itchy pustules left by the horrible insects. We were quite worried about him and just hoped he wouldn't get malaria. Dion had got a dreadful cough particularly during the night. If we weren't going to get some sort of an illness from this trip, it would be a miracle. We certainly wouldn't get fat! Thank goodness we could have a wee 'nip' in the evenings. Good thinking at the Duty Free shop.

The people in this village looked terribly poor, quite the worst so far. We gave some painkillers to an old man with malaria. There was an old crone sitting beside a fire outside, who was absolute skin and bone, but from whom I bought a beautiful hand made, naturally dyed *bilum*, the local stretchy string bag, woven from grass and used to carry all sort of goods – including babies. I was very pleased with it, and use it still today for shopping.

Later, in the middle of nowhere, we came upon a market. There were about thirty canoes pulled up on the river bank. Most of what was for sale was sago and both fresh and smoked fish and prawns, green ginger and betel nut, all wrapped up in leaves. I watched one beautiful girl walking around hawking her wares from a *bilum* hanging from her forehead down her back. Nearly everyone was wearing ragged Western clothes.

When we arrived in Tangunjamb, the water was gin-clear. The rains should have been clearing by now when gradually the whole river would become translucent. A tiny green frog leaped out of the river, landing on my foot and a beautiful blue and turquoise butterfly hovered round the boat, landing on each of us, enjoying the salt on our skins. Lots of swifts or maybe skimmers, whizzed over the water, scooping insects from its surface.

We were quite a way down-river from Ambunti, specifically to visit some of these magnificent *haus tambaran* with their distinctive high, forward-leaning roofs. After a while we arrived at the beautifully painted *haus* that we were looking for. We had to climb a long ladder up to the first floor where we were delighted to find lots of lovely but quite expensive carvings for sale.

Haus Tambaran

(No stuffed heads nowadays). I bought a carved gourd and a ceremonial baton, and Trish bought one piece. Then we were told that not only do we have no lunch, but that we had also run out of water. Now that we were nearing the end of our trip, there seemed to be a certain lack of incentive on board. Ah well, this is Papua New Guinea – as Beatrice remarked – Land of the Unexpected.

Back at Ambunti I felt so sad that our fantastic river trip was over. We went to visit the local mission here which is quite beautiful. It is a modern building designed on the same lines as the *haus tambaran*. The ceiling and altar pieces were painted in traditional designs by local people, and are fabulous works of art.

We met up with Alois again and over cold beers, talked to two Australian chaps from the World Wildlife Fund who were hoping to curtail much of the logging, and attempting to introduce eco-tourism, offering the local people an alternative source of income while maintaining their habitat. They asked us about river conditions, i.e. accommodation, food, water, etc. They were delighted that we had seen the birds of paradise and suggested covered walkways to where their display trees were! Oh dear. Thank goodness we saw part of this amazing country before anyone started to 'sanitise' it. We had a delicious dinner that evening, yet again against a back drop of torrential rain and dramatic thunder and lightening

The weather had cleared by the morning, and again we enjoyed our flight low over the Sepik River and back to Wewak. We had time to kill before our flight to Port Moresby so found a little shop where we had drinks and a cake each. The shop was interesting in that I was able to write in my diary everything that was for sale: – there was a fridge with drinks, a cake, one bar of Sunlight soap, one tube of Colgate toothpaste, some guitar strings, a ball of string, a dozen cards of bias binding, some airmail envelopes, a thermos, a cat (alive and cleaning itself) one packet of sugar, some tins of mackerel and luncheon meat, tobacco, matches, pots and sieves and seven or eight dresses. Quite an eclectic selection.

Beatrice and Sogeri, 1923

At home in Port Moresby, Beatrice spent the rest of 1923 writing her next book. Wherever she went, she would take notes and use her experiences – particularly her surroundings – as background material for her novels. By then, with the publication of *Nobody's Island*, Beatrice had in excess of eighteen novels under her belt.

Yet again, around 1923/24 Beatrice built another cottage on the Sogeri Plateau, describing it as 'one of the most beautiful places in the world'. Her cottage was approached by a flight of steps, at the top of which you would come to a stile, and a fence to keep the goats out from the garden which overlooked the majestic Rouna Falls. Here Beatrice could enjoy the excellent health that she had observed in the other white residents of the district. The Sogeri Plateau, at the foothills of the Owen Stanley Range, and at over 3,000 feet, was an escape from the scorching heat and humidity of Port Moresby. The plateau was inhabited by the Koiari people, whose ancestors were fierce warriors. They lived in treetop houses as protection from enemy raids.

Beatrice's Rouna Falls home soon became a place of pilgrimage for visitors to Papua. For many miles around, the white house with its red roof was visible. By the middle of 1924 a 'motor' road existed along the twenty miles from Port Moresby to Rouna Falls. As soon as the road was finished, Beatrice was able to travel in her motor-car, driven, not by herself as she 'hated machinery', but by her Papuan chauffeur.

In August 1924 Nichola, Beatrice's younger sister, and Doctor Howard Sinclair, arrived from England to stay with her at Sogeri.

Here was a little bit of scandal brought to my notice by a friend who was writing about the yachting prowess of Doctor Sinclair. In 1896 he had been awarded the Royal Cruising Club's prestigious Cruising Club Challenge Cup in his four-ton cutter, *Brenda*, and again in the following two years. After this he was never again mentioned in the club's history. Why not? Some time later, my friend discovered in the *Yachtsman's Manual and Who's Who* of 1938/39 that Doctor Sinclair had gone to live in Torquay in Devon. But why?

As mentioned earlier, he had married Maud Grimshaw, and her younger, unmarried sister Nichola had been living with them. Maud had died in 1923 leaving Howard and Nichola free to marry. However, it was considered totally immoral and quite scandalous for a man – especially a doctor – to marry his sister in-law. Hence all the secrecy surrounding the doctor's whereabouts, and the couple's quiet marriage in Papua. Having travelled out as 'Dr' and 'Miss' in separate cabins, they travelled from Papua to Sydney and back to the UK as 'Dr and Mrs' – in a shared cabin. How they were received back in England, history does not relate.

On the Move

By October 1924, Beatrice had had two more books published in London, and had visited Cairns and Kuranda.

Kuranda is situated on the Atherton Tableland, above Cairns, in northern Queensland. The town was first settled in 1885, and with the construction of the railway from Cairns it had become a popular tourist destination by the time Beatrice visited. It was both the rainforest and the local Aboriginals which attracted her to the area.

Beatrice followed this with a visit to Darwin where she gave a lecture entitled 'Among the Savage Head Hunters of the Sepik River in New Guinea'. Then, while she was in the Northern Territories, she travelled to Bathurst Island, off the north coast of Australia, where she attended a very fine corroboree – an event where the Aboriginals interact with the Dreamtime through dance, music and costume, their bodies painted in different ways, and wearing various adornments, only worn on special occasions.

Back in Papua, Beatrice went house-hunting again, purchasing a house from the Honourable LL Bell, the retired Commissioner of Native Affairs. Beatrice's books had become best-sellers in the UK and the US, and many had been translated into other languages. Beatrice had become a wealthy woman.

The two-storey house was on Port Road, Port Moresby, and was said to have been the finest residence in the town. It was a spacious house, with wide tropical verandas, standing in its own grounds, high above Port Road which encircled the bay. A climb of about thirty steps brought one to the front veranda, from which there was a fine view over the harbour and surrounding hills.

Thursday Island

Thursday and Tuesday Islands

Beatrice had already been to Thursday Island for the pearl fishing in 1908. This time – most likely in November 1925 – she travelled from Daru to Thursday Island where she describes the hotel she stayed in:

> the hotel was a mad hotel, but not unpleasant. There were beds, and meals, and for the rest you looked after yourself; your boy could do your wash and hang it in the sight of society and the Island along the front veranda, without hindrance; you might (and did) find lunatics, and gentlemen politely the worse for liquor, in your own quarters at unholy hours, without anybody, even yourself, being much perturbed about it ... there were no doors to shut, ... sometimes late at night unauthorised visitors simply walked in and up, and unannounced, slept in the best bedrooms, as the tumbled state of the rooms next morning proclaimed. Nobody worried, and the manageress smiled through it all.[114]

Beatrice recounts having had great trouble securing any sort of a boat to Tuesday Island. Eventually however, she found a boat, and with a white captain and her friend Mrs Leigh, set off, intending to go camping.

However, the cutter, after rocking and rolling in the difficult tides in the Torres Straits, sailed up to a pair of uninhabited islands, with creamy-white beaches, and dropped anchor – the captain and his passengers happy to go ashore.

On the following morning, however, the captain was anxious to get going as he thought a storm might be coming. Beatrice was reluctant to leave, not taking him very seriously, but when they arrived back at Thursday Island and noticed the sheltered harbour full of small sailing boats, she accepted his advice, and began to consider ways of returning to Port Moresby. The ladies' indecision was solved by their trusty cutter captain, who suggested they stay with him as he was going to go there anyway.

The weather had become very still and Beatrice and her friend decided to go with the captain. It was indeed a pleasant morning; 'the lull before the storm'. But the day rapidly worsened, with the little boat leaping about in the rising waves. It became impossible to remain on deck with nowhere to sit, so the ladies retreated to the hold where cases, bilge-water and cockroaches sloshed around, inducing both of them to be repeatedly sick.

By night the wind increased to a gale – and worse:

> The storm yelled in the rigging, the cutter staggered helplessly through mountainous seas. Only our faithful little Kelvin engine kept us going and fighting.

114 *Isles of Adventure*, pp. 80–1. Thursday Island is one of the Torres Strait Islands archipelago located approximately 39 kilometres north of Cape York Peninsula, Queensland. I have been unable to find Tuesday Island anywhere off Australia. Perhaps now under another name.

> The mast had cracked in a fierce gust of wind, and it began to look as if the Torres Straits, notorious as a swallower-up of ships, were going to make a mouthful of one more.[115]

The hatch cover was only partly closed, letting in both rain and seawater below. Nobody wanted it completely closed; they had the vague idea – and misplaced belief – that when the cutter finally turned turtle, they might be able to crawl out in time, and survive. The captain could no longer see where he was going until, as things went from bad to worse, Two Brothers Island looming up out of the dark and rain, and a few native boats became visible, moored in the shelter of the island. Here they stayed for the night. Nobody slept – the captain and his crew of two Papuans, staying on deck, afraid they would drag anchor and break their mooring lines.

The weather was as bad as ever when the grey light of dawn crept over the sheltering island. The captain preferred to go on and take their chances. So off they went. Running for Daru Island and the comforting bulk of Papua. Gradually the storm moderated, and by ten a.m. it was as fair a sea and sky as any sailor could want. A little before sundown, the brave little boat, her captain and passengers, quietly glided up the narrows that led to Daru.

An English periodical invited Beatrice to write an article on whether it was better for a woman to be married or single:

> 'I have been asked to tell the public what I think of the solitary life, gipsy wanderings, clearing, building, planting in the great forests, coupled with literary work, as against the home life of a married woman and mother' writes Beatrice Grimshaw, the famous novelist, in the April edition of 'Pearson's Magazine'. Miss Grimshaw, whose far distant home is in the South Seas, continues:
>
> 'The comparison is somewhat futile. One does not think that any woman, since time began, ever weighed the one method against the other, and deliberately chose what seemed to her, the best. Fate does the choosing ...'
>
> 'If you meet love early in life, and settle down, as so many of our mothers did, just after leaving school, you are sure all your days that you 'chose' right, even though you never chose at all. Even though the big world calls and Spring winds sow disquiet for evermore.
>
> 'We all know the wedded gipsies who may never roam. The children hold them; the man holds them. They know well they have missed something...they suffer a little ache when salt winds blow. They feel their eyes grow dim at the sound of an anchor chain. But the sound of the gate letting in father drowns it, the smell of the family roast in the oven over-powers the dreamy whiff of the sea.

115 *Isles of Adventure*, p. 90.

'It is getting dusk; Rouna, the giant waterfall near my home in Papua, is lifting her voice louder and louder. On the three hundred foot of white tossing water, the moon begins to fall. The forest smells like spring narcissus. My native attendants have gone. I am alone'.

'Is it good?' 'Yes'.[116]

Mrs Effie Sandery, a visiting journalist, 1925

Mrs Sandery was a freelance journalist based in Adelaide, who wrote for *The Saturday Journal* and *The Register*, under the pseudonym 'Kircaldy'. She also wrote for *The Townsville Daily*, Queensland.

Having heard about the famous writer, Effie was delighted when she was invited to stay at Beatrice's lovely home at Rouna Falls. The two writers sat for some time on the veranda, talking about their exploits and chatting about the glorious views. When approached about her career as a writer, Beatrice immediately replied that she was not an explorer, and that it was incorrect to be called one. She considered her work as a pioneer more important than that of a writer, mentioning some of her experiences of the vanilla plantation near Samarai, and the clearing of the trees at her forest plantation. They then turned to the subject of publishing. Originally Beatrice had used an agent as she had had no idea about the publishing business, but by the time she met Effie, she sent all her work – including her writing for periodicals – under contract, to one big combine who sorted it out between the various publishers in London, New York and Sydney.

During a tour of the lodge, Mrs Sandery was fascinated by Beatrice's curios from all over the world. Amongst all the curios, Effie came across a large photograph of a lovely old ivy-covered house, its windows looking straight out at one without the verandas she was used to. She discovered it was her hostess's old family home in Ireland, and gazing upon the picture recognised an almost forgotten mounting block at the foot of the steps, so unnecessary now, in the present days of motorcars.

116 'Solitude or Marriage', Cornwall County Times (England) 16th April 1925, p. 3.

Chapter 19: The Fly River

A Widow's Weeds: Fly River

The Fly River poured out enough water each day to supply everyone in the world with forty gallons. In 1926, after eighteen years mostly spent in Papua, Beatrice eventually had the opportunity to go up the Fly River that February with her friend, Sir Hubert Murray – the Lieutenant-Governor. Also on board was Leonard Murray whose father was Hubert Murray's half-brother. Leonard was the Lieutenant-Governor's private and official secretary, and who, on his many travels along the coast and on inland patrols with Hubert, had gained a detailed knowledge of Papua. A keen sailor, Leonard served as navigator on the government ship, *Elevala*, and as master of the *Merrie England* and the 150-ton *Laurabada*. Mr Waldron was the engineer.

The river had been explored almost as far as the headwaters – over six hundred miles up. Captain Blackwood of the HMS *Fly* named it when he stopped briefly at the delta in 1842. The Italian, d'Alberti, explored it in three successive trips, 1875, 76, and 77. In 1885 Captain H.C. Everill took a party a short way up the Fly. By 1926 the government had made the river environs much safer, nevertheless, Beatrice's party on board the *Laurabada* carried firearms 'just in case'.

The first night on the Fly brought a welcome relief from the hoards of mosquitoes which had plagued everyone on board. The boat had visited the solitary Madiri Rubber Plantation, run by a planter/missionary couple – the 'Freshwaters'(really?). The hard-working pair were pathetically sad to see the boat leave. Tide Island, 160 miles upstream, marked the end of tidal influence, the boat now having to creep gently forward for fear of running onto a sandbank. There was complete silence on board, just the low throb of the engine, and the monotonous call of the leadsman constantly singing out the depths; '...and a half – quarter less five – by de mark – half two – quarter less two...' Then the bridge instructions, 'half speed astern'. The tension was palpable. But the *Laurabada* got through alright.

One night, when they were lying at anchor, Beatrice heard a strange sound on the far bank – maybe a mile away. A curious eerie trumpeting made her realise she was hearing the famous cassowary 'drum'. There must have been several of them, their resounding call intensified across the river in the otherwise silent night.

It took two days from Madiri to where the Fly branches into the Strickland River – only discovered in 1913, and the *Laurabada's* route – and on into Lake Murray, strewn with islands and inhabited by an equally unknown and warlike tribe.

Up until then, their journey had been comparatively swift and uneventful but now began the odd sightings of humanity – small clearings with a few deserted huts and trees cut down.

There was always plenty of food to be had around the rivers; fish, fowl, and sago as well as wild bananas and other fruits. The sergeant on board explained:

> 'This feofle he eat fig, wallaby, cassawy,' (volunteered the old sergeant). Flenty kai-kai (food). Flenty pish he stop along river, this man he catchem pish all de time.'[117]

With less current now, they were making really good time and on the third day since leaving Madiri, the river began to widen all around – the forests thinned, and finally disappeared. The boat was surrounded by vast flocks of flying birds, shrieking, quacking and calling. Before long the mainland had shrunk to a vague purple line on the horizon. The *Laurabada* was now surrounded by the blue waters of Lake Murray, dotted with bright green islands, and stretching far into the distance.

In no time the canoes appeared – the natives totally unafraid of this enormous ship in their midst. They were most curious about the vision on the foredeck – a woman no less – a creature they had never seen before. They were also very keen to do some business in trading; beautiful painted and carved paddles, ornamental dancing clubs and arrows – every one a work of art. Also, human heads and jaws. The Fly River preserved heads were famous all over New Guinea, with perhaps the ablest exponents of this doubtful art from the Lake Murray district. The scalp would be opened at the back, removing and curing the skin into thick, soft leather. This would be stuffed with grasses, lacing it all up again with strips of cured skin. After painting it black, red and white, the nose was elevated with a small piece of bamboo, and the open mouth filled with white stones representing teeth. The finishing touch was the hair made from long locks of fibre, sometimes with feathers added. The natives had all these works of art for barter against a metal knife, some beads, or a length of cloth.

The one big drawback was, of course, no common language – even with the other Papuans onboard. Wild and shy as these people were, they were exceedingly courageous having no fear of the great ship.

117 *Isles of Adventure*, p. 107.

They hovered all round, darting about in their canoes like water-flies, shouting unintelligible talk. How Beatrice wished she could understand these natives whose work she admired so much.

Presently a small launch was slung out, and Hubert, Leonard and Beatrice, along with four native police, set off to explore, travelling some distance before seeing a small village on one of the islands. They knew it had been visited before, when the natives had been aggressive, but nevertheless they made for it in the hope was that this visit would be peaceful.

As the boat approached the island, the men came running down to the water's edge. As they neared the land, they were helped in through the mud, most of the islanders yelling with excitement.

They were a fine-looking lot, naked – but decorated with shells and feathers, wearing long artificial hair down their backs. It became apparent that the villagers were happy with the visit, particularly with the strange white woman who they crowded round, touching, and excited by the softness of her skin. Everyone was curious about each other, but yet again, without a common language, nothing was learned about anything.

Eventually the old sergeant explained by sign language that Beatrice would like to see the womenfolk. After some minutes, they appeared from a different island, sobbing and wailing, and refusing to go any closer until Beatrice went to meet them. The men, Beatrice noticed, were kind to their wives, assuring them that there was nothing to be afraid of. Although these people were head-hunting savages they knew how to treat the women better than those of the peaceful tribes on the coast. These girls were quite plump and good-looking and bore no signs of hardship.

However, it was not all as peaceful as it had seemed. Beatrice had already noticed an excess of excitement boiling up, and began to be afraid it might boil over. The men had started yelling, not in a casual way, but in a concerted chant that usually meant trouble.

The party walked calmly down to the launch, boarded the boat and away. Nobody was attacked. The visit was, in fact, rather barren as nobody could converse. However, it was at least, a visit of good will.

As is most likely to happen with boat engines – it stopped. Luckily the group were out of sight of the village, hidden behind an uninhabited island. As it happened, almost all the local natives were clustered round the *Laurabada*, and did not notice the predicament of the white party's smaller boat.

At last, safely back on board the *Laurabada*, they found it swarming with excited natives anxious to do some trading. One big native had found his way towards Beatrice's cabin when one of the policemen found him and dragged him away.

Nobody seemed to have missed anything until the Lieutenant-Governor discovered that someone had entered his cabin and stolen a pair of trousers, and the amazing choice – a 'History of Ireland' – in Gaelic! It might as well have been in Double Dutch, but it gave the travellers a good laugh.

They lay at anchor all night. In the morning it was clear that nobody had come to disturb the passengers during the night, as they started downstream – the current, this time being with them. It was a drama-free journey until the ship encountered the notorious Fly River tidal bore.

There was always something of a bore on the Fly at high tide, but with a spring tide it became most formidable. The victory of the sea over the river as it swept up the Fly driving back – for a while – the river, built a terrace of water from bank to bank, eight or nine feet above the level of the sea. Anything caught by the bore wave was in for trouble.

Beatrice was reading in the lounge when she was roused by one of the men to come up on the bridge as there was a bore coming:

> looking with glasses across the huge space of the lower river, at a thin white line advancing with amazing swiftness from the far-off sea. The bore came on as fast as a galloping horse; whether one could hear its ugly roar or not from the safe distance that we kept – half a mile in deep water – I cannot say, but some of us fancied we did. It was not in the least like a sea-wave; it came on fiercely, tossing its head in a peculiar, angry fashion, like that of a very vicious horse. Small wonder the natives personify it and fear its approach above any other of the dangers of this most dangerous river.[118]

With the *Laurabada*'s powerful engines they had nothing to fear, but the engineer told Beatrice that even the *Laurabada*, if caught unawares by the bore, could be stripped of every deckhouse and probably stove-in forbye.

Back in Port Moresby – now illuminated by electric light, Beatrice was interviewed by *The Sydney Morning Herald* about her new book '*The Paradise Poachers*' based on the Sepik River; and about her recent travels up the Fly River. When queried about native taxation, she said she was in favour of it, as the proceeds of the taxation went entirely to native welfare such as education – especially in technical instruction, and also providing medical treatment for all Papuans.

118 *Isles of Adventure*, p. 134.

Chapter 20: A World Tour

By August 1926, and although not short of local adventures, Miss Grimshaw set off to spend a year travelling round the world, planning to visit New Zealand, Panama – where the marvellous canal had now been open since 1914 – America, the UK, South Africa and Samoa. She set sail from Port Moresby on August 10th on board the redoubtable *Morinda* bound for Sydney.

Here she was to have been a guest of honour at a dinner at the new premises of the Lyceum Club in Hunter Street. However, she fell victim to her old foe – an attack of malaria, and was unable to appear. Miss Cox-Taylor, the chairperson and some friends brought a beautiful bouquet of sweet-peas to Beatrice's hotel bedroom. She was also booked to speak at The Feminist Club, but was still too unwell.

She was well enough, however, to continue her journey onward a few days later, on board the SS *Ulimaroa* to Wellington, and from there, on 24th August, now on board The SS *Athenic*, across the Pacific, through the Panama Canal making a stop in Colon. There it picked up two 2nd class British passengers: William Hull, an engineer, and Harry Whitewood, a dredge master. Both were also recorded as having been resident in the Republic of Colombia, so it seemed possible that they had been working on the canal. Beatrice as usual was a 1st class passenger.

October, 1926

The *Athenic* docked in Southampton, and as usual, Beatrice stayed a few days with her relatives on the south coast before going to London. Here, again, she was guest of honour at London's Lyceum Club in Piccadilly. The room was reported to have been filled with a crowd of famous authors of the day, including Henry de Vere Stacpoole, Mrs Philip Champion de Crespigny, and Sir John Foster Frazer. Beatrice gave a short address on Papua and the conditions of living there.

I think she must have gone to Ireland again. There were still a few relatives here, including the Beresford family of Portrush, whose daughter Constantia was married to Beatrice's brother, Osborne. It must have been discussed that perhaps it would be possible for another Beresford daughter – the unmarried, fifty-three-year-old, Selina Augusta known as Lena – to return to Papua with Beatrice and live with her as a companion. In any event, that is what happened.

The Wreck of the Redwing, another novel was published in London by Hurst and Blackett in January 1927, and on the evening of 1st February, at 7 p.m., Beatrice gave a talk on the fledgling BBC, entitled 'Up the Fly River'.

Beatrice remained in the UK until 1st March, when she and Lena departed on board the SS *Ulysses*, via Las Palmas and Cape Town, to Fremantle and Australia.

However, by June she found time to take a short sortie to New Caledonia, and on board the SS *Dupleix*, away she went. We don't know if she brought her 'companion' with her, but as she is never mentioned, I think probably not.

New Caledonia

In the afternoon, four days out from Sydney, Beatrice spied the mountain tops of New Caledonia, lying southwest of Vanuatu, and about 750 miles east of Australia. This group of islands were again first discovered by Captain Cook in 1774. He named it 'New Caledonia' as part of the island reminded him of Scotland. (Strange how these tropical islands reminded him of Scotland!) From then until the 1840s, only a few sporadic contacts with the archipelago were recorded, and in 1849, the crew of an American ship was killed and apparently eaten by the *pouma* clan.

By May 1864, the island had become a place of exile for French common-law prisoners, when 248 men disembarked from the ship, SS *Ephigénie*. The prisoners on board – confined in cages – had endured the voyage to New Caledonia for between 80 and 140 days. Exercise and rations were very limited, meaning that on arrival many prisoners were ill.

Penal transportation laws of 1854 meant that any male prisoners aged over sixteen and sentenced to over eight years were forbidden to return to France. Prisoners convicted of sentences of less than eight years were to endure *doublage*, which made residence in New Caledonia compulsory for a period equal to the duration of their sentence. Then known as *libérés* they were still not free from the confines of the penal colony. When it was officially closed in 1922, the penal colony still held 2,310 prisoners.

After her ship docked, Beatrice made her way by car to a hotel to relax and enjoy the view. The food was good, and cheap. The French residents were courteous, and one was assured everywhere that New Caledonia's past was over and done with; even the old prisons had been torn down and it all seemed perfectly delightful. But nevertheless...

In the middle of the harbour was another island with buildings on it. It was Île Nou, the famous prison, and still not empty. Beatrice had already noticed the thin, old, grey-haired men – barefoot and dressed in rags – shuffling around the town. If you asked anyone who they were, the subject was quickly changed. They were, of course, the *libérés* – those convicts never to be totally free, and never to return to their home country of France.

For a couple of weeks Beatrice saw all that she was permitted to see. Then a French friend persuaded her to go a bit further afield by taking the local bus. It would only cost a few shillings and she would get a real insight into the country.

The motor-bus was mostly very sociable, except for a quiet libéré sitting at the back. As for the rest, according to Beatrice they were all just a little bourgeois, but very jolly. There was one passenger who Beatrice named 'Porthos' – black-moustached, debonair, and full of laughter, he was always on the lookout for any pretty young girl at whom he would call compliments. Porthos was very good-looking and wonderfully aware of it. Modesty was not part of his vocabulary. His flirting had the whole bus rocking with laughter. Beatrice decided that more cheerful folk you could not wish to find – certainly not among the better classes, where so much reserve caused such well-bred dullness.

They sped along, stopping for lunch where Beatrice shared a table with a travelling salesman and his wife and children, telling each other about their lives – up to a point. Then, refreshed, the company proceeded on their way.

They drove through valleys of sugar cane and bananas, until at last they arrived at the mountain town of Bourail. The quiet tree-shaded streets were full of pretty bare-footed girls, in fashionable short skirts, while now and then big carts of local produce clattered along, drawn by a team of silky oxen.

Although these attractive convict girls were frequently taken by the officials as their *droit du seigneur*, it was understood that they would have to marry convict men, and live with them in government-assigned farms, Bourail being the setting for these mass marriages. Some sort of informal selection would take place in the village church where they all went on Sundays, and where, instead of Holy Communion, lots of body-language communion went on between the two sexes. Quick matches were made, to be followed by marriage, followed again by great parties with feasting and drinking. Surprisingly, some of the marriages were more or less successful, while others split up.

At the inn where Beatrice went to stay, the food was excellent, cooked by a Chinese chef. But the hotel had been a prison, and the six bedrooms all still had barred windows. The walls and floor were solid stone, so although rather stark, it was cool. Beatrice recalled having already spent a few nights in the Laloki native jail when she first arrived in Papua in 1908, but she preferred this one in Bourail as being so comfortable – and weather-proof.

Back in Noumea, Beatrice had hired a launch to take her and a young Frenchman, to the Isle of Pines. The owner of the boat and his wife were glad to have another man on board in case they hit bad weather. So off they went, starting in dead of night, the seventy-odd miles to the island.

The quartet covered the miles over a calm, blue sea, and it was nearly noon when they arrived at the Isle of Pines. The beaches of the island were sparkling white sand, but it was a surprise for Beatrice to find it covered by dark, tropical pines, standing motionless in the still air. From the sea, it looked almost like a beach resort with white villas here and there, behind a magnificent sea-wall, built of cut stone, with a jetty to match it where they landed. The little party stood together looking at the empty roadway and listening to the silence. There was nobody now living there.

This island had been one of the most celebrated penal stations. All the fine stonework had been cut by convicts, many of them political prisoners. And so, rather subdued, the new arrivals sallied forth to find a villa, owned by a Noumea merchant, who had generously loaned his little house to Beatrice for a few days.

There were plenty of rooms in the villa, but very little furniture. The four of them sat on benches around a long refectory table – nobody willing to do any cooking. However, the two men went out and shot a few pigeons, and the boat-owner caught a few fish, but it was left to Beatrice to prepare dinner as best she could.

The meal was a great success, the fine talk enlivened by a bottle of fine wine, thoughtfully brought by the young Frenchman, who had a fund of stories about the sea. Some years previously when he had been very poor and shared a small boat with some others, he spied one day, on a rock, a dirty-looking greasy mass that smelled unpleasant. His companions were against taking the stuff into the boat, but he insisted. Back in Noumea, it was exactly what he thought it was – ambergris, and worth, at that time, a lot of money. The huge profits were shared, and our hero took himself to France where he met and married his little Parisian wife. Returning to New Caledonia he bought a good launch of which he was the sole owner.

The party wandered round the Isle of Pines, finding that the most interesting place was the old settlement. There were abandoned walled gardens, graceful stone staircases leading nowhere, ancient roofless houses with *Lantana* flowers running riot over the ruins. Oranges and papayas hung from overgrown trees, all forsaken and silent.

Beatrice admitted to not having written much about the natives of New Caledonia. She did however know of one chief – Atai – who became friendly with the widow of an official. The widow was quite pretty and frequently invited Atai for coffee and to discuss social questions. The natural result followed when Atai fell in love with her and eventually asked her if she would marry him. She, however, having encouraged him up to this point, was furious, rejecting her dark lover with more scorn than was necessary. Atai left with rage in his heart against the entire white race. The revolt that quickly followed may or may not have been as a result of Atai's rebuff, but certainly many white settlers were massacred.

Chapter 21: Back on Papua New Guinea

Beatrice's House, and Staff

Beatrice arrived back in Port Moresby at the end of July 1927. Greeting her on her return were good reviews of her latest published books; *The Wreck of the Redwing, Black Sheep's Gold*, and *Eyes in the Corner and other Stories*.

The film of Beatrice's book, *Conn of the Coral Seas* was being made on location in Fiji under the title, *The Adorable Outcast*. The American producer was Norman Dawn, and the leading cast of Edith Roberts, Edmund Burns, and Walter Long were engaged in Hollywood. This trio represented the strongest group of artists yet placed under contract for Australasian Films Ltd.

On the island of Bau, 300 natives were employed building the exterior of a native ceremonial house. Spectacular scenes abounded. One would depict two thousand native warriors dancing in full war dress with clubs and spears, and one of the biggest scenes to be filmed would contain five hundred war canoes. King Ratu, who was watching the filming, pronounced the scene as having been reproduced with thrilling realism.

When the outdoor filming was completed, the company moved to studios in Sydney for the indoor shots. Some of the big sets included an enormous living room built in tropical Javanese style of architecture. Beatrice was there for three months to give assistance and ideas about the scenery.

By the summer of 1928, the film had its premiere in the Tivoli Theatre in Brisbane. The directors of Union Theatres were so delighted with the completion of *The Adorable Outcast*, that no stone was left unturned to present it in a manner befitting its greatness, and nine big Fijian natives – all natural players of steel guitars, were brought to Australia to lend atmosphere to the proceedings.

Having spent just a little over a year as Beatrice's so-called companion, Lena Beresford had decided to return to Ireland, finding the climate too hot and humid.

Meantime, Beatrice, heard that two ladies were claiming to be the first white women to ascend the Fly River, spent no time in sending the following radiogram from Port Moresby:

> Two ladies who claim to have recently ascended the Fly River, claim also to be the first white women to accomplish the journey. My own journey up the Fly River in 1926, when I also visited Lake Murray, was the first to be accomplished by a white woman!

Beatrice's output of writing was phenomenal. She was still travelling, helping make a film, and having frequent guests at her homes both at Port Road and at Rouna Falls. At the same time she had published about twenty-five books, some through different publishers, using alternative titles, and in many editions. She had also written numerous articles, endless short stories, and various pamphlets.

Researching Beatrice, I was frequently amazed, not only by the amount of writing she did, but also the amount of travelling.

She was very pleased at the arrival of the *Morinda* into Port Moresby in September 1928, bringing three Ford cars, one of which was for Beatrice – a Model A Tudor Sedan.[119] Even though there were only about twenty miles of made up roads, as Beatrice said, one had to be *'a la mode'*.

By then sixty, Beatrice was at least doing slightly less 'difficult' travel, departing for New Zealand on 24th December 1930, spending January, February and March revisiting Wellington, the Cook Islands and Tahiti before arriving in San Francisco at the end of March.

She took time visiting Hollywood before crossing the States to New York, leaving there at the end of July for Liverpool, on board the SS *Baltic*. She stayed with her sister and brother-in-law in Torquay much of the time she was in England. Always describing herself on the ship's manifest as Irish, Beatrice eventually departed from Southampton in November 1931 on board the SS *Christian Huygens*.

Hull Daily Mail - 6 Jul 1932 Great advert for Beatrice's stories in "The Best All-Story Magazine" carried in at least a couple of other Papers in July 1932 (Yorkshire Evening Post and Nottingham Evening Post)

119 *Cairn's Post*, 29th September 1928.

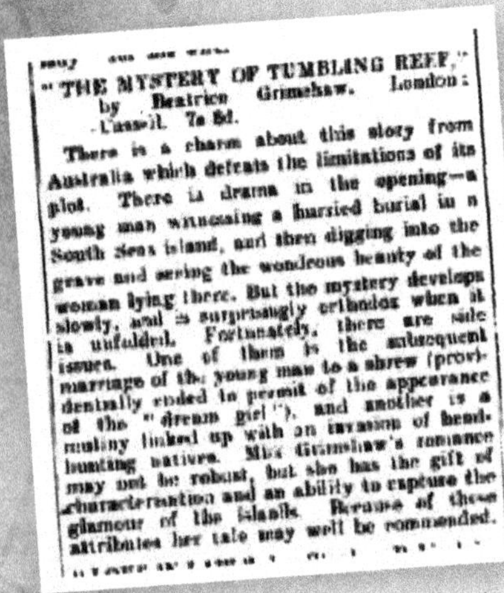

"THE MYSTERY OF TUMBLING REEF," by Beatrice Grimshaw. London: Cassell. 7s 6d.

There is a charm about this story from Australia which defeats the limitations of its plot. There is drama in the opening—a young man witnessing a hurried burial in a South Seas island, and then digging into the grave and seeing the wondrous beauty of the woman lying there. But the mystery develops slowly, and is surprisingly orthodox when it is unfolded. Fortunately, there are side issues. One of them is the subsequent marriage of the young man to a shrew (providentially ended to permit of the appearance of the "dream girl"), and another is a mutiny linked up with an invasion of head-hunting natives. Miss Grimshaw's romance may not be robust, but she has the gift of characterisation and an ability to capture the glamour of the islands. Because of these attributes her tale may well be commended.

"The Mystery of Tumbling Reef" published by Cassell about October 1932

"THE MYSTERY OF TUMBLING REEF"by Beatrice Grimshaw. London: Casseil 7a 6d.

There is a charm about this story from Australia which defeats the limitations of its plot. There is drama in the opening - a young man witnessing a (hurried burial) in a South Sea Island, and then digging into the grave and seeing the wondrous beauty of the woman lying there. But the mystery develops slowly, and is surprising orthodox when it is unfolded. Fortunately, there are side issues. One of them is the subsequent marriage of the young man to a shrew providentially ended in permit of the appearance of his "dream girl", and another is a mutiny linked up with an invasion of head-hunting natives. Miss Grimshaw's romance may not be robust, but she has the gift of characterisation and an ability to capture the glamour of the island. Because of these attributes her tale may well be commended.

Tobacco Farming

Through her contacts in Ireland, Beatrice had heard of Professor Thompson Flynn who lived in Belfast, where he served as the Chair of Zoology at Queen's University from 1931-1948. His son, Errol Flynn – later the film star, only lived briefly in Ireland while his father was teaching at Queen's University. But he was living in Papua in 1933 where he apparently owned the Laloki tobacco plantation with his partner Trelawney Adams. The plantation was near Rouna Falls – the perfect site for growing tobacco.

In the 1930s although growing its own, Papua was importing tobacco at the rate of £25,000–£30,000 per annum. A stick of tobacco was standard issue for all local labour.

Although tobacco farming should have been a remunerative business, it appears that the young Mr Flynn left too much for his boys to do instead of working the plantation himself; the resultant crop, when it arrived in London, was mildewed.

So it was that Beatrice heard that the plantation was for sale, and, hoping that her brother Ramsey by now living in Oberon New South Wales, would come and manage it for her – she bought the plantation. She had given the project great thought, declaring that she thought it was better to put capital into something in Papua rather than outside.

By June, Ramsey Grimshaw had driven to Sydney from Oberon, and, shipping his car on board the SS *Montero*, arrived in Papua to take over managing the tobacco plantation.

Wau

Wau is a town in the province of Morobe, and is situated at an altitude of around 3300 feet. It was near the site of a gold rush at Edie Creek during the 1920s and 30s when prospective gold diggers arrived at the coast and struggled inland up through the dense bush. It is a little vague exactly why Beatrice visited the gold fields at Wau in November 1933. Perhaps she was just curious, or wanted first hand information which might provide the background for another book. Whichever, she was a passenger on board the *Macdhui* en route for Salamaua, the staging post into the inland areas, making for the goldfields via the rough Black Cat Track.

When the miner, Bill Royal, washed up the first dishes of gold from Edie Creek in 1926 it became obvious that there was a need for a faster and easier way to reach the gold mining area. It was an exhausting six hour trek to get supplies of food and equipment up to the camp from sea level, and to transport the thousands of ounces of gold back down again.

An important date in prospecting and gold mining came in 1927 with the first aeroplane flight to Wau. Guinea Airways Ltd was registered on 4th November 1927. During the next few years the company was to become the world's leading freight operator, carrying huge loads by 1930s standards, including complete motor cars. With a fleet of four aircraft, Guinea Airways could carry around sixteen tonnes a day.

Having arrived at Salamaua, Beatrice rode up the Black Cat Track to Edie Creek on the famous 'bitzer' lorry. She spent a couple of months in and around Wau and Edie Creek viewing all that was possible. Then, instead of the trek back down to the sea port and waiting for the arrival of the *Macdhui*, she enjoyed her first flight – returning home by aeroplane.

Beatrice leaves Papua New Guinea, 1935

Quite suddenly, everything seemed to be changing for Beatrice. Her recurrent attacks of malaria and the heat were taking their toll. The advent of cars and now aeroplanes had brought tourism to Papua. Cruise ships visited the island with alarming frequency, bringing eager tourists, who, as they went ashore, made straight for the aerodrome where they boarded a small aircraft.

The flight took them around thirty miles inland to the Rouna Falls – Beatrice's hideaway. As the plane swooped down, here of course was a wonderful view of the river, the falls, and the celebrity's house. Beatrice had become a victim of her own success – and how she hated this intrusion of her privacy.

By August 1934 she is reported to have said she was leaving Papua for good, and was disposing of her interests in the Territory:

> Captain A.S. Fitch, managing director of the Steamships Trading Company, Ltd., has purchased her comfortable home as it stands (the Port Road house); Dr W. M.

> Strong has bought the 15-mile property on the Laloki River, where Miss Grimshaw has been growing tobacco.[120]

Whether Strong, a medical administrator, also bought the cottage at Rouna Falls is unclear. *The Cairns Post*, 31st August 1934, goes on to say that Miss Grimshaw would be making her home in Sydney for a few months, after which she would visit America for about eighteen months, and that it was likely she would eventually make her home in England, only visiting Papua briefly.

I don't think she did either of these trips – certainly not the journey to England, as she was in Sydney by December 1934 at the Society of Women Writers luncheon, and as guest of honour at The Australian Fellowship of Writers in the Art's Club, Sydney.

Even with all this upset in her life, Beatrice continued writing, and *Victorian Family Robinson*, *Nobody's Island* and *Pieces of Gold and other Stories* were all published in London during 1934.

The last straw for Beatrice was when her other brother, Osborne Grimshaw, who had been living and working for the government for twenty years in Papua, retired early in 1935. Along with his wife, he left the country for ever, on board the *Montoro* bound for Sydney for a few months' stay in Australia, after which the couple would reside in England.

Beatrice left just one thing behind when she departed Papua – a Church Bell. She had donated the bell inscribed with her name, in 1924 to the Catholic Church in Port Moresby. According to Hugh Laracy in 'Pride and Prejudice in Papua', in 1977 it was hanging in the Roman Catholic Cathedral.

Diana's Departure from Papua New Guinea, 1995

Having flown from Wewak to Port Moresby, Trish, David and I made our way to The Gateway Hotel where we were staying the night before our departure from Papua New Guinea.

120 The *Cairn's Post*, 31st August 1934.

David and Our Tiny Airplane

The hotel was quite expensive and modern with lots of glass and chrome and air conditioning.

Where are you Moses and the Sepik?

We had a very comfortable room for three, but I felt strangely depressed. Suffering from anti-climax? I wasn't hungry and just did not want to be there. Some other British tourists had dinner with us, but they had not been anywhere like where we had been; they had stayed all the time on a cruise ship on the lower Sepik, and only ventured out in a motor launch by the day. They thought they had been so adventurous, but what a lot they had missed; going upriver in a dug-out canoe and over-nighting at local villages with the native people. Although they were very interested in what we had done, and amazed at our experiences, I simply didn't want to talk to them and somehow felt guilty for feeling superior. No doubt I would get over it all in time.

The End of the Affair

(Having written my diary about Papua New Guinea in 1995, reading it now, twenty-one years later, I remember vividly how I felt.)

Of course no bags had arrived with us that night. Maybe they would arrive in the morning, or maybe, if they didn't turn up we would have to stay longer. Maybe?

They did turn up at the airport just half an hour before we were due to fly.

We flew to the UK via Japan where we had to spend another night, near the airport at the Nikko Narita Hotel. Of the little we could see of this country, it was immaculate – even the hub-caps of the buses were clean. The flower beds were pristine and there was no litter. It seemed almost sterilised.

What a far cry from the colour and wild exuberance of Papua New Guinea.

Chapter 22: Australia

By March 1935, Beatrice was in Australia, staying with her brother Ramsey, at his home in Oberon NSW, and by April she had gone to stay at the Royal Hotel Bathurst, not far from Oberon, with the view to moving there. She loved the situation of Bathurst, declaring it one of the prettiest places she had ever seen. Certainly, arriving there from the heights of the Blue Mountains, the view was spectacular; the road winding down the long hill beside the railway tracks, into the green and bosky Macquerie River Valley – and it was cool. Maybe it reminded her of Ireland!

However, she wasn't going to rush into anything, and in order to find atmosphere for her next book, she went travelling again, spending three months in Tonga and Samoa. Beatrice arrived back in October on board the *Mariposa* at Sydney, where she went to live in an apartment at the magnificent Hampton Court, King's Cross.

While being interviewed in Sydney, Beatrice still seemed intent on visiting England the following year.

But by 1936 the possibility of another war was being discussed, and I could find no ship's manifest, or any other travel papers, with Beatrice's name on it. So it appears that although she had not done visiting the South Pacific islands, she never went back again to England or Ireland. Instead, she soon went to live in Bathurst, initially renting a little single-storey cottage at 222 Seymour Street, across the road from Saint Stanislaus College. She had bought a house in Kelso, about a mile from Bathurst, and was having it renovated.

Beatrice's first home in Bathurst

The property she had bought was an historic inn, originally built over a century earlier by ex-convict Thomas Kite in 1823, and which, sometime later was used as an officers' mess. The building was situated on four acres of land and boasted four rooms, a narrow hall, kitchen, bathroom, laundry and veranda. Beatrice's renovations were to be quite elaborate, but happily the tap-room would still exist as her lounge. She named her new home 'Wayside', and was soon able to move in.

A Miss Mary Ann McMenamin had been appointed to the job as post mistress in 1914, and was still in the position when Miss Grimshaw was at Kelso. Miss McMenamin, a devoted Catholic, would sometimes accompany Beatrice to church.

Beatrice came and went a good deal, probably by train, between Kelso and Sydney – sometimes for social events and sometimes on literary business, usually making the Hotel Metropole her headquarters in Sydney, but was certainly back in Bathurst in 1937 for the September social highlight of the year – the Debs Ball, held in St Vincent's Hospital.

Everything possible was done to ensure that the occasion was one of total brilliance. Flower arrangements were on every table, and some four hundred dancers crowded the hall to the strains of Monty's Full Orchestra. Six debutantes made an attractive picture as they proceeded up the hall to be presented by Mrs Jack Harris to Beatrice Grimshaw where, elegantly dressed in black velvet, she took the presentation of the girls at this sparkling event.

In order to avoid the Bathurst winter of 1938, and for colour for her next book about the pearling industry, Miss Grimshaw disappeared off, on board the *Merker*, to spend some weeks away in the north at the already familiar Thursday Island in the Torres Strait, arriving back in 'Wayside' at the end of winter.

The Sydney Morning Herald ran an amusing feature by a representative of the Women's Supplement:

> The way of an interviewer is hard. A misplaced word, a suggestive smile – even a knowing wink – will sometimes place the interviewer on queer street – ruefully rubbing his trousers! That is almost what happened to me when I called upon Beatrice Grimshaw, the celebrated novelist, at her home near Bathurst recently.
>
> I was passing through Kelso, a charming little village on the outskirts of Bathurst, when I was attracted to a small square house, standing on a hill.
>
> The roof was red and the eaves fitted snugly to the walls, like a lid on a chocolate box. Having been told who lived there, and would I like to meet her, I answered in the affirmative.
>
> We opened the gate and made our way up a pretty winding path bordered with whitewashed stones, followed by a fox-terrier which had scurried in before I could lock him out.
>
> Miss Grimshaw answered our knock and bade us enter. A rather tall woman with a commanding figure, her hair is a silver sheen streaked with black. Her eyes are large and blue, and twinkle at you from behind ultra-thick glasses.
>
> No sooner were we introduced and seated than there was a terrific din outside. The fox-terrier was attacking – as only fox terriers can – a cat.
>
> Like all men I love a fight. I smiled unconcernedly.
>
> The smile was still-born!
>
> Miss Grimshaw jumped to her feet. Her lips twitched nervously. 'My pets, my poor pets', she screamed, 'save them!'
>
> Outside, cat and dog were racing round a shrub, tearing at each other savagely.
>
> Urged on by Miss Grimshaw's frantic shouts and excited gesticulations, I endeavoured to catch the dog. Soon I was just another piece of rubbish in a gyrating circle of cat, dog, pieces of stick, and dust. Round and round we went. Now I had the dog, now I didn't. Now I had the cat, now I didn't.
>
> Eventually the cat, after clawing the dog viciously, climbed a nearby tree and snarled down at her aggressor. The dog was unceremoniously thrown out.
>
> My hostess, her face scarlet with emotion, confronted me.
>
> 'How dare you set your beastly dog onto my pets!' she screamed, pointing an accusing finger at me. 'Take your dog and get out of here'.
>
> Very embarrassed, I explained that the dog wasn't mine.

Immediately she apologised. Phew, that was a close call.

Miss Grimshaw loves animals – with the possible exception of fox terriers. She gently lifted the cat off the tree and caressed it.

'You know' she said 'poor pussy was only protecting her family'.

A timid meow revealed a tiny kitten in the undergrowth.[121]

With everything calmed down, the interview continued, with Beatrice telling this impressed reporter about her life, from being born in Ireland, to all her travels around the South Pacific, to living for twenty-seven years in Papua, and now living in Kelso. She said she had come to Australia because she was suffering from some unidentified tropical disease as well as malaria, but that now, thanks to the splendid climate, she was well again and in perfect good health.

As the reporter was leaving, he heard a dog bark. He started to run, when he heard Miss Grimshaw calling, 'Don't let any dogs in!'

The start of the Second World War in Europe, is generally held to be 1st September 1939, beginning with the German invasion of Poland, with Britain and France declaring war on Germany two days later. It was a frightening and depressing time, and with everyone wanting to contribute in some way to the war effort, in October 1939 a branch of the Red Cross Society was formed at Kelso with Beatrice joining.

As history recalls, Beatrice never stayed at one place for any length of time, and true to form, although now seemingly happy in Kelso, and aged almost seventy, she put her lovely little house, 'Wayside' on the market. However, the house did not sell immediately.

Continually motivated to try new ways of promoting her books in order to make a living, in June 1940 she became involved with broadcasting on the radio. The existence of Australian – and in this case Irish – writers was gradually becoming known to readers, and soon also to listeners. Through the initiative of a New South Wales woman, Joan Hardy, a regular radio feature came into existence with a programme on 2UE when authors would be interviewed and their books discussed. Among the Australian/Irish authors, came Beatrice Grimshaw, whose latest book, South Sea Sarah was discussed.

Beatrice, who was elderly and living in Australia, was now a famous writer throughout the world. (Photo courtesy of State Library of NSW, Australia)

121 *The Sydney Morning Herald*, 13th February 1939.

Chapter 22: Australia

As well as this book, during 1940, Beatrice had published in London, *Murder in Paradise, Lost Child,* and *The Woman in Black*.

Another programme, on three successive Sunday afternoons – the 9th, 16th and 23rd June 1940, Beatrice recalled thrilling accounts of her life in Papua, the first of the series of three was entitled *Away From it All*. The next two were *Cannibal Friends* and *The Humours of Papua*.

Then, when these programmes were such a success, her book, *The Lost Child* was made into a play for radio. The story dealt with the pearl divers and various cosmopolitan characters of Thursday Island. *The Lost Child* was heard at 9 p.m. on Thursday evenings.

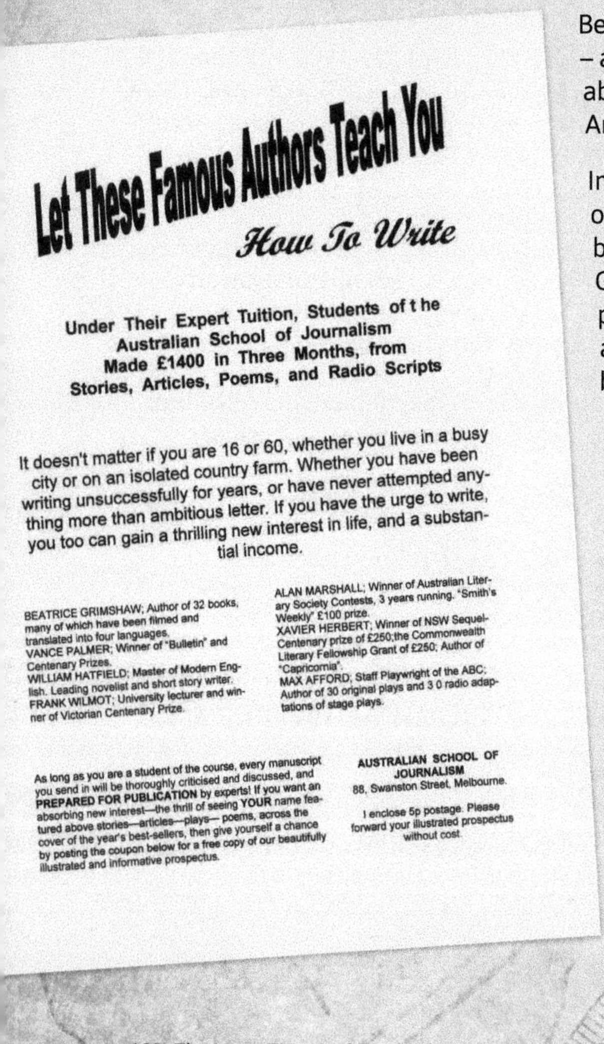

Beatrice had become so well known that even – and most surprisingly – there was a piece about her in *The Larne Times*, from County Antrim, Northern Ireland:

> In the literary field proper, I will mention only one Ulster-born writer who deserves to be better known here (in Ireland) – Beatrice Grimshaw. A new book by her has just been published. Her first appeared as far back as 1907, and since then she has produced between 40 and 50 volumes.[122]

It goes on to tell about Beatrice's education in Belfast and then about her travels, noting that she was especially interested in tropical colonisation.

At the end of May, 1941, Beatrice's home was placed on the market in Bathurst, with Clements and McCarthy and F. Glasson and Company. In mid-June an auction was held to sell many of Miss Grimshaw's effects. But Beatrice's health was still a problem, and may again have been a contributing reason for leaving Kelso and going initially to stay in Sydney for the milder winter weather, and where she found the solitude necessary for writing.

122 *The Larne Times*, 9th November 1940, p. 4.

Throughout the early 40s, Beatrice was a member of The Australian School of Journalism, teaching writing. She was also still writing – now mostly articles for magazines and the press. One of her amusing articles was a ghost story, published in *The Sydney Morning Herald*, January 1942. It was titled, 'The Ghost Horses of Malaya'. The story starts:

> Everyone knows the Phooka legend of Western Ireland; the story firmly believed by Ireland's peasantry, of the wild ghost horses that gallop on the stormy headlands, luring unwary travellers to their death in the seas below.
>
> There is a ruined little palace in the Maluccas, not far from the place where our soldiers are now on guard, that owns a legend even more terrifying than the myth of the Phooka. And more real, for I heard the thing myself – perhaps.[123]

Beatrice goes on to tell of how, while she was staying in the little palace, alone, she heard from time to time strange noises like a baby crying, or the call of an owl. Then sometimes there was the sound of the wind. It was perhaps thunder that she heard one night, or the low throb of a volcano. But what she heard sounded quite close by – possibly in the palace compound. She went out in the moonless night to look from the veranda.

'The wind arose, and came galloping past, with a noise like a stampeding cavalry, and a long whistling scream' She had never heard anything like it before. She retreated back into the house and bed and drew the mosquito net, tightly round her.

The following morning she told a Malay woman about her night adventure. Neither spoke the others language very well, but what she did gather from the woman's husband was this...

It was a fact that a tragedy had taken place in that compound that marked it out as dangerous. A young sultan and his wives had lived there, but one of the wives did not love him, but loved somebody else. She would meet up with her lover at the gate of the compound at night, and return at dawn.

The sultan found out, but said nothing as he thought of a punishment. He owned some young fiery horses which he let loose in the dark compound. The erring wife was returning at dawn and let herself in through the gate. When she heard the sound of galloping horses, she tried to get back out through the gate but it was locked. They found what was left of her in the morning. The story was that the wild horses still haunted the compound on certain dark nights. You could never see them, but if you met them it meant certain death.

123 'The Ghost Horses of Malaya', *The Sydney Morning Herald*, 17th January 1942.

It may have been the wind, or the sound of the volcanoes. Anyone can believe what he likes. But Beatrice did not stay much longer in the little ruined palace.

'The Revolting Daughter'! Was the catchy title to a piece written by Beatrice in *The Sydney Morning Herald*, later in 1942; writing at some length, and holding forth on the subject of women's emancipation. It had become possible for women to go to university and take a degree in medicine, to leave home and get a job, and live in chambers:

> The wheel has come full circle; the once 'revolting daughter' has nothing now left to justify rebellion. It began in the eighteen sixties and seventies ... the girl demanded freedom; she wanted to ride in hansom cabs alone, to climb to the top of omnibuses, to take tea by herself in restaurants, and even, to leave home and engage in clerical work. A popular music hall song expressed it well:-
>
> I handle the ribbons – I smoke my cigar,
> I polk till Aunt Jane looks aghast.
> I swim like a fish, ride like young Lochinvar,
> In short, I am fast, I am fast.[124]

By now, Beatrice's home was with her brother Ramsey, at Inglis Cottage in Oberon. The Inglis were an old Oberon family who were of Irish descent. They owned a house, Dulcie Domum, and had a boarding establishment on their farm. It was known as the Irish settlement in Oberon. Later, by early December, Beatrice was admitted to the Bathurst District Hospital – malaria, was making itself felt again.

Beatrice was now seventy-three, and although the spirit was willing, the flesh was letting her down, and in June 1944, illness again prevented her from attending Oberon's CWA (Country Women's Association) exhibition.

In 1945, at the end of the Second World War, Beatrice's final book, *The Missing Blondes* was published in Sydney.

Beatrice had always been curious about the different types of native she met, from Tahiti westwards to Papua; the varying characteristics of facial features, and the types of hair. Where did they originate, and how did they get to these remote islands? She would, I think, have been extremely interested in Thor Heyerdahl's Kon Tiki Expedition in 1947, when Heyerdahl journeyed by raft from Peru to the Tuamotus proving that the straight-haired people of Eastern Polynesia could have originated in South America.

I was always fascinated by the final paragraph in Beatrice's short biography, 'How I Found Adventure' where she writes:

124 *The Sydney Morning Herald*, 26th December 1942

> Romance? Yes, such I have never written, and never will write. Sorrow, and death; a spot in an island graveyard where 'the mossy marbles rest' upon the bravest heart that Papua ever knew.
>
> One adventure remains: the last, an adventure, and a meeting.[125]

So it would appear that she did have a special man in her life – William Little perhaps, who had died in 1920? From her words, one would assume that she believed death would be her 'last adventure' and that she would 'meet' William again.

William Little had been a good friend of Hubert Murray. He was a well-known and respected miner and surveyor, and had been voted a Member of the Legislative Council for Papua in 1906, representing the Northern Division.

In June 1908, *The Sydney Morning Herald* had reported the departure of an expedition into the interior of Papua. The explorative group was the brain-child of one, Donald Mackay, who wanted to find new places to explore. Having decided that Papua was about the only place left, he decided to go there, financing the expedition from his own pocket.

He needed, of course, to gather together a good team of men. Along with some other doughty gentlemen, Mr William Little MLC was recommended to him, whose knowledge would be invaluable, and who would be responsible for finding a number of bearers. The purpose of the expedition was to map part of the interior.

William Little seemed, on the face of it, exactly the sort of man attractive to Beatrice.

A little more evidence to the story was written about Beatrice living in Papua. One paragraph caught my eye:

> One is permitted to wonder mildly why she (Beatrice) made this wild region her home in preference to the more gracious lands of Polynesia. Perhaps it is because she met the love of her life there. Judge Hubert Murray...had a close friend – William Little, explorer, gold miner, pioneer. Miss Grimshaw and he fell in love. He was, she says, a typical Australian and through him she gained her admiration of the Australian people. They became engaged, but before they could marry he died of some obscure and undiagnosed tropical fever. Beatrice remained single, but she still treasures Little's ring of Papuan gold.[126]

And finally, having read *Conn of the Coral Seas*, published in 1922, just after William's death, I found it hard to believe she could have written such an explicit love story without having experienced it herself.

125 How I Found Adventure – The *Blue Book* of 1939

126 *The Pacific Islands Monthly*, 18th February 1947.

I am sentimental enough to hope she did have a lover in her life.

As Beatrice was now writing less and doing a little teaching, she applied in 1948 for an Australian pension. Although she was not entitled to a regular old-age pension, she was awarded a Literary Pension from the Commonwealth Literary Fund.

By 1949, Beatrice's health was failing badly. In May she was taken by ambulance into Oberon District Hospital, and then again in March 1950 Beatrice and her brother Ramsey were both admitted to hospital where Ramsey died in May of that year.

In 1953, *The Illawarra Daily Mercury* reported a most agreeable meeting with Beatrice:

> The travellers, Horrie Charleton (an artist), and David Aspeden who had just returned from a holiday at Oberon, tell me that sitting at their table was an amazingly interesting personality – Beatrice Grimshaw, the authoress. Her many books give you the idea she is a vital person, and the boys say that in her eightieth year, she still is that.[127]

That summer was an important and happy time for the British Empire. In May, Edmund Hilary and Tensing Norgay reached the summit of Everest, and the 2nd June saw the Coronation of Queen Elizabeth II. However, it was a sad day in Bathurst on 30th June, when Beatrice Grimshaw was taken again from Macquarie Homes to St Vincent's Hospital where she died.

There were countless obituaries. *The Sydney Morning Herald, The New York Times, The National Advocate* (Bathurst). A long and interesting piece in *The Daily Mercury*, (Mackay, QLD). And from *The Times*, London, the obituarist gave her no more that justice when he remarked that her 'long sequence of novels and short stories achieved high competence'.

Beatrice had written a Will in 1951, appointing a priest, the Reverend James Joseph Nolan of Oberon:

> aforesaid Clerk of Holy Orders, sole Executor and Trustee of this my Will. I GIVE, DEVISE AND BEQUEATH all my Estate both real and personal of whatever nature and wherever situate to my Trustee UPON TRUST for the Roman Catholic church at Oberon, to be applied for such uses as my Trustee in his absolute discretion may think fit, etc, etc.

The church inherited a little over £750 – in today's money about £7,800, not a huge amount, but surely enough to give Beatrice a headstone. However, rather strangely, on 1st July, after Requiem Mass at 7 a.m., and a funeral service held, not at Oberon, but at St Michael and St John's Cathedral in Bathurst, Beatrice was buried in the Roman Catholic section of Bathurst Cemetery.

Her grave remained unmarked until 11th January 2017.

127 *Illawarra Daily Mercury*, 7th February 1953.

Diana in Australia, 2017

After shadowing Beatrice through Fiji and Vanuatu, Joyce and I flew back to Auckland. Here Joyce would stay with her family for Christmas, while I flew onwards to Sydney and Adelaide.

I spent Christmas 2016 with all my family – my three children, their partners and my grandchildren, at my son Neil's home in Adelaide. It had been a very special time, all of us together for Christmas, the first time in many years. This was something that Beatrice never experienced, although it is clear she was close to her siblings.

Before leaving home, Graeme Hill, chairman of the Bathurst Historical Society had kindly invited me to be guest of honour at the unveiling of a plaque on Beatrice Grimshaw's unmarked grave. I planned to fly from Adelaide to Sydney and then take a bus to Bathurst on 10th January, the day before the ceremony. I was to come closer to Beatrice than I ever could have imagined at the start of my search for her.

The bus journey to Bathurst through the Blue Mountains was boring to start with, along a dual carriage-way with two lanes of cars endlessly coming into Sydney. However, when we got higher up I could see the mountains really were blue. As we neared Bathurst, and now winding along beside the railway tracks – a journey frequently taken by Beatrice – I was looking down into the green grassy Hartley Valley on one side of the Macquerie River, and the Megaloong Valley on the opposite side.

Dianne Barnes and her husband who had invited me to stay in their lovely old wooden house, were very welcoming.

The following morning a crowd of us were taken on a bus tour of Bathurst and Kelso to places which Beatrice would have known. It had been carefully put together by Alan Mc Rae, the local historian who also narrated the trip.

We all clambered up into the bus and trundled off down the long hill and across the Macquarie River up to Kelso – named after Kelso in Scotland.

We took a road off to the left towards Holy Trinity Church, standing sentinel over commanding views. This historic church holds a unique honour – that of being the first church built west of the Blue Mountains.

A little further along the road stood the grand house of 'Woolstone'. The house is situated almost opposite where Beatrice's house 'Wayside' would have been before sadly being demolished. The new street where houses have now been built, is called Wayside Court.

The little Store where Beatrice shopped

Situated round the corner from 'Wayside', and unchanged since Beatrice's day, stands the Kelso Hotel opposite which are the Kelso Corner Shops. This row of little shops – including the post office – remain exactly the same as in Beatrice's day and where she would have been able to do all her shopping. It was here that I met Carol Churches who was born in Kelso in 1937. She remembered Beatrice quite well, her house being close to where Beatrice lived. She was still at school when Beatrice died, but she remembered being given an egg cup with rabbits on it one Easter, and still had the image of her as she walked around the shops at Kelso always dressed in black. All a long, long time ago.

Back in the bus, and returning to Bathurst we passed 222, Seymour Street, opposite St Stanislaus College (both still standing). This is the little house Beatrice rented when she arrived in Bathurst in 1936.

We finished our tour at the Roman Catholic Cathedral. Bishop John Francis Norton was bishop here when Beatrice Grimshaw came to Mass when there were no services at Kelso.

We all repaired to the Irish Pub for beer or soft drinks and lunch, and looked at a small collection of items left by Beatrice after she died, now belonging to Alan McRae.

The main event in Bathurst turned out to be a huge success.

The unveiling ceremony was at the local Roman Catholic graveyard where the committee had erected three gazebos to protect us from the sun. It was a good turn-out with about forty-five people attending, plus TV cameras, and a reporter and photographer. Then Graeme Hill, in his position as mayor, and I, performed the unveiling of a very nice black marble stone. The local Irish priest, Father Paul Devitt gave a blessing, and spoke a few words, and then I had to say a few words as did Graeme.

It was quite emotional for me being so close to Beatrice's remains; this remarkable woman whom I had followed across the world, at last recognised with the inscription:

IN MEMORY OF
BEATRICE ETHEL GRIMSHAW
BORN IRELAND 3.2.1870
DIED BATHURST 30.6.1953
TRAVEL WRITER, PUBLICIST,
AUTHOR, BUSINESS WOMAN &
PLANTATION MANAGER IN PAPUA

Beatrice unveiling

It was here that her journey – and thus mine – ended very fittingly in the Roman Catholic cemetery in Bathurst, New South Wales.

Bathurst. Stone Masons at Beatrice's Memorial

Afterword

The next morning I took off from the little local airport for my flight back to Sydney, arriving at a small country terminal some distance from Terminal 1. Here I became totally lost trying to find transport to the main terminal. Eventually I found a bus – right outside where I was standing! Having duly arrived at the correct check-in and got rid of my huge luggage, not surprisingly I collapsed on to a bar stool making short work of a large Bloody Mary.

So the project was over. The ordinariness of sitting squashed into a tourist class aircraft seat was so mundane following three months' excitement doing my detective work. What was it about Beatrice that had sent me half way around the world? My own curiosity as an Irish woman and traveller, I suppose; wanting to see what and where she found so new and exhilarating – and would I?

I did indeed. But a lot has changed in the hundred odd years since Beatrice's days in the South Pacific. As I write, there is talk about mining under the Bismarck Sea off Papua New Guinea, killing acres of ancient corals and millions of fish. Mass tourism has brought pollution, with Beatrice's clear blue Pacific water thick with plastic rubbish, and global warming raising sea levels covering some of the low-lying islands.

And the erstwhile pristine Fly River? As my nephew Andrew reported back to me – since Beatrice was there some of the changes she would notice include discharging tailings and waste rock into the river, significantly impacting the riverine ecology. Today's widespread exploration for oil and gas; logging of pristine rainforest, and massive human population growth, with the replacement of sago palm roofs on bush huts with tin roofs. And of course, the inevitable appearance of cell phone towers along the river, with everyone now in mobile phone contact.

A proposed large-scale copper and gold mine situated in the mountains above the Sepik will irreparably harm the relatively pristine Sepik and Frieda Rivers, and devastate the region's primary rainforests and indigenous cultures.

However, there are a few positive changes. Education is available to everyone, modern medicine has obliterated many diseases, and traditional cultures of the indigenous peoples are no longer viewed simply as primitive.

The country's rich biodiversity has long been recognised – Papua New Guinea having its own environmental protection legislation and conservation areas; joining the Ramsar Convention (Protection of Wetlands of International Importance) in 1993. Species such as the tree kangaroos, singing dogs, birds of paradise and various butterflies are recognised as unique, and are protected.

Before knowing about her, I had already visited some of the places that Beatrice had explored in Papua New Guinea. Since knowing about her, I have followed her to her old home, Cloona; to Dublin; France; New Zealand, some of the most outlandish islands in the South Pacific, and finally Australia.

Besides learning a lot about the Pacific Islands while shadowing Beatrice Grimshaw, it was a surprise and a joy how much interest and participation I received from local people.

I have loved every moment of my peregrinations.

Bibliography

Non-Fiction:

"From Fiji to the Cannibal Islands."
(Eveleigh Nash. 1907)
ditto as *"Fiji and its Possibilities."*
(New York: Doubleday. 1907

"In the Strange South Seas".
(Hutchinson. 1907)
ditto (Philadelphia: Lippincott). 1908

"Three Wonderful Nations." (Dunedin, New Zealand: Union Steamship Co. 1907)

"In the New New Guinea."
(Hutchinson, 1910)

"Islands of the Blest." (Dunedin New Zealand: Union Steamship Co. 1911)

"Isles of Adventure."
(Herbert Jenkins. 1930)
ditto (Boston: Houghton Mifflin. 1931)

Novels:

"Broken Away".
(John Lane. 1897)

"Vaiti of the Islands".
(Eveleigh Nash. 1907)
ditto (New York. Wessels. 1908.)

"When the Red Gods Call."
(Mills & Boon. 1911)
ditto (New York. Moffat. Yard. 1912)

"Guinea Gold."
(Mills & Boon. 1912)
ditto (New York. Moffat. Yard. 1912d

"Red Bob of the Bismarks."
(Hurst & blackett 1915)
ditto as "My Lady of the Islands."
(Chicago: McClurg. 1916)

"Nobody's Island."
(Hurst & Blackett. 1917)
ditto (New York: Doubleday, Page. 1923)

"White Savage Simon."
(Sydney, Australia. Blackstaff. 1919)
ditto (Newnes 1924)

"Queen Vaiti."
(Sydney Australia: Blackstaff. 1920)
ditto (Newnes 1921)

"The Terrible Island."
(Hurst & Blackett. 1920)
ditto (New York, Macmillan. 1920)

"My South Sea Sweetheart."
(Hurst & Blackett. 1921)
ditto (New York. Macmillan. 1921)

"Conn of the Coral Seas."
(Hurst & Blackett. 1922)
ditto (New York Macmillan. 1922)

"The Sands of Oro."
(Hurst & Blackett. 1924)
ditto (NewYork, Doubleday Page. 1924)

"The Wreck of the Redwing."
(Hurst & Blackett. 1928)

"Black Sheep's Gold."
(Hurst & Blackett. 1927)
ditto (New York, Holt. 1927)

"The Paradise Poachers."
(Hurst & Blackett. 1928)

"My Lady Far Away."
(Cassell. 1929)

"The Star in the Dusk."
(Cassell. 1930)

"Helen of Man o' War Island."
(Pearson. 1931)

"The Mystery of Tumbling Reef."
(Cassell. 1932)
ditto (Boston: Houghton, Mifflin. 1932)

"Victorian Family Robinson."
(Cassell. 1934)
ditto (Boston: Houghton Mifflin. 1932)

"Rita Regina."
(Herbert Jenkins. 1939)
ditto (New York, Arcadia House. 1940

"Lost Child."
(Herbert Jenkins. 1940)

"The Missing Blondes."
(Sydney, Australia: Invincible Press. 1945)

Short Stories & Series Collections:

"The Sorcerer's Stone."
(Hodder & Stoughton. 1914)
ditto (Philadelphia: John Winston. 1914)

"Kris Girl."
(Mills & Boon. 1917)

"The Coral Queen."
(Sydney, Australia: Bookstall. 1919)
ditto (Newnes 1921, Abridged Library Series.)
ditto (Newnes. Expanded Edition. 1925)

"The Coral Palace."
(Mills & Boon. 1920)

"The Little Red Speck."
(Hurst & Blackett. 1921)

"The Valley of Never Come Back."
(Hurst & Blackett. 1923)

"The Candles of Katara."
(Hurst & Blackett. 1825)

"Eyes in the Corner."
(Hurst & Blackett. 1927)

"The Beach of Terror."
(Herbert Jenkins. 1930)

"The Long Beaches."
(Cassell. 1930)

"Pieces of Gold."
Cassell. 1935)

"Red Gods Calling."
(Sydney Australia: Ayres nd. 1939)

"South Seas Sarah" & *"Murder in Paradise."*
(Sydney, Australia: New Century Press. 1940)

"The Island Queen." (Todd, 1943)

"The Woman in Black."
(Sydney, Australia: Admiral's nd.)

Diana Gleadhill was born in County Down, Ireland, where she still lives. She worked as a professional librarian who dabbled in decorative art. Driven by her natural curiosity, and sense of adventure, she has explored destinations as diverse as Kenya, Uganda, South America, Kamchatka Peninsula, and Central Asia. She is a Fellow of the Royal Geographical Society

Her previous publications are:-

Kamchatka: A Journal and Guide to Russia's Land of Ice and Fire.

"Handsomely illustrated, compact guide – the first to the region"..... Longitude Books

"A fantastic production – I couldn't put it down. With the fascinating text, and the wonderful pictures, it really is one of the best travel books I have ever read".....
Brian Black, Byword TV

"A breathless account of an intrepid, unmistakably Irish traveller, thrilled with living and moving at the edge of her comfort zone, written with irrepressible good humour, and boundless energy".....
Irish Times

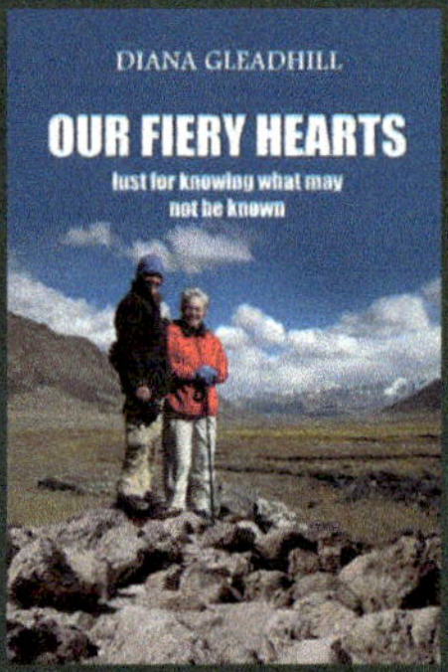

Our Fiery Hearts: Travels in Central Asia.

"Wonderful, adventurous and intrepid. An extremely interesting read".....
Michael Palin, BBC

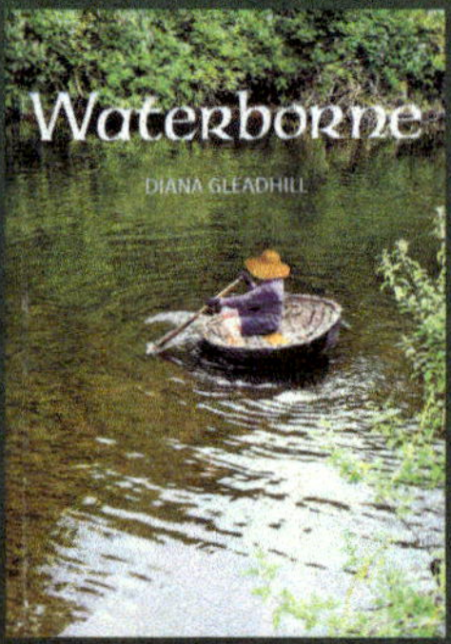

Waterborne: A collection of 'watery' memoirs.

"The book takes the reader from sailing and swimming in the author's familiar, and much-loved Strangford Lough in County Down, to sailing with friends round the globe, and by canoe, up the remote Sepik River, in Papua New Guinea. Brilliant".....
Brian Black, Byword TV